The MoveOn Effect

OXFORD STUDIES IN DIGITAL POLITICS
Series Editor: Andrew Chadwick, Royal Holloway, University of London

News on the Internet: Information and Citizenship in the 21st Century
David Tewksbury and Jason Rittenberg

*The Digital Origins of Dictatorship and Democracy: Information Technology
and Political Islam*
Philip N. Howard

The MoveOn Effect

THE UNEXPECTED TRANSFORMATION OF
AMERICAN POLITICAL ADVOCACY

DAVID KARPF

OXFORD
UNIVERSITY PRESS

OXFORD
UNIVERSITY PRESS

Oxford University Press, Inc., publishes works that further
Oxford University's objective of excellence
in research, scholarship, and education.

Oxford   New York
Auckland   Cape Town   Dar es Salaam   Hong Kong   Karachi
Kuala Lumpur   Madrid   Melbourne   Mexico City   Nairobi
New Delhi   Shanghai   Taipei   Toronto

With offices in
Argentina   Austria   Brazil   Chile   Czech Republic   France   Greece
Guatemala   Hungary   Italy   Japan   Poland   Portugal   Singapore
South Korea   Switzerland   Thailand   Turkey   Ukraine   Vietnam

Published by Oxford University Press, Inc.
198 Madison Avenue, New York, New York 10016

www.oup.com

Oxford is a registered trademark of Oxford University Press

Library of Congress Cataloging-in-Publication Data
Karpf, David, 1978–
The MoveOn effect : the unexpected transformation of American political advocacy / David Karpf.
     p.   cm.—(Oxford studies in digital politics)
Includes bibliographical references and index.
ISBN 978-0-19-989836-7 (hbk. : alk. paper)—ISBN 978-0-19-989838-1 (pbk. : alk. paper) 1. Political
participation—Technological innovations—United States. 2. Internet in political campaigns—United
States. 3. Internet—Political aspects—United States. 4. Blogs—Political aspects—United States. I. Title.
JK1764.K37   2012
322.40973—dc23   2011042905

Printed in the United States of America
on acid-free paper

Contents

Tables, Graphs, and Illustrations

Preface

This book stands at the intersection of two knowledge traditions—academic and practitioner. It has drawn from both and seeks to contribute to each in kind. My graduate education began in the fall of 2003. One week before moving to Philadelphia, I was asked to serve as the Sierra Club's National Vice President for Training. The Sierra Club is a volunteer-run, federated political association, the nation's oldest and largest environmental organization. I had held various roles in its national leadership since high school. I also decided to run for a position on the organization's Board of Directors in 2003–04, part of an internal mobilization called "Groundswell Sierra" that was attempting to prevent a hostile takeover of the organization's Board.

My graduate department chair was understandably less than thrilled by these commitments. As I was soon to learn, doctoral training requires a tremendous amount of time and intellectual discipline. It is hardly the right time to join a working Board. The years that followed were marked by a hectic tension—writing research papers during Board meeting lunch breaks, rushing to finish conference calls before teaching class. At the start of a Board meeting I would be beset by cognitive dissonance, as I reminded myself to stop talking like a grad student and instead talk like an organizer. Those years were also marked by tradeoffs, as I continually sought to balance my academic and organizational responsibilities. It was only in the final few years of my time on the Sierra Club Board that I learned to treat those stressful overlaps as an asset rather than a burden. In many ways, this book is the result.

The fall of 2003 was a momentous time for the Internet and American politics. The Dean juggernaut was at its zenith. Tens of thousands of volunteers were attending "Meetups"—web-coordinated local events—and donating millions of dollars to boost the obscure Vermont governor to frontrunner status in the Democratic presidential primary. Those were heady days, when the Internet seemed to be rewriting the rules of campaign politics. The campaign's eventual collapse in an Iowa cornfield was still distant and unimagined. And to my eyes, as a political organizer, the Dean phenomenon represented a marvelous puzzle.

Several months earlier, in January 2003, my old college friend Aaron Leavy had phoned, asking for advice on meeting facilitation. He was in Minnesota and fully expected that dozens of people would turn out to a winter event for this unknown presidential candidate simply because it had been posted on some website somewhere. I offered what advice I could, while keeping my honest, haughty opinion to myself: organizing doesn't *work* that way! People don't magically appear to a meeting just because you posted it on a website. Potential volunteers aren't floating in the ether, waiting to connect with one another if only you establish a coordination point. It takes relationship building and reminder calls and dozens of mundane-but-essential tasks to build a volunteer apparatus. I counted myself as an early Internet skeptic, because (up until the Dean campaign) there was little evidence that the lowered transaction costs of the web made much difference for the practical work of mobilizing citizen political power. By the fall of 2003, I knew I had been wrong about the Dean campaign, and I wasn't the least bit certain why that was the case.

The Dean phenomenon provides a backdrop to this book. The research presented here is focused on what came next. The Dean for America campaign turned into Democracy for America, a neo-federated political association that quickly became a powerful organizing force in my adopted city of Philadelphia. MoveOn. org was likewise moving beyond e-petitions, becoming the proverbial 800-pound gorilla within progressive politics. The blogosphere was developing an organizing capacity as well, apparently moving beyond the "just a bunch of chatter" label that I had previously applied to it. These were new political associations, and they were impressive in size and ability.

From my vantage point on the Sierra Club Board, a parallel course was unfolding. On the plus side, the medium was making a variety of "backend coordination" tasks much easier. E-mail is faster and cheaper than phone calls. Computer databases are a lot more useful than boxes of index cards. The hard, boring work of internal coordination—setting up meetings, licking envelopes, reminding people about events—had become far more efficient. These are small matters to the detached social observer. They are revolutionary for practitioners. But at the same time, our annual budget sessions were a maze, full of discussions about "unrestricted revenue" versus "restricted revenue." Changes in the communications environment were altering some well-established nonprofit fundraising strategies.

Sierra Club members pay annual dues. In return, they receive a set of solidary incentives (a backpack or a calendar) in addition to a magazine and various newsletters. The more active members participate in a massive federated volunteer structure, including local group and state chapters. The new political associations—most obviously MoveOn.org—had subtly redefined membership as a nonfinancial transaction. MoveOn's "members" often don't even know that they are members; they just know that they receive a lot of e-mails from the organization, and sometimes they take action (online or offline) or give money to a particular targeted activity.

At issue, essentially, was a major disruption in nonprofit revenue streams. Major donors and foundations were still supporting our work, but average Americans weren't opening their mail as much. The trend was toward online bill payment. Direct mail, which had served as the bedrock of a healthy nonprofit's fundraising strategy for decades, was being replaced by a different style of online giving. Major donors and foundations give large gifts to support specific projects. Members give small gifts (dues) to support the organization as a whole. Decrease the dues and you suddenly face a troubling scenario in covering overhead costs—even if your organization remains well-respected and effective. MoveOn and Democracy for America were small and nimble, using the Internet to engage in organizing on the cheap. The Sierra Club was hefty and deliberative, a throwback to a bygone era when organizations had volunteer entities in every town.

The Internet's effect on political associations—what I term the organizational layer of the American public sphere—was neither simple nor direct. Academic attention to lowered transaction costs, "organizing without organizations," e-petitions, and social networking sites was orthogonal to the transition I was seeing. Rather, a second-order effect was underway, with much broader consequences. Changes in membership and fundraising regimes advantage a new generation of political organizations and put "legacy" groups like my own in a precarious position.

Therein lay an opportunity to combine my competing responsibilities. My role with the Sierra Club yielded an interesting puzzle. My training as a political scientist yielded the tools and professional incentives to solve it. As a result, this book is a hybrid endeavor, designed to appeal to communities of political practitioners and social scientists alike. The text has been written with both communities in mind, and it is my sincere hope that each will find something of value in the pages that follow. It draws upon a wide range of scholarly fields—political science, communication, sociology, social movement studies, and Internet research—and attempts to offer something to each of these fields in kind. The professional field of political advocacy is changing thanks to new communications technologies. Those changes hold important implications for the organizational basis of citizen political engagement. I hope to shed some new light on the subject.

The intellectual debts I have accrued in the course of this study are many. I owe deep thanks to my dissertation committee at the University of Pennsylvania, Rogers Smith, Jack Nagel, and John Lapinski. All of my good intellectual habits stem from their tutelage. Rogers Smith offered tremendous clarity and mentoring in every stage of the project, from its murky early moments, to first putting pen to paper, to refining the several loosely joined chapter drafts into a cohesive whole. My lengthy and ongoing conversations with Jack Nagel have improved both my thinking and my writing. My perspective on methodological pluralism borrows much from our discussions about "the parable of the drunken search." My understanding of interest groups and political participation would be severely lacking without his influence. John Lapinski provided a professional lodestone of sorts throughout the dissertation process, keeping me focused on how my research contributes to political science as a discipline. For a topic that so easily can become disjointed from the major disciplinary themes, this proved a necessary, valuable, and oftentimes lengthy service.

The project also benefited from the insights of friends and colleagues. Lokman Tsui and I spent a year holding weekly meetings to discuss our weird Internet-related ideas. David Faris offered a comparative perspective on blogs, as well as a frequent friendly ear and careful editorial eye. Rasmus Kleis Nielsen and Daniel Kreiss have challenged and improved my thinking about campaigns and social movements. Kevin Wallsten, Amber Davisson, C.W. Anderson, and Aaron Shaw have all given generously of their time and patience. Each has deeply influenced the direction of my thinking, and this text is far better for it. Chris Warshaw and Hahrie Han, my fellow Sierra Club political scientists, have likewise had a profound influence throughout the course of this work. Sahar Massachi and Rachel Haynes provided valuable feedback on earlier drafts of this manuscript, long before it was fit for public consumption.

Within the political "netroots," my debts are many. Among the bloggers, I am particularly thankful to Natasha Chart and Chris Bowers. Among the Drinking Liberally community, Jeremy Meyer in Philadelphia; Chris Blazjewski and Ben Jones in Providence; and Jen Johnson, Jennifer Suh, and Justin Krebs in New York have been outstanding hosts. My time in researching Philly for Change was greatly enriched by Hannah Miller and Anne Dicker. Among MoveOn's far-too-busy staff, I cannot thank Natalie Foster, Noah Winer, Matt Ewing, Daniel Mintz, and Matt Smucker enough. Stephanie Taylor of the PCCC may be the hardest-working progressive in America. That she makes time to share insights over our frequent breakfast meetings in DC is both a treat and a surprise. I wish she would take a vacation, and I am glad that she does not.

The work on this manuscript spanned appointments at several universities. The dissertation was completed while I was a fellow-in-residence at the Miller Center for Public Affairs at the University of Virginia. The Miller Center provided a welcome academic environment, and I am thankful to Brian Balogh, Sid Milkis, and Jeff Jenkins, for both the fellowship support and the academic community they provided. Henry Farrell agreed to serve as a mentor during that yearlong fellowship, providing critical feedback and identifying some key flaws in the earlier work. I likewise owe thanks to Stuart Shulman, Bruce Bimber, Andrew Chadwick, Matthew Hindman, Siva Vaidhyanathan, Marshall Ganz, Matthew Kerbel, Richard Davis, Ken Rogerson, and Chris Bosso for reading and commenting on drafts of Chapters 2 and 3 in particular.

The Membership Communications Project was conceived, designed, and implemented during my postdoctoral fellowship at Brown University's Taubman Center for Public Policy. Key concepts in this book—"beneficial inefficiencies," in particular—came out of vigorous discussion with the undergrads and masters students who took my Internet and Public Policy seminar. Alexandra Filindra and Susan Moffitt were particularly insightful colleagues during my time in Providence.

I have enjoyed a Visiting Fellow position with the Yale Information Society Project in 2010–11, and the vigorous give-and-take of ideas in those lunchtime sessions has added much, particularly influencing Chapter 1. Laura DeNardis, Jack Balkin, Perry Fetterman, Daniel Kreiss, and C.W. Anderson have all been a treat to work with. My colleagues at Rutgers, both in the School of Communication and Information and at the Eagleton Institute for Politics, have provided an intellectual home and collegial support. I am lucky to have found such a good community.

Ronald Kahn, Harlan Wilson, and Paul Dawson of Oberlin College are responsible for getting me into academia. They knew I was headed to grad school long before I did and steered me in the right direction at every turn. My parents have been the finest of influence. (My father deserves special commendation as Research Assistant on the Blogosphere Authority Index!) Finally, I'd like to thank my colleagues and mentors in the Sierra Club. All of my instincts about political organizing were forged through "The Club." Bob Bingaman, Larry Bohlen, Kim Mowery, Robbie Cox, and Baird Straughan did right by me. My normative preference for "neo-federated" organizations stems from the healthy appreciation for democratic participation I learned from one of the last great federated organizations. The Sierra Student Coalition remains my greatest source of pride. I hope that the findings of this book are a service to that community as well. Or that they at least find it interesting.

To the extent that the reader finds this text accessible, all credit is due to my editors at Oxford University Press—both Angela Chnapko and Andrew Chadwick—and four anonymous reviewers. All mistakes and impenetrable language are of course my own.

The MoveOn Effect

1

The New Generation of Political Advocacy Groups

"Political mobilization is seldom spontaneous. Before any large
element of the population can become a part of the American
political process, organizations must be formed, advocates must be
trained, and the material resources needed to gain the attention of
national policy-makers must be gathered."
—Jack Walker, *Mobilizing Interest Groups in America, p. 94*

This book is a study of the Internet's effect on American political organizations. Current research about the Internet and politics holds two competing claims to be true. First, the new media environment has enabled a surge in "organizing without organizations." We no longer need organizations to start a petition, create media content, or find like-minded individuals. Second, many fundamental features of American politics—from the average American's lack of political knowledge or interest to the elite nature of major political institutions—remain unchanged by the new media environment. Everyone can now speak online, but surprisingly few can be heard.

I offer a third claim that modifies both of these perspectives: changes in information technology have transformed the *organizational layer* of American politics. A new generation of political advocacy groups has redefined organizational membership and pioneered novel fundraising practices. They have crafted new tactical repertoires and organizational work routines. "Political mobilization is seldom spontaneous," and the organizations that mobilize public sentiment have changed as a result of the Internet. The real impact of the new media environment comes not through "organizing without organizations," but through organizing *with different* organizations.

Though Internet-mediated organizations have played a prominent role in American politics for a dozen years, we still know very little about their operation.

MoveOn.org, the best known of these groups, has historically been tight-lipped about their strategies and operating procedures. Major political blogs like DailyKos.com function as quasi-interest groups but have generally been regarded as sites for citizen journalism. To add to this, there has been surprisingly little research on the ways in which the Internet impacts political organizations.[1] For example, Democracy for America (DFA), the sedimentary offspring of the Internet-fueled Howard Dean presidential campaign, has attracted minimal inquiry. Yet many of DFA's local groups have launched a renaissance of place-based organizing, supporting the very type of citizen engagement that Internet critics have long dismissed as unfeasible. Amidst all the attention to trends in social media, the transformation of political organizations has gone overlooked.

This book is a descriptive analysis of the new generation of advocacy groups. Based upon several years of network ethnography, key informant interviews, content analysis, and text analysis, it provides a detailed look into the operations of these new organizations and their impact on the broader advocacy group system. It offers insights into three distinct models for "netroots" (a portmanteau of "Internet" and "grassroots") advocacy organizations: Internet-mediated issue generalists, online communities of interest, and neo-federated organizations. It also charts the development of netroots infrastructure organizations—groups that combine technology and political expertise to fill new supportive niches in the advocacy group system. Finally, it analyzes the surprising failure of conservatives to build equivalent online organizations, concluding that such failures can be explained by *outparty innovation incentives*. This theory holds that the adoption of new technologies primarily occurs within the party network that is out of power.

By way of introduction, this chapter highlights the important role that netroots political organizations play in American politics today. The story begins in icy conditions, in the midst of a harsh Wisconsin winter. For three and a half weeks, from February 16th through March 9th, 2011, Wisconsin was home to the largest American labor protest in a generation. Unlike the Egyptian uprising that occurred mere weeks beforehand, public observers did not attribute a causal role in the Wisconsin protests to social media—no one believes Twitter caused the Wisconsin standoff. The Internet did play an essential mediating role, however. And it is through such large-scale events that the important niche now filled by a new generation of political advocacy groups becomes clear.

#WIUnion

The labor protests in Madison began as a local reaction to a state policy matter. On February 15th, 2011, recently elected Republican Governor Scott Walker unveiled his budget repair proposal. Included in the bill was a provision that would dramatically curtail the collective bargaining rights of public employee unions. Under the guise of a short-term budget crisis, the new governor was attempting to cripple a core constituency of his Democratic opposition. Unions are not only reliable sources of Democratic-leaning votes; they also provide key organizational support during election seasons. As such, weakening the union movement is in the long-term electoral interests of the Republican Party network. With Republican majorities in Wisconsin's State Senate and State Assembly, Walker had every reason to expect his bill to pass quickly into law. Democrats were outraged, but they had few bargaining chips. The entire 14-member Democratic State Senate Delegation (quickly dubbed "the Wisconsin 14") decamped to neighboring Illinois, forestalling an immediate vote. Local union members turned out by the thousands, setting up a massive peaceful demonstration within and around the capital building, and the national labor movement—organizations like the AFL-CIO and SEIU—quickly joined these protesters.

The labor movement was not alone in this conflict; the netroots also immediately joined the fray. MoveOn.org reached out to their 5 million members, generating 150,000 notes of support for the Wisconsin 14 in a matter of days, and DailyKos, Democracy for America, and the Progressive Change Campaign Committee (PCCC) all launched fundraisers for the State Senate delegation. On February 27th, a netroots-led coalition held solidarity rallies in every state capital, drawing 50,000 attendees and additional press attention nationwide. Meanwhile, Madison became "ground zero" for netroots organizers. Bloggers and field campaigners arrived in the state capital to help coordinate logistics, organize pressure tactics, and cover the details of the struggle. Armed with flip cameras, they interviewed local protesters and rapidly compiled issue advertisements. They then quickly turned to their national membership base for funding and placed the commercials on local television.[2]

The nearly month-long, continuous protest was the "largest continuous demonstration for workers rights in decades."[3] Daniel Mintz, MoveOn's Advocacy Campaign Director, remarked, "What happened around Wisconsin showed the most energy since 2008 and, in a non-electoral context, since the start of the Iraq War."[4] Though the governor obtained passage of his bill on March 9th, by then the damage had been done. His public approval ratings plummeted, and the Republican governor of nearby Indiana decided against pursuing a similar bill due to fear of public reprisal.[5] An energized coalition of local and national progressive organizations immediately announced recall campaigns against six vulnerable State Senate Republicans. Democracy for America alone hired 35 field staff to work full-time on those recall efforts. The August special elections succeeded in unseating two of those senators, considerably narrowing the Republican Senate majority.

There are three important lessons about the Internet and political advocacy that we should take from Wisconsin. The first is that Internet-enabled political organizing moves *fast*. Prior to the protests, netroots organizations like the PCCC and DFA had no developed staff capacity in Madison. Yet, within 48 hours of the day Governor

Walker unveiled his bill, they diverted their attention away from the federal level, re-tasking key staffers, educating their membership, crafting online petitions, and raising funds. Over the following two weeks, they organized mass protests in 50 state capitals. In an era of 24-hour news channels, blogs, and Twitter updates, news cycles move fast, and netroots organizations have fashioned themselves to keep apace.

The second lesson is that the interest group ecology associated with the Democratic Party network has changed. The liberal coalition has for decades been composed of single-issue groups that remain concentrated within their "issue silo." The ACLU and the Sierra Club may agree in spirit with the Wisconsin protesters, but they aren't going to mobilize staff and financial resources to support them. Members donate to these groups to represent their interest in civil liberties or environmental protection. Their annual dues provide a reliable basis for lobbying staff and policy experts, both in Washington, D.C., and in states across the country. The netroots define membership differently, disassociating it from financial transactions. Instead, they rely upon a fluid fundraising model based on targeted, timely action appeals. As a result, the netroots become "issue generalists." Staff structures and tactical repertoires are all built *around* the Internet. This yields new work routines, communications practices, and broad strategic assumptions. While other left-leaning interest groups remained focused within their traditional issue silos, the netroots swarmed to Wisconsin, providing a nationwide cavalry and expanding the scope of the conflict.

The third lesson is that Internet-mediated political organizing is hardly limited to blog posts and e-petitions. Critics who dismiss Internet activism as mere "clicktivism" focus attention on particular digital tactics and argue that historic movements for social change require deeper commitments and stronger ties than those found on Facebook or Twitter.[6] Some proponents of Internet activism, also focusing on these digital tactics, argue that they are a new form of action and should be treated as "social movement theory 2.0."[7] Neither of these perspectives captures what we saw in Wisconsin, where a new generation of large-scale organizations demonstrated their capacity to mobilize substantial resources over a sustained time period. By ignoring the organizational layer of the public sphere, we have missed important developments in American political engagement.

Divergent Internet Effects: Organizing without Organizations, Political Normalization, and the Organizational Layer of American Politics

The argument presented in this book is meant as a rejoinder of sorts to a pair of divergent research traditions, one within Internet studies and the other within political science. Within Internet studies, there is a popular line of thinking concerned with "organizing without organizations," "open-source politics," or "social movement theory 2.0."[8] According to this strand of theory, the traditional logic of collective action has been fundamentally altered by the lowered transaction costs of the new media environment.[9] Formal organizations are no longer necessary since individual tactics like e-petitions can now be organized online and information can spread virally through social media channels like blogs, YouTube, Facebook, and Twitter. In other words, we are all our own publishers and political organizers now.

The "theory 2.0" tradition has made a substantial contribution in identifying the significant implications of lowered online transaction costs. Indeed, "mass self-communication" is now possible in a manner unlike ever before.[10] And social network-based communication occasionally spirals into collective action, leading to online protest actions and offline political scandals. In the language of social movement scholars, we have seen the birth of new "repertoires of contention."[11] Online groups can form through Facebook. Offline meetings can be organized cheaply through Meetup.com. Political campaign commercials can be remixed and posted to YouTube, garnering millions of views. Media content is now spread through Twitter and the blogosphere, bypassing traditional gatekeepers. The costs of engaging in many individual acts of political speech have become infinitesimal, particularly in a stable democracy like the United States, where citizens do not face the looming threat of government reprisal.

The "theory 2.0" tradition is also steeped in the Science and Technology Studies practice of identifying the "affordances" of a new technology. As Jennifer Earl and Katrina Kimport define it, technological affordances are "the actions and uses that a technology makes qualitatively easier or possible when compared to prior technologies."[12] Computers and websites do not directly affect political systems. Rather, they advantage certain actors and social practices. Technology does not deterministically change society—people *using* technology do so. The "leveraged affordance" approach, as a challenge to technological determinism, has added valuable nuance to our understanding of the Internet and society. Online media incentivize some novel political behaviors, but it is the people who make use of this new technology that affect the contours of political speech.

But critically missing from this line of research is the notion of *scale*. Lowered transaction costs have made individual political actions far easier. Yet sustained collective action continues to require organization. Indeed, every large-scale example of "open-source organizing" or "commons-based peer production," be it the Linux operating system or Wikipedia, develops an organizational hierarchy of some sort.[13] Linux is run by Linus Torvalds and his "lieutenants," and a large proportion of the edits to Wikipedia come from a core group of volunteer administrators. The political arena is no exception. Large-scale contests over political power, such as occurred at the Wisconsin state capital, require organization. Changes in communications technology alter one set of organizing constraints by dramatically lowering the marginal cost of communication. But another set of political fundamentals remains unchanged.

Largely in response to the "organizing without organizations" line of research, a set of critics has emerged, dismissing online activism as mere "clicktivism," or "slacktivism."[14] According to their arguments, the Internet's effect on political institutions is minimal, and may even have deleterious unintended consequences. Malcolm Gladwell suggested, in a widely read *New Yorker* essay, that "The revolution will not be tweeted." He argued that social media tools fail to promote the type of strong interpersonal ties necessary for successful social movement organizing. Stuart Shulman has warned that waves of e-petitions and online public comments will swamp federal agencies in "low quality, redundant, and generally insubstantial commenting by the public," drowning out more substantive citizen participation.[15] Evgeny Morozov dismisses most digital activism as "slacktivism" and argues, "Thanks to its granularity, digital activism provides too many easy ways out."[16] Waves of new online communications tools lower the costs of citizen input, and this in turn unleashes waves of low-cost symbolic actions with little or no political impact. Underlying these observations is a deeper concern that, to the extent that e-petitions and Facebook clicks substitute for deeper citizen engagement, they may breed resentment and increased apathy toward government action. When all that clicking produces no change, they reason, citizens will turn bitter or tune out.

The clicktivism critics are right to question the value of an individual e-petition or Facebook group. Judged from the standard of traditional power analysis, which Robert Dahl classically defined in 1957 as, "A has power over B to the extent that he can get B to do something that B would not otherwise do,"[17] the average e-petition is a shallow intervention indeed. Powerful actors are unlikely to choose a different course of action solely on the basis of a digital signature list. But it is also only a single tactic. As we saw in Wisconsin, such tactics hardly capture the extent of online organizational ventures. Furthermore, as we will see in the following section, such criticisms lose their sting when placed within the context of political advocacy organizations. The average e-petition is indeed of minimal value, viewed in isolation. But so is the average written petition. Digital activism is not a replacement for the Freedom Riders of the 1960s; it is a replacement for the "armchair activism" that arose from the 1970s interest group explosion.

NORMALIZATION AND POLARIZATION

While Internet scholars have focused on these "theory 2.0" phenomena, political scientists have focused upon two trends: political normalization and political polarization. In response to an initial wave of research in the 1990s predicting Internet-driven political revolution, several scholars have documented the limited effects of new media tools. First among them were Michael Margolis and David

Resnick, who argued that the gains of potentially revolutionary new technologies are subverted to serve the interests of existing political elites, muting their overall impact.[18] The value of new communications technologies tends to be appropriated by existing political institutions. Rather than prompting wholesale political renewal, they reinforce elite institutional politics.[19]

The normalization theme has been roundly supported across a range of fields. Bruce Bimber and Richard Davis have demonstrated that political campaign websites are visited mostly by existing supporters rather than by undecided voters. As such, the utility of these sites for building third-party challenges or persuading undecided voters is minimal. Sidney Verba, Kay Schlozmann, and Henry Brady have shown, through survey data, that those citizens who engage in online political action are, from a demographic perspective, essentially the same citizens who previously engaged in offline political action.[20] Darrell West has noted that "interactive democracy" is the last stage of e-government adoption, and one that is rarely reached by public agencies focused on narrow improvements to service delivery.[21] Richard Davis noted that elite political bloggers act as "agenda seekers," fitting themselves into the broader system of political and media actors rather than subverting or fundamentally altering it.[22] Matthew Hindman has convincingly argued that, in the face of the lowered transaction costs and information abundance found online, "paradoxically, the extreme 'openness' of the Internet has fueled the creation of new political elites."[23] In all of these areas, the hopes of early Internet enthusiasts can be reasonably dismissed. In sum, America's governing political institutions and mass American political behavior (the two overarching fields of inquiry within American politics research) have not been transformed by communications technology.

Meanwhile, a line of inquiry in political communication research has highlighted the Internet's potentially troubling implications for civic discourse. Cass Sunstein first wrote in 2001 about "cyber-balkanization." Citizens tend to moderate their views when presented with evidence that challenges their biases, and they tend to radicalize when presented with evidence that supports their biases. As news-filtering technology improves, it becomes increasingly easy for citizens to avoid countervailing facts and opinions, polarizing the public sphere.[24] Eli Pariser argued a decade later that the problem has gotten worse, driven by companies like Google and Facebook who view undesired facts as an engineering problem, solvable through better search algorithms.[25] Philip N. Howard highlights the massive expansion of political data and resulting microtargeting practices. As he has argued, political consultants can now effectively engage in "political redlining," separating the population into refined categories based on their interests and voting tendencies, then hypertailoring their messages.[26] Joseph Turow found that banks and commercial firms are already mining our purchase data and turning it to alarming (and unregulated) ends in the marketplace.[27] The Internet is far from an idyllic, egalitarian space where everyone has an equal voice.

In political communication, there is a well-established tradeoff between political deliberation and political participation. Diana Mutz strongly argues that the countervailing facts obtained through "cross-talk" discussion tend to demobilize political participants.[28] There is a debate within the research community as to whether deliberation or participation is more desirable. Morris Fiorina finds partisan activity to be problematic, moving policymakers away from the moderate preferences held by the average American citizen.[29] Alan Abramowitz counters that increased participation from the subset of "engaged citizens" is arguably a good thing. A polarized government that represents their preferences offers clearer choices to all voters, yielding a stronger democracy.[30] As we will see, these tensions take on new life with the new generation of political organizations. Netroots political associations have an improved capacity for detecting and representing the preferences of their membership. That membership is itself polarized, though—there is no MoveOn or DailyKos for disinterested moderates. Increases in Internet-mediated political participation look nothing like the idealized New England town meetings of old.

The trend toward political normalization occurs because of fundamental attributes of the American political system. Elections occur biennially, decided on a single-member, simple-plurality basis (also termed "first past the post"). National legislation requires the support of 60 senators to overcome a filibuster. Separation of powers and federalism were designed long before the Pony Express or electricity, much less flash mobs and crowdsourcing. Even the most radical changes to communications systems must be channeled through those structural constraints in order to impact traditional political outcomes. What's more, American citizens have historically displayed low levels of interest in governmental affairs. The move to a "post-broadcast" media environment has allowed disinterested individuals to ignore the nightly news, widening the knowledge gap between well-informed and ill-informed members of the populace.[31] New channels for political speech fit into an existing system of powerful actors and institutions, and this affects the shape of communications technology.

THE ORGANIZATIONAL LAYER OF POLITICS

An intermediary layer exists between government institutions and the mass citizenry. My interest lies in this often-overlooked corner of political communication research—the organizational layer of American politics that facilitates interaction between government elites and mass publics. Studies of political organizations have a grand pedigree in political science, dating back to the early pluralists who viewed government as a neutral arbiter in the battle between organized citizen interests.[32] As we have learned more about the fundamentals underlying political institutions and political behavior, organizational studies have drifted into isolation. Part of the problem is methodological: it is nearly impossible to establish the immediate impact of such groups. The field of interest group competition rarely features unambiguous wins. As Baumgartner et al. recently demonstrated (2009), identifying who wins and who loses amongst interest groups is a daunting proposition in its own right, with no "magic bullets" among the various tactics and strategies.[33] Merely estimating the size of the interest group population is a devilish problem.[34]

The organizational layer of politics is not particularly large.[35] Compared to the size of the national population, issue-based political mobilization is miniscule. The largest day of protest in Wisconsin drew approximately 100,000 citizens, a fraction of the state population of approximately 5,600,000. Tea Party protesters at each of the 2009 Health Care Congressional Town Hall meetings numbered in the dozens, yet those dozens drove a national media narrative. MoveOn's 5 million members represent less than 2% of the American population. These are numbers that would vanish within the margin of error in a nationally representative survey.

Yet there is good reason to believe that the makeup of the organizational layer matters a great deal for broader political concerns. Theda Skocpol has found that the late-20th-century decline in American social capital is likely tied to the disappearance of cross-class federated membership associations during the 1970s. Until that time, social capital was built and maintained through civic organizations. Those organizations changed when membership and fundraising regimes, along with the broader government opportunity structure, shifted to favor professionalized, DC-based advocacy groups.[36] It stands to reason that the new wave of Internet-mediated organizations will also play an intermediary role in defining civic beliefs and citizenship ideals.[37]

In a similar vein, recent scholarship documents the central role that political organizations and informal party coalitions play in public policy decisions. Steven Teles documents the central role played by conservative organizations like the Federalist Society in fostering a broader conservative legal movement that has reshaped the federal courts.[38] Jacob Hacker and Paul Pierson argue that American economic policymaking has been driven firmly to the right by a network of conservative think tanks and advocacy organizations founded in the "lost decade" of the 1970s.[39] Seth Masket argues that the deep polarization of legislative politics is driven by informal party organizations at the local level that control resource flows around political primaries.[40] Political party networks are composed of both individuals and organizations. Changes in the composition and ideological position of these party networks affect the content of American policymaking.

The makeup of the organizational layer of American politics has substantial implications for both American institutions and American political behavior. Yet, as noted earlier, research concerning the Internet's impact on political organizations has been slim. With a few noteworthy exceptions, political organizations have been absent from our analysis.[41] The debate over "clicktivism" has focused largely on social network sites like Facebook and "warehouse sites" like petitiononline.com. Studies of the Internet and political campaigning have largely been placed within the political normalization framework. The new generation of political advocacy groups has received practically no attention. Yet, a sustained look at these new political associations helps to illustrate some key transitions within the organizational layer of politics. As a guiding example, consider the Progressive Change Campaign Committee.

THE PROGRESSIVE CHANGE CAMPAIGN COMMITTEE

The Progressive Change Campaign Committee (PCCC) is the newest of the large-scale netroots advocacy groups. In the aftermath of the 2008 election, three longtime netroots professionals chose to launch a new organization "to elect bold progressive candidates to federal office and to help those candidates and their campaigns save money, work smarter, and win more often."[42] The organization's name is a subtle dig at the Democratic Congressional Campaign Committee (DCCC). While the DCCC exists to support and elect Democratic officials, the PCCC exists to support and elect "bold progressives" (sometimes referred to as "not more Democrats, but better Democrats"). Combining professional expertise in electoral field campaigning, issue campaigning, and software development, the cofounders explicitly sought to challenge dominant centrist elements of the Democratic Party network. In the first two years of its operation, the organization managed to attract over 750,000 members, raising over $2,000,000 to fund its legislative and electoral efforts. The PCCC has received awards and recognitions from the New Organizing Institute ("Most Valuable Organizer" award in 2009) and *The Nation* ("Most Valuable Online Activism" in 2010).[43] The organization is a model example of how "Internet-mediated issue generalists" operate in the new media environment.

The presence of the Obama administration factors heavily into the PCCC's mission and organizational niche. Their launch in 2009 makes the organization unique amongst its netroots peers. MoveOn.org was founded in 1998 and rose to prominence during the 2002/2003 Iraq war buildup. Democracy for America was formed in the aftermath of Howard Dean's 2004 presidential primary campaign. Political blogs like DailyKos developed advocacy group-like qualities from 2004 through 2006, in response to the perceived failings of Democratic Party elites during the years of unified Republican governance. We will see in Chapters 5 and 6 just how important these "outparty" conditions can be for driving innovation and bringing new voices into the party network. The conditions for building new advocacy organizations and challenging entrenched interests within a party network are much more favorable during periods of opposition.

The PCCC has carved out a niche as the outlet for leftwing criticism of Obama administration policy. On issues like the "Public Option" in the Affordable Care Act, the PCCC was almost solely responsible for keeping leftwing policy options active in the public debate after centrist Democratic leaders had abandoned them.[44] The organization worked with progressive Democrats Jared Polis (CO-2) and Chellie Pingree (ME-1) to launch a House sign-on letter that attracted 118 signatories. It then partnered with Democracy for America to help raise $124,000 for the two champions' reelection efforts through the ActBlue.com fundraising portal.[45] The group employs a "hybrid" tactical repertoire, mixing the tactics traditionally associated with interest groups (lobbying and letter-writing), social movements (protests and rallies), and political parties (candidate fundraising and field mobilization).[46] It uses the Internet to engage members both actively, through member surveys and requests for input, and passively, through analysis of e-mail open-rates and action-rates that reveal member preferences. Having attracted a large membership of motivated partisans, these participatory tools further reinforce the organization's progressive issue positions.

The PCCC's first high-profile action provides a window into how netroots political associations operate. In April 2009, after several months of legal challenges, Democrat Al Franken was declared the winner of the 2008 Minnesota Senate race. Franken had won the November 2008 election by a narrow enough margin that a recount was required, but Republican Norm Coleman contested the recount through a series of long-running court challenges, preventing the Senator-elect from being seated. By April, it was clear that Coleman's challenge served primarily as a delaying tactic, preventing the Democratic Party from adding a 60th Senate vote. Thus, the Democratic Senatorial Campaign Committee (DSCC) chose to launch an e-petition calling on Coleman to end the legal challenge.

Blogging at OpenLeft.com, a top-25 progressive political blog, PCCC cofounder Adam Green offered a withering critique of the DSCC's action alert:

> "Working for MoveOn from 2005–2008, I wrote lots of e-mails inviting people to take action. . . . I'll never fault anyone for trying weird, wacky new things [in e-mails]—even if they fail. With one caveat: Every activist e-mail must have a plausible 'theory of change.' People should see some concrete theory about why taking action could lead to a desired result. But some people choose to inflame people's passions just to get their e-mail addresses (and more likely than not, to fundraise from them—as opposed to later engaging them in quality activism). This sullys [sic] the online activism process for the rest of us.
>
> . . . if you think about it, why on earth would Norm Coleman listen to the DSCC? Can you think of a less credible messenger than the DC committee whose sole role is to defeat Senate Republicans like Coleman?"[47]

Green then brainstormed an alternate message, proposing a "Norm's Democratic Dollar a Day" fundraiser. Supporters would be invited to pledge $1 to the

DSCC for every day that Coleman delayed Senator Franken's seating. Every day that Coleman held out would directly contribute material resources to the future election of Democratic senators. In the blog post's comment thread, one reader replied, "So, um, why don't you go ahead and make that a thing?" The PCCC did so, raising over $200,000 in the process and attracting national media attention.

The organization's membership list is a direct consequence of these actions. The membership base has developed through sedimentary waves, consisting of the residual list of partisans who acted upon the PCCC's request for donations. Choosing a timely issue and offering a simple-but-meaningful opportunity for participation attracts waves of engagement. Every individual who signs a petition, forwards a message, or makes a donation is defined as a PCCC member. The more timely the issue, the more likely it is that new participants will chose to take action. One advantage of this "headline chasing" is that it often leads the organization to be an issue generalist, mobilizing around time-sensitive topics that fall into the cracks between traditional issue silos. A timely, well-crafted action can receive extra publicity through top political blogs, social network channels, and mainstream media coverage. That coverage in turn yields a larger, participation-based member list.[48]

The PCCC illuminates five core themes that we will revisit through this book. First is that, just as "organizing without organizations" theorists have predicted, lowered online transaction costs do indeed play an essential role for netroots political associations. A blog post can now lead to a campaign tactic, and that campaign tactic can provide a surge of funding and membership growth. The pathways and processes for developing an advocacy campaign have changed. Legacy advocacy groups, by comparison, historically have relied on resource-intensive and slow-moving direct mail and canvass programs to build their membership base. The barriers to entry for new advocacy organizations have been steeply reduced, and this proves essential to early group-formation processes.

Second, not all digital tactics are created equal. The central problem with "clicktivism" arguments is that they paint with too broad of a brush. *Even the leading online organizers* are frequently critical of e-petitions and Facebook activism when poorly constructed. As we will see in Chapter 5, netroots organizing constitutes a professional field, with supportive infrastructure organizations, semiformal backchannel communications listservs, and network forums where they discuss and debate best practices in the emerging tactical repertoire. One can simultaneously be underwhelmed by the average e-petition or social media gadgetry and still hold that the Internet represents a major transformation at the organizational layer of the public sphere.

Low barriers to entry are only part of the story, however. The third theme holds closely to the political normalization tradition: the online environment can support only a limited number of large-scale netroots groups like the PCCC. While anyone can start their own online petition, the benefits of a large organizational membership are vital to the PCCC's sustained mobilization efforts. This is a variant of findings established by Matthew Hindman in another context. Hindman has conclusively demonstrated that there is an essential difference between the ability to speak online and the ability *to be heard* online. The sheer abundance of information available online leads to the development of heavily skewed power law distributions in web traffic—a digital "elite."[49] While a blog post at the Huffington Post or DailyKos routinely receives hundreds or thousands of reader comments, the average blog receives zero comments per post. While the average online petition receives at most a handful of signatures, an e-petition cosponsored by the PCCC, MoveOn, and Democracy for America will draw hundreds of thousands of signatures. In the realm of the Internet, *big is different than small.*[50] And there can be only a handful of big organizational players.

In layman's terms, power law distributions feature a "short head" and a "long tail."[51] As the PCCC has grown, the value of being big—of being one of the hub sites that emerge in the short head of a power law distribution—has reaped additional benefits. A *culture of analytics* pervades the PCCC's day-to-day organizational practices. When deciding between competing issues, tactics, and message frames, the group can settle internal debates through *testing.* Their member list is large enough to support randomized segmentation, feeding back comparative results based on the membership's revealed preferences. Which issues are most important to PCCC supporters? What issue frames will lead them to pay the most attention? What action requests will they respond to? These are questions that all membership-based political associations ponder. They are questions that everyday motivated citizens have no means of evaluating. The scale of the PCCC's member list yields sophisticated new tools for deriving answers.

An intriguing fourth theme emerges, related to the literature on cyber-balkanization: polarization through participation. The PCCC's testing practices allow it to isolate sentiments among its membership. This membership is large in comparison to other advocacy groups, but small in comparison to the nation's population. As one example, fewer than 30,000 people, in a country of 310,000,000 individuals, took part in the "Dollar a Day" fundraiser. Later PCCC campaigns have aimed at pressuring centrist Democrats, supporting members of the Congressional Progressive Caucus, and holding the Obama administration accountable when it adopts Republican policy positions as part of compromise legislation. Since the PCCC's membership is made up of engaged partisans, its tactics appeal to the sentiments and interests of those partisans. The organization is hardly made up of radicals, but neither is it made up of the centrist median voters who have long been a fixation of political strategists and media consultants. Confrontational tactics are popular with a member base that often feels taken for granted by the Democratic Party establishment. Listening to the partisan membership reinforces the organization's partisan position. Internet tools let motivated partisans increase their political voice.

A fifth and final theme concerns *what the PCCC cannot do*. The PCCC is an "Internet-mediated issue generalist." They work primarily on issues of national importance, responding to micro-level opportunities that arise through the rapidly shifting media agenda in an era of 24-hour news channels, news blogs, and Twitter posts. The size and activity of their membership, combined with an artful flair for creative and influential tactics, provides the basis of the group's power. They engage in both online and offline activities, merging issues campaigns and electoral campaigns. But when the PCCC speaks, they speak with one voice. Much to the chagrin of early proponents of "open-source democracy,"[52] the core of the PCCC is a small set of skilled political professionals. The organization has tools for receiving input from its 750,000 members, but does not provide a space for those 750,000 to interact with one another. Commons-based peer production or open-source politics, this is not.

Even more importantly, the PCCC has no local units, no standing structure through which its "bold progressives," at the local level, can exert independent influence upon city and state policymaking. A comparison to labor organizations is particularly apt: the PCCC is never going to sit across the table from management and negotiate a new collective bargaining agreement. This is one critical reason why netroots groups like the PCCC invested so heavily in the 2011 Wisconsin protests. Netroots organizers are well aware of the limitations of their niche. Most (such as PCCC cofounder Stephanie Taylor) have work experience with labor unions and traditional electoral campaigns. They know there are capacities that legacy organizations are better able to provide.

Unfortunately, the change in membership and fundraising regimes—what I term "The MoveOn Effect"—advantages groups like the PCCC while undercutting many of the traditional capacities of legacy organizations, a topic we will return to in Chapter 2. The MoveOn Effect does not lead inexorably to all advocacy groups converging toward the Internet-mediated issue generalist model. Chapters 2, 3, and 4 will detail three divergent netroots organizational models. But all netroots organizations define membership similarly, fundraise in similar manners, and have dramatically lower overhead costs than their legacy organizational peers. The technological affordances that groups like the PCCC take advantage of carry a menacing undertone for the existing advocacy group population. The new media environment fosters a *disruption* of the broader interest group ecology of American politics.

The Internet and Disruption Theory

The concept of disruptive innovation features heavily in this narrative. The Internet has been fruitfully described as a "sequence of revolutions."[53] Because innovation continues at such a rapid pace on the Internet, it has proven to be an enduring challenge for those studying its effect on politics. YouTube did not exist during the 2004 election, yet it was a fixture by 2008. The microblogging service Twitter was still in its infancy in 2008. It is a fixture of the media landscape today. Now that mobile web devices like the iPhone and Android phones are rapidly gaining market penetration, new social experiments with geolocational data are being devised. In the time that elapses between my completion of this manuscript and its physical arrival upon a bookshelf, another major innovation or two is likely to be heralded for "changing everything."

Partially for this reason, I have chosen to deemphasize individual social media tools in this study. There is no chapter on "Facebook politics" in this book. Readers who are interested in best practices in Twitter activism have likely realized by now that this is not the book for them. These social media are still diffusing; our usage practices with them are still maturing. How we use Twitter or Facebook today tells us little about tomorrow, just as how we used web pages in 1995 told us little about how we communicate today.

But, as we have seen in communications industries such as book publishing, newspapers, and music, the Internet exhibits a tendency toward fostering *disruptive* forms of innovation. The new media environment has set traditional commercial sectors into disarray. It is a classic example of what Clayton Christensen calls the distinction between "disruptive" and "sustaining" innovations. Sustaining innovations offer incremental performance improvement in an existing field of production. Disruptive innovations foster the rise of a competing field of production. In so doing, they undercut existing market forces.[54] Under such circumstances, the advantages of traditional organizational bases of production are undermined; the stable revenue streams that supported those organizations became unreliable. Moments such as these tend to exhibit a generational character. Old industrial leaders decline and new industrial giants emerge.

We are now witnessing the same pattern unfolding in the nonprofit advocacy sector. A generation of advocacy groups emerged from the "interest group explosion" of the 1970s. They defined membership through the act of annual checkwriting and relied on that stable revenue stream to develop an infrastructure (offices, staff, lobbyists, and organizers) for pressuring decision-makers around specialized issue topics. Today, those revenue streams have been undercut. As I will detail in Chapter 2, direct-mail fundraising is a dying industry. Though legacy advocacy groups certainly still exist, their influence has been eclipsed in many areas by the netroots, and they are facing increased pressure to cut infrastructure costs.[55]

For readers who are familiar with works such as Bruce Bimber's *Information and American Democracy*, Andrew Chadwick's "Digital Network Repertoires and Organizational Hybridity," or Mario Diani's "Social Movement Networks Virtual and Real," this point about industrial disruption will be the book's most noteworthy contribution.[56] These authors are among the few who have deeply investigated the Internet and organizations, and their work has heavily influenced the theoretical underpinnings of this study. But whereas Bimber, for instance, argued in 2003 that "traditional advocacy organizations and parties are moving to extend their dominance to the new realm of information technology,"[57] I find that there are important generational differences between the ways that netroots and legacy organizations use information technology. Digital innovations have taken on a disruptive, rather than a sustaining, character.

Nature of the Study

Stephanie Taylor is one of the PCCC's cofounders. On November 3, 2010 (the morning after a massive electoral defeat for the Democrats and the network of progressive organizations that support them), Stephanie set her Google Chat status message to simply read, "Back to Work." This book is about how that "work"—the day-to-day activity of American political associations—has been altered by the new communications environment. Each chapter details a different type of netroots organization, highlighting the ways that they use technology and mobilize segments of the public. I selected the organizations on the basis of their "hub" status—one benefit of the power law distribution of online traffic is that it renders the largest organizations easy to identify.

Studying "work" among Internet-mediated organizations is a complicated matter. Their "offices" are often coffeehouses or apartments. Interactions occur through Google Groups, G-chat, and conference calls rather than around water coolers and boardroom tables. The site for ethnographic observation is a mixture of online and offline activity. The research in this book is thus rooted in a variant of the political science tradition of "soaking and poking" as practiced by Richard Fenno. The study is modeled upon works like Philip Howard's "network ethnography" and Joseph Reagle's "historically informed ethnography," albeit with a more informal style.[58] My own position on the Sierra Club Board of Directors (2004–2010) provided a key space for theorizing some of the changes to advocacy group organizing, creating a natural rapport in interacting with netroots organizational leaders. The specific techniques that I used to gather data included key informant interviews, ethnographic observation, and detailed content analysis of e-mails, blog posts, and other texts produced by new and old organizations alike. I have endeavored to observe and interact with the leading netroots organizations, speaking with their leaders, observing their campaigns, and watching their interactions at conferences and other network events. These qualitative observational tools are augmented in places by two large-scale original datasets: the Membership Communications Project (for e-mail analysis, in Chapters 2 and 4) and the Blogosphere Authority Index (a blog ranking mechanism, used in Chapters 3 and 6). Both datasets serve to illustrate the broader empirical picture, allowing us to look beyond the small set of hub organizations that animate this study. Readers interested in the details of my methodology are encouraged to explore the research appendix.

Outline of the Book

I have identified three distinct models for how large-scale netroots organizations use the Internet to mobilize their membership. Groups like MoveOn and the PCCC rely primarily on e-mail for member communication. Their web pages are sparse, and when they do engage in web-based actions (such as the PCCC's "Call Out the Vote" distributed GOTV program), they frequently develop separate web sites for that purpose (www.calloutthevote.com).[59] Major community blogs like DailyKos and FireDogLake, meanwhile, operate as web-based gathering places for an *online community-of-interest*. The DailyKos community (self-described "Kossacks") consists of thousands of active diarists who contribute content to the site. Such online communities can have major political impacts, particularly when they direct their joint attention to a shared political priority or candidate, resulting in waves of donations and campaign actions. Meanwhile, *neo-federated groups* like Democracy for America (DFA) use e-mail to communicate with members, but those communications center around announcements of upcoming offline events, offering "online tools for offline action."

These three types of communication—organization-to-member/online; member-to-member/online; and member-to-member/offline—are nonexclusive categories. There are DailyKos "meetups" and local MoveOn Councils. DFA frequently collaborates with the PCCC on national e-mail actions, and DailyKos started collecting visitor e-mail addresses in August 2010. Democracy for America's blog, "Blog for America," was one of the early influential political blogs,[60] and Adam Green of the PCCC routinely writes diary posts for DailyKos and OpenLeft.com. The book thus uses these organizations as guiding case examples to explore the three organizational models, emphasizing the dominant features and political implications of each in turn. All of these organizations provide an *organizational substrate*, or a venue through which political mobilization can occur across a wide range of issues. They all are *sedimentary organizations*, building their membership lists and reputations through waves of heightened citizen interest and enthusiasm.[61]

The following three chapters provide an analytic treatment of the three netroots organizational models. Chapter 2 uses MoveOn to illustrate changes to membership and fundraising regimes and to highlight the disruptive nature of the current change to the political economy of advocacy groups. Chapter 3 turns to the political blogosphere and the networked community of online political activists who self-describe as the "netroots." Sites like DailyKos function as

quasi-interest groups. They engage in similar mobilization practices to more traditional advocacy groups: choosing priority issue campaigns, endorsing and
fundraising for candidates, pushing issue frames, challenging party leaders, and
highlighting the flaws of opposing arguments. Chapter 4 turns attention to neo-
federated organizations. It begins with an analysis of Democracy for America's
local group in Philadelphia, PA, Philly for Change. Yet Democracy for America
includes only a dozen or so groups of Philly for Change's size and strength; much
of its national work is patterned like an Internet-mediated issue generalist.
Through an investigation of *proto-organizational forms* (online organizations
that develop before the relevant technology is ripe) and a discussion of the
growing potential of the mobile web, the rest of Chapter 4 lays out some of the
likely paths for development within this ideal type. It also features a discussion of
Organizing for America (OFA), the associational offspring of the Obama presidential campaign that is now housed in the Democratic National Committee.

Chapter 5 turns our attention to a range of non-membership Internet-mediated
organizations. Focusing upon the particular circumstances present after the 2004
election, it highlights five different forms of "infrastructure" that help advocacy
groups new and old adapt to the new political opportunities presented by information technology. The New Organizing Institute serves as a "network forum" of
sorts, a training institute where the professional community gathers, shares best
practices, and formulates new strategies.[62] ActBlue.com provides a nonprofit
fundraising platform—critical infrastructure for groups like PCCC and DailyKos
when they want to facilitate member donations to candidates. ActBlue lowers the
costs, both in legal and technical support, necessary for networks of individuals
to mobilize their community-of-interest. A set of for-profit consultancies, or "vendors," provide similar support around a range of new media tools. Nearly all of
these vendors were founded by alumni of the Howard Dean and Barack Obama
campaigns, evidence of the shifting forms of power within the party networks
themselves. Living Liberally, meanwhile, provides a very different type of "infrastructure," establishing a large network of progressive social events around the
country, through which netroots participants can build up a reservoir of social
capital within the movement. A set of *network backchannels*—Google Group listservs such as TownHouse and JournoList—allow netroots participants and other
professional networks to establish a space for internal discussion and coordination away from the public spotlight. Such lists offer a key insight into *how* the
public sphere has changed as a result of the Internet. Whereas in previous generations professional networks were *publicly visible but closed*, today these networks
are increasingly *publicly opaque but porous*. The organizational layer of American
politics remains the province of a limited subset of the populace, but the means
through which people engage with that layer have changed substantially.

Absent from the case examples in Chapters 2 through 5 is any representation
of conservative political associations. Chapter 6 offers a detailed explanation of

the reason why, as well as a theory of *outparty innovation incentives* that helps to explain the partisan adoption of technological innovations over time. Simply put, the main reason why conservative groups are absent from this study is because, from 2004 through early 2009, what was most noteworthy was the relative dearth of online conservative political institutions. Recognizing the success of groups like MoveOn and DailyKos, conservative political leaders continuously attempted to build equivalent organizations. Their efforts failed time and time again. Even after 2009, with the rise of the Tea Party movement, conservative attempts to build a parallel infrastructure have continued to produce mostly failures.

Rather than employ a false equivalence, choosing weak conservative analogues to the robust new organizations on the left to "balance" the study, I instead endeavor to investigate the roots of this failure. I argue that the two party networks experience relatively few overlaps, and that the adoption of Internet tools and development of Internet institutions occurs in a partisan manner, with the outparty facing stronger incentives for growth and change. We lack a robust conservative netroots not because conservatives are ideologically incongruent with the "bottom-up" Internet, but because conservatives were already winning elections and thus saw little reason to advance dramatically different tools and organizations (and the new actors who lead them).

Chapter 7 offers concluding observations, returning to a broader set of questions regarding the effect of the organizational layer upon political behavior and elite political institutions. It provides a series of final observations, including the drivers of continual change within systems of political competition, what we should make of *dis*organized political content on social media platforms, and a few reasons for hope and concern in an era of Internet-mediated citizen politics.

2

The MoveOn Effect

Disruptive Innovation in the Interest Group Ecology
of American Politics

"Membership as we know it is a myth of the past."
—Interviewee comment, *Monitor Institute "Disruption" Report, 2010.*

I first encountered MoveOn.org unexpectedly, in the spring of 2000. I was the National Director of the Sierra Student Coalition (SSC) and, like so many of my Sierra Club colleagues, had developed a healthy dose of skepticism toward the assorted attempts to apply dot-com era enthusiasm for all-things-digital to political organizing. While attending a national conference on youth civic engagement, a colleague and I happened upon Peter Schurman, a former SSC staffer. We spent 20 minutes in conversation discussing politics, organizations, and individuals. I had to sublimate my reaction to his new job, working with some startup organization that had launched an e-petition around the Clinton impeachment hearings. As Peter talked about combining technology and politics, engaging supporters online, and learning from successful tech startups, I nodded politely and said little. But as he walked away, I turned to my colleague and muttered, "e-petitions . . . what a joke. That organization will never amount to anything."

Six years later, while conducting background research for my doctoral dissertation, I ran across another reference to Schurman. His organization, whose name had promptly fled my memory, turned out to be MoveOn.org. Peter had served as their first Executive Director. The subtitle of this book is in part a reference to that early conversation. The use of the Internet by political associations has changed from the time I was an advocacy professional to today. Groups like MoveOn played a central role in facilitating that development, and neither political practitioners nor political scholars were quite able to see clearly as the change unfolded. Unexpected transformations indeed.

Today, it would be nearly impossible to dismiss MoveOn as I did over a decade previously. With an e-mail-based member list of over 5 million and 2008 election year expenditures in excess of $90 million, MoveOn.org stands as arguably the single largest interest group in American politics today. Founded by a pair of technology entrepreneurs, the organization has maintained its commitment to campaign tactical and communications innovations, creating field-defining shifts in membership engagement and small-dollar fundraising practices along the way. MoveOn is an essential case example, not only for understanding new groups like the Progressive Change Campaign Committee that mimic its structure, but for more broadly assessing how the underlying political economy of American political associations has been altered by the new communications environment. It was MoveOn's successful experimentation with new organizational structures, communications practices, and campaign strategies that signaled to longstanding political associations that the Internet was useful for something more than placing petitions and clearinghouse information into a more accessible medium. What's more, the new organizational practices MoveOn has pioneered have been fundamentally disruptive in nature, yielding greater utility to newly formed organizations than to legacy groups with existing reputation and influence.

This chapter explores the structural and tactical innovations that have led to MoveOn's meteoric rise in American politics.[1] Drawing upon previous works detailing the history of civic associations in America, it argues that the changes in membership and fundraising regimes introduced by MoveOn are similar to the changes witnessed in the late 1960s and early 1970s—changes that led both to an "interest group explosion" and to the replacement of a previously dominant organization-type with a new modal organization-type.[2] It provides a detailed account of the "Internet-mediated issue generalist" model, as typified by groups like MoveOn and the PCCC. Such groups span multiple issue spaces, function with greatly reduced overhead costs, mobilize their community-of-interest around the daily political headlines, and utilize data-rich "analytics" tools to obtain *passive democratic feedback* from their online memberships.

The chapter also explores the systematic impact of changing communications technology on existing advocacy organizations—"the MoveOn Effect." To be clear, the MoveOn Effect is not a reference to the immediate effectiveness of the organization itself. Rather, it refers to the second-order impact of changes in membership and fundraising regimes—changes successfully pioneered by MoveOn.org—on an organizational population built in response to older membership and fundraising regimes. Based on a combination of in-person observation, elite interviews, e-mail content analysis, and secondary source literature review, the chapter delves into nonprofit fundraising, a topic that often remains obscured from view by organizational firewalls and confidential data-sharing agreements. Simply put, it is commonly known that direct-mail-based fundraising is in decline. American citizens have increasingly turned to online bill payment. Response rates to direct-mail solicitation drop as a result. As a recent Monitor Institute study put it, "The expense of direct mail is going up, the yield rate is going down, but there is no replacement strategy."[3] Online fundraising provides an alternative, but one that better serves "headline chasing" groups with minimal overhead costs. The large staffing and office expenses of legacy organizations are based in a *beneficial inefficiency* of the old fundraising environment, ill-supported by targeted online fundraising techniques. The more efficient online communications medium comes at a cost for the old generation of political associations, just as the rise of direct-mail fundraising in the 1970s contributed to the decline of a previous generation of civic associations and enabled the rise of single-issue, professional advocacy organizations.

This chapter has four parts. It begins with a discussion of the historical analogues to the MoveOn Effect, drawing upon important research contributions by Theda Skocpol and Bruce Bimber in particular. It then offers a brief discussion of MoveOn's history. The path from forgettable 1998 startup to left-wing juggernaut includes several important lessons regarding the partisan adoption of technological innovations. The third section will provide a detailed analysis of the "MoveOn model," which approximates the Internet-mediated issue generalist model. Here I detail MoveOn's staff structure, membership relations, engagement practices, and fundraising strategies. This section relies both on interviews with current and former MoveOn staff and on the Membership Communications Project (MCP), a large-scale analysis of six months of e-mail appeals that I collected from 70 major progressive advocacy groups (see Methods Appendix for details on the MCP data collection process). The final section will use MCP data along with secondary-source information on nonprofit fundraising techniques to highlight the disruptive character of the new fundraising practices, highlighting the "generational" nature of the current transition.

The Historical Analogue: Information Technology and the "Interest Group Explosion"

Theda Skocpol offers a key historical analogue in her 2003 book *Diminished Democracy*. Writing in response to Robert Putnam's argument about the decline of social capital and civic engagement in 20th-century America, Skocpol argues that much of the drop can be attributed to the transformation of the organizational layer of American politics. Detailing the long history of cross-class federated membership organizations in American civic life, Skocpol demonstrates that a crucial shift "from membership to management" occurred in the late 1960s and early 1970s. That time period saw an explosion in the number of DC-based registered lobbying organizations, but also saw a substantial decline among federated membership organizations that had long provided an institutional basis for

American civic participation.[4] Skocpol attributes this shift to a number of important factors, including the rights-based issue framework emerging from the Civil Rights Movement, the governmental opportunity structure that placed a premium on expert lobbying opinion over citizen input, and a change of membership regimes from membership-as-participation to membership-by-mail.[5]

This final point bears particular elaboration: the very *concept* of organizational membership changed. Membership in federated civic groups consisted of attending meetings, holding office, and otherwise forging an identity-based attachment as an "Elk" or a "Rotarian." Such identity-based membership is evident in a host of historical artifacts from early generations, from ribbons and marches to gravestones and eulogies. It is also a necessary antecedent to the dues payments that early civic associations required for sustenance. Skocpol offers rich examples of early organizational founders traveling from city to city, developing the tapestry of local group affiliates necessary to fiscally sustain a national organization. The new generation of professionally managed political associations relied instead upon direct mail (and, later, door-to-door canvass operations) for their membership recruitment.[6] This created a new category of "armchair activists" who, incentivized through some combination of solidary, purposive, or other selective incentives, gave financially without participating locally.[7] Armchair activists agreed with the issue focus and broad purpose of a political association, without directly participating in its activities. Such issue-based membership attachments were *easier* in a host of ways, requiring less time and commitment on the part of the individual and requiring less maintenance and attention on the part of the organization. However, the easier membership model also created far fewer attachments, making them less useful as "laboratories of democracy" and generators of social capital.

Writing contemporaneously with Skocpol, Bruce Bimber offered a valuable insight into the technological underpinnings of this sea change in organization type. Bimber's *Information and American Democracy* describes the development of political associations in American politics over the course of four "information regimes." Bimber's central argument is that major changes to the costs and availability of information directly affect the political economy of association-building. Simply put, organizations prior to the late 1960s *had* to engage in the costly task of developing local infrastructure, because the mainframe computing database technology necessary for financially viable direct-mail appeals had not yet been invented. The falling costs of information, broadly defined, facilitate novel developments in membership and fundraising regimes, in turn encouraging the growth of new types of political associations. Skocpol makes brief note of these technological underpinnings but otherwise remains mute on the role of information technology in structuring decisions about the management, structure, and financing of nonprofit political and civic associations.[8]

Bimber goes on to discuss the Internet as a "fourth information regime" and describes the features of "postbureaucratic" advocacy groups that he expects to emerge in that system. Figure 2.1 summarizes these predictions, combining elements of Skocpol's and Bimber's work to highlight what we can think of as three "generations" of political associations in America. Centrally, the common thread between Skocpol's and Bimber's work is the contention that changes in membership and fundraising can produce a generational shift among advocacy organizations. In the language of population ecology researchers such as Virginia Gray and David Lowery, changes to membership-based funding streams affect the available "energy" in an interest group ecosystem, altering the arrangement of organizational niches and displacing the dominant organization-form.[9] Organizational sociologist Debra Minkoff highlights that these generations are not monolithic—rather, she and her colleagues have found that the DC advocacy group system features multiple clusters of organization types.[10] Not all legacy advocacy groups rely on direct-mail support and armchair activism. What's more, Elisabeth Clemens has traced the roots of modern interest group politics back to the late 19th and early 20th century reform movements.[11] The Generational concept is a heuristic device, a means of highlighting developments that affect which organizations gain resources and political influence—"market share," so to speak.

Era	First Generation (1800s-1960s)	Second Generation (1970s-early 2000s)	Third Generation (2000-present)
Membership Type Typical Activities	Identity-Based Attending Meetings, Holding Elected Office, Participating in Civic Activities	Issue-Based Mailing Checks, Writing Letters, Signing Petitions (Armchair Activism)	Activity-Based Attending local meetups, Voting online, Submitting User-Generated Content
Funding Source	Membership Dues	Direct mail, Patron donors, Grants	Online appeals, Patron donors, Grants
Dominant Organization-Type	Cross-Class Membership Federations	Single-Issue Professional Advocacy Orgs	Internet-Mediated Issue Generalists

Figure 2.1 Core Features of Three Generations of Political Associations

They are only a rough tool for measuring the organizational diversity within an advocacy group system.

While decades of scholarship from the interest group and social movement traditions detail the "interest group explosion" of the 1970s, Skocpol and Bimber lead us to reflect specifically on changes among *membership associations,* a particularly vital, particularly public form of interest group.[12] The very notion of organizational membership changed in the 1960s and 1970s, both as a response to the social movements of that era and as a response to advances in information and communications technology. New revenue streams emerged, and old ones decayed, leading not only to more political associations but also to an ecological change in the prevalent type of organization. Bimber predicted that a similar change would occur in response to the Internet. He viewed it as a sustaining (rather than a disruptive) innovation, based upon the early organizational case examples available at the time. As we see in the following section, MoveOn.org's organizational model likewise revolves around a redefinition of associational membership.

The Growth of MoveOn

MoveOn.org was founded by Joan Blades and Wes Boyd, a married couple who made their fortune in the mid-90s tech boom when they created, among other things, the highly popular "flying toasters" screen saver. In 1998, during the midst of the Clinton-Lewinksy affair, the two grew tired of scandal politics and started a simple website where visitors could sign a petition asking Congress to censure Clinton and "move on." Attention to the website diffused virally, and within a week 100,000 people had signed the petition, eventually attracting 500,000.[13] When the petition failed to make an impression on Congressional decision-makers (as online petitions are wont to do), Blades and Boyd reached out to their list and invited people to engage in citizen lobbying and other pressure tactics. The group attracted a fair amount of media attention as a new, Internet-mediated interest group, but was viewed mostly as an odd anecdote rather than a game-changing powerhouse.[14] Blades and Boyd's experience as technologists have left an essential imprint on MoveOn's organizational philosophy, leading the group to adopt and adapt the practices of a tech startup rather than the practices of legacy political associations. The result has been a culture of ongoing experimentation and technological innovation in the hopes of "bringing real Americans back into the political process."[15]

In the aftermath of the Lewinsky scandal (and around the time when my own incidental encounter with Peter Schurman occurred), MoveOn remained an Internet-mediated organization, albeit one that lacked a particularly clear mission. It boasted a large e-mail list and a nimble, virtually networked staff that required few overhead costs, but the organization's niche within the "interest group ecology" of the American Left was unclear. This is, in fact, part of a pattern that we will see duplicated in later chapters—a feature of the partisan adoption of technology I refer to as the outparty innovation incentives thesis. The year 1999 featured a Democrat in the White House, facing off with intransigent Republican opponents in the House and Senate. What should a generally progressive/liberal "call to action" focus upon in such circumstances? Which issue demands immediate action, and what clear message should citizens send to their representatives? To be clear, I am not suggesting that new organizations are *formed* only during periods of oppositional politics, but rather that nascent organizations are being created at all times, and the circumstances that allow an organization to build a large membership, sustainable fundraising, and reputational authority are weighted toward periods of counter-mobilization.

Indeed, it wasn't until the post-September 11th lead-up to wars with Afghanistan and Iraq that MoveOn would emerge as a leading voice for self-identifying progressives in America. Eli Pariser, then a college student at Simon's Rock College, built a similarly large list around his website, 9–11peace.org.[16] Blades and Boyd recruited Pariser to join MoveOn's staff, merged the two large e-mail lists, and the three of them quickly brought the organization to the forefront of the burgeoning anti-war movement (Pariser would become MoveOn's second Executive Director in 2004). Michael Heaney and Fabio Rojas find that MoveOn emerged as a central hub of anti-Iraq war mobilization activity.[17] Whereas the political agenda for left-wing organizations in 1999 was fractured and opaque, the political agenda for the American left in 2003 was obvious: "Stop the War." Over the following half-dozen years, MoveOn would master this responsive, oppositional style of political engagement. The Bush administration set the national political agenda (and could count on supportive Republican congressional majorities from 2002–2006). MoveOn reacted to that political agenda, "chasing the headlines," so to speak, with timely calls to action.

MoveOn's e-mail-based appeals quickly moved well beyond the simple e-petition the organization had been founded upon. In the lead-up to the 2004 Democratic primaries, MoveOn launched its own "MoveOn primary," in which supporters could vote online for the candidate they felt the organization should endorse. Occurring during a lull in the campaign cycle, while political reporters were thirsting for a new angle on the impending Iowa caucus and New Hampshire primary, the primary attracted substantial national media attention. Howard Dean earned a plurality of these votes (and Dean's vocal online supporters thusly were added to MoveOn's member roles), but, lacking a majority, the organization made no endorsement. Also in 2004, MoveOn would host its "Bush in 30 seconds" competition, soliciting user-generated political commercials, encouraging supporters to vote on the best one, and then inviting those supporters to donate and help air the commercial during the Super Bowl[18]. Through exhaustive message-testing and the development of several innovative campaign tools, MoveOn developed a capacity for generating millions in small-dollar contributions, launching online and offline oppositional tactics to the latest Bush administration efforts, and continually building its list of occasional-to-frequent left-wing political participants.

In the 2008 election, MoveOn's e-mail member list ballooned to over 5 million, much of it based on eye-catching viral videos and offers of free Obama/Biden merchandise. MoveOn members donated over $88,000,000 to Barack Obama, and 933,800 of them volunteered a combined 20,841,507 hours to his campaign. Much of this occurred through "online-to-offline organizing," with the help of the organization's system of location-based "MoveOn Councils" that act as an Internet-mediated equivalent to the local chapters of Skocpolian civic associations. In non-priority states, the group organized web-based "Call for Change" phone-banks, with members in Vermont downloading a list of members in, for instance, Virginia, calling them, and inviting them to join the local organizing efforts. Far from the "clickstream" petitions often bemoaned by scholars and public intellectuals, the Call for Change program allowed MoveOn's network of political partisans to directly engage in one of the most traditional "offline" political tasks—Get-Out-the-Vote election phone calls. In battleground states, it also developed direct partnerships with the Obama campaign field system.[19] The political advocacy start-up had become a well-established feature of the political advocacy system.

The MoveOn Model

MoveOn's success in establishing itself as a major organization in 21st century American politics is undeniable. The organization has become a touchstone among the new generation of advocacy groups, spawning spinoffs such as ColorofChange.org, Momsrising.org, Avaaz.org, and (to a lesser extent) the PCCC. Former MoveOn staff play major roles in other central political organizations, including the Democratic National Committee (through Organizing for America, discussed in Chapter 4), the New Organizing Institute (discussed in Chapter 5), and legacy political associations. Its tactics and organizational practices have also been mimicked by a variety of Internet-mediated issue *specialists*—niche organizations that focus their attention on a specific issue area. As the organization moved from nascent political startup to central political hub, elements of its successful "model" received intense interest from the rest of the advocacy community—from public intellectuals, consultants, major donors and grantmakers, and peer organizations. The workings of that model can be divided into four categories: organizational structure, membership, engagement practices, and fundraising.

MoveOn Organizational Structure

Three features of MoveOn's organizational structure represent significant departures from traditional political associations. First is the small size of the core staff itself—despite having over 5 million members and being one of the most prominent political organizations in America, MoveOn's staff size fluctuates between 20 and 35. This core staff is augmented by a *phantom staff* numbering in the hundreds—short-term employees brought in to organize in election season, for instance. Second is the lack of physical infrastructure—there is no MoveOn central office, an organizational policy referred to as "radical decentralization." Third is the set of networked, hybrid organizational practices that the staff size and radical decentralization promote. Whereas older organizations, in line with Mario Diani's early predictions, have used the Internet to modestly increase the efficiency of intra-organizational communication, MoveOn and other newly founded organizations assume a radically different structure, made possible by the technical affordances of Internet communication.[20]

MoveOn's staff is remarkably small. Whereas other major nonprofits in America have professional staffs in the hundreds, MoveOn had only 21 full-time staff members in 2008. (Some organizations have this many people in their human resources department alone!) The organization has since increased staff size to support offline volunteer activism, primarily through MoveOn Councils discussed in a subsequent section. The organization's staff structure has often been misunderstood by researchers. Noriko Hara for instance, conducted volunteer and staff interviews in a study of MoveOn's 2004 "Leave No Voter Behind" campaign, but was able to gain access to only short-term staffers brought on for that particular campaign.[21] These "phantom staff" occupy a limited space in the organizational hierarchy. Whereas the 20–30 core staffers are in frequent, active communication with one another, the hundreds of additional task-specific campaign workers are given much more limited roles. Hara draws the conclusion that "within the organization, MoveOn appeared to struggle with yielding control to some paid staff."[22] In actuality, MoveOn actively involves their core staff in wide-ranging organizational decisions (one of the benefits of keeping its core staff so small). The larger group of task-specific staffers is accorded an equivalent lower level of decision input. The phantom staff is a key modification of Bimber's "post-bureaucratic" organizational form. Rather than employing a large staff and developing a bureaucratized departmental structure to manage their performance, the organization invests in a limited set of networked participants, hiring short-term organizers as needed.

The second key feature is the organizational policy against any established MoveOn offices. The organization eschews traditional overhead costs of office space, management staff, and paperwork support. There is a standing policy *forbidding* the creation of MoveOn field offices. Natalie Foster, who worked as

Deputy Field Network Director from 2006–2008, explains the philosophy as follows: "If there are no offices, there's no water cooler talk. Offices create satellite offices. MoveOn wants to keep the organization flat, with no hub offices and no organizers stuck on the periphery."[23] Rather than a human resources department, MoveOn has Chief Operating Officer Carrie Olson, who has worked with Blades and Boyd since their time in the software industry. Olson turns to outside vendors for larger tasks, further leveraging the "phantom staff" system. MoveOn's core staff communicate with each other throughout the day via Google Chat, e-mail, cell phone, and conference call. They physically work from home offices or coffeehouses, though, a policy that flattens intra-organizational communication while lowering the overhead costs necessary for sustaining the organization.[24]

The staff size and infrastructure policy enables MoveOn to operate as a "networked nonprofit" in ways that older organizations cannot.[25] When interviewing current and former core staffers, the common response to "what is your job title" was some variation on "job titles change a lot/I've played a lot of different roles." The frequent communication and regular in-person staff retreats foster a style of network-oriented participation that cannot occur in larger organizations. Following the logic of the "birthday paradox," arranging a meeting of 20–30 people is a much different undertaking than arranging a meeting of 200–300.[26] This contributes to the continuous tactical experimentation and innovation that we see from the organization. Staff teams can bridge multiple skill sets. Departmental hierarchies can remain fluid, allowing key individuals to be retasked to an emerging issue or political opportunity. Founded by technology entrepreneurs, MoveOn has borrowed from the "start-up" culture of the software industry, keeping the staff small *so that* the organization can remain nimble. That "nimbleness" infuses the membership, engagement, and fundraising practices of the organization as a whole.

MoveOn Membership

Membership in MoveOn is the singular most disruptive feature of the group's model. Much as the direct-mail pioneers redefined organizational membership from "participant" to "small donor," MoveOn redefines membership from "small donor" to "message recipient." The organization chose to decouple the member-donor linkage, counting all e-mail recipients as "members." As a result, many of the organization's members remain unaware that they merit such classification.[27] If you have never given money or taken political action with the organization, but you once forwarded a funny election video of theirs to a friend, is "member" the right term for your involvement with the group?

For MoveOn's purposes, unlike the purposes of the large political advocacy associations that predate it, the breadth of their "membership" is justifiable. For

MoveOn, there is virtually no downside to having an expansive list. Matt Bai makes this distinction in his book, *The Argument*, terming it "The Power of the List": "In a virtual world . . . few things [are] as valuable as a massive list—that is, a database of names and e-mail addresses that could be identified with a single need or interest, and thus could be mobilized with the push of a button."[28] The distinction here lies in the dramatic reduction in transaction costs online. When organizations communicate with their membership through the mail, a large, disorganized list consumes too many resources. This is because the savings through economies-of-scale are minimal: the postage on 1,000 pieces of mail is 10 times the postage on 100. Online, however, an e-mail to 100 consumes the same resources as an e-mail to 1,000 or 10,000.[29] When the marginal cost of communicating with an additional member is greater than 0, there is an incentive to cultivate narrower and more responsive lists. When the marginal cost of each membership communication approximates 0, there is an incentive to cultivate broader lists, regardless of responsiveness.

The infinitesimal marginal costs of e-mail give rise to the "culture of analytics" or "culture of testing" found in MoveOn and other netroots organizations. MoveOn is able to engage in elaborate forms of message testing on a day-to-day basis. The organization actively monitors data on "open rates" (how many recipients open the e-mail), "clickthroughs" (how many readers click on the "ask"), "action rates" (how many readers sign the requested petition, forward the message, donate, etc.), and "removal" (how many recipients ask to be removed from the list).[30] Test messages are sent out to subsets of MoveOn's list, often with varying issue frames and political "asks," in a methodology that approximates a randomized field experiment.[31] Only those messages that receive acceptably high open and clickthrough rates are distributed to MoveOn's entire list for action. Such practices, known as "A/B testing" originated with direct-mail fundraising but take on a different texture in the new medium.[32] Whereas testing a direct-mail package takes weeks to yield results and carries with it significant financial expenditures, testing an e-mail produces results within hours and incurs no incremental expense. Likewise, the low costs of information storage and retrieval allow MoveOn to parse their list in a variety of ways, identifying high-activity and low-activity members, as well as members who display or report interests in specific issue areas. If even the lowest-involvement "member" takes one action per year, MoveOn captures additional value from their membership redefinition. And if such members never take action, the costs to the organization nonetheless hover close to zero.

The change in membership regimes favors Internet-mediated "issue generalists" like MoveOn over single-issue organizations focused on environmental protection women's rights, civil rights, or other specific topics. Issue generalists can attract supporters interested in all of these topics, engaging in *headline chasing* when the subject is ripe for political action. In 2010, the organization worked on health care, climate change, women's rights, labor issues, tax policy, Wall Street reform, net neutrality, gay rights, and the midterm election.[33] They frequently partnered with single-issue legacy organizations on these actions. But while the legacy groups appealed to supporters only around their singular issue topic, regardless of the media agenda, MoveOn pivoted only when the issue was ripe for action. The practice of headline chasing is particularly well suited to changes in the news environment, matching the well-established newsroom trend toward more event-driven news.[34]

The organization also selects a handful of priority campaign issues each year, serving as a bulwark against the limitation of headline chasing. The downside of headline chasing is that it is a purely reactive activity. Those topics that receive active media attention are at the "top of the head" for message recipients, and thus receive greater clickthrough rates.[35] The danger is that an organization that bends with the political winds will have little capacity for setting the broader political agenda. In selecting priority campaigns, MoveOn seeks to take a more active role in setting the political agenda. As the following section describes, those MoveOn supporters who participate most actively in the organization are given some small franchise in setting the course of its activity through the priority campaign process.

MoveOn also launched a new initiative in 2011, SignOn.org, which allows members to create their own petitions. Though still in beta testing as this book goes to press, SignOn is designed like a "warehouse" site such as PetitionOnline and Change.org. Any supporter can craft their own e-petition through SignOn. org. MoveOn includes a disclaimer, taking no responsibility for the content of the petition. MoveOn monitors petition traffic to SignOn and selects popular topics to forward on to segments of its national membership.[36] It thus allows for a "trickle-up" mechanism, in which activists around a local or peripheral issue can demonstrate the popularity of the topic, increasing the issue's exposure in turn. Headline chasing may typify MoveOn's Internet-based membership, but it is not the sole feature.

MoveOn Engagement

What does membership actually mean within MoveOn? How does the organization engage supporters, and what does it ask its members to do? Four elements of MoveOn's membership engagement are particularly worthy of discussion. First is the set of activities in which the organization invites its membership to participate. Among the critics of "clicktivism," MoveOn often is invoked as an organization that sends out a near-constant stream of e-petitions.[37] As part of the Membership Communications Project (MCP), I analyzed six months' worth of action alerts from the organization, categorizing them by action type. The results reveal a far more varied tactical repertoire. Second is the process of *passive demo-cratic engagement* enabled by the pervasive presence of A/B testing. Such engage-ment is a major benefit of the activity-based membership regime, solely available to organizations that have embraced this new conception of group membership. Third is the prevailing philosophy of "Strong Vision, Big Ears" that leverages var-ious opportunities for *active* democratic input, albeit only under circumstances selected by the central staff. Fourth and finally, there is the MoveOn Council sys-tem—a limited version of the "neo-federated" organizational model that we will explore in detail in Chapter 4.

The "clicktivism" critique of MoveOn maintains that the organization engages its 5 million members through simple online e-petitions and other tactics that ask little of the membership and thus have little effect. Looking at the organization's actual e-mail trail leads to a very different perspective, however. From January through July 2010, I collected these e-mails through a dummy e-mail account as part of the MCP dataset. Seventy progressive organizations were included in the data analysis, based primarily on their inclusion in Erica Payne's *The Practical Pro-gressive*, a book that profiles a network of organizations supported by the Democ-racy Alliance donor community (see Chapter 5 for further discussion). It is important to note that, because of the A/B testing practices, the messages col-lected in the MCP *do not* constitute the entirety of MoveOn's membership e-mail. MoveOn tests its messages with random segments of its overall list. It also sends weekly member input surveys to random segments of the overall list and sends additional e-mails to MoveOn Council members. The data provides a member's-eye view of e-mail practices, providing a useful baseline for comparison, but it is not technically an exhaustive list.

MoveOn's e-mail practices display a mix of online and offline action requests. The organization sends, on average, between three and four e-mails per week. These messages include informational updates, funding requests, action alerts, event announcements, and requests for member input. Of the 99 messages received between January and July 2010, 77 featured a call to action. Figure 2.2 provides a breakdown of those action requests. While 18 of these action alerts were indeed e-petitions, an equal number were requests to attend a local event—usually a house party or a rally. MoveOn also asked its membership 14 times to e-mail or call Congress, and 16 times asked its membership to donate to a political candidate they were supporting in the Arkansas Democratic Senate primary. Twice it asked members to make Get-Out-the-Vote (GOTV) calls for that candi-date, and once it asked members to contact President Obama.

MoveOn's tactical repertoire also includes more-participatory forms of engagement. In 2004, for instance, it announced the user-generated "Bush in 30 Seconds" advertisement contest. MoveOn members submitted potential videos highlighting their opposition to Republican policies, voted among the submis-sions to select a winner, and then were invited to donate $25 to help put that video

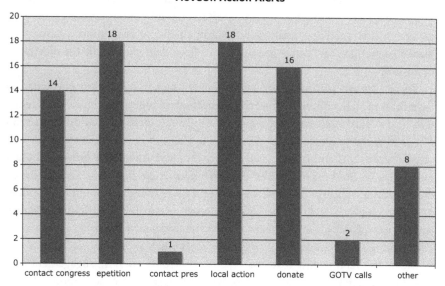

Figure 2.2 MoveOn Action Requests

on the air. This contest—the first of its kind—soon faced two problems, however: a "spatial voting" problem and a "merry prankster" problem.

The spatial voting problem is as follows: If issue ad submissions run the gamut from centrist to hard left, an online voting process should winnow to the median policy preference *of a MoveOn member.* As MoveOn members are, by definition, engaged partisans, this policy preference will be far to the left of the median American voter . . . the eventual audience of such commercials. Indeed, there is anecdotal evidence that this flaw creates practical issues, as with a 2008 campaign spot titled "Alex." The commercial featured a young mother with her baby, named Alex, asking John McCain, "When you say you would stay in Iraq for 100 years, were you counting on Alex? Because if you were, *you can't have him.*" Comedian Jon Stewart previewed the campaign ad on *The Daily Show,* and Stewart followed it with the punchline: "That ad of course brought to you by MoveOn.org, ten years of making even people who agree with you cringe."[38] The spatial voting problem is a variant on the *polarization through participation* issue referenced in Chapter 1.

The merry prankster problem will receive full attention in Chapter 6, but we see a preview of it in the Bush in 30 Seconds contest. Out of the thousands of videos submitted for consideration by MoveOn members, two of them labeled President Bush a war criminal and drew unfortunate comparisons to Adolf Hitler. MoveOn did not select this video or endorse the message, as its voting membership did not support either video. Nonetheless, conservative activists seized upon these ads as proof of the organization's radicalism. Seven years later, prominent conservatives continue to (falsely) claim that MoveOn *produced* an advertisement comparing President Bush to Hitler.[39] MoveOn took greater care in vetting its 2008 "Obama in 30 seconds" user-generated content contest and has otherwise eschewed such tactics, a recognition that open-source or commons-based production practices can carry serious risks when deployed against a motivated opposition.

There are several MoveOn engagement activities that offer less participation than Bush in 30 Seconds but more than the standard e-petition. These include the web-based "call for change" program, which enables members to host and attend Get-Out-the-Vote house parties by allowing them to download a voter list in a target state and then use their cell phones at a local member's house to hold a no-cost phone banking event. The "Bake Back America" bake sale is another such online/offline venture. In 2004, it involved 14,000 members holding a national bake sale, raising $750,000. The organization also coordinates nationwide "house parties," planned around campaign-related videos (such as Michael Moore's *Sicko* and Al Gore's *An Inconvenient Truth*) and events (such as presidential debates).

MoveOn's A/B testing fosters a type of passive democratic engagement that represents a major advance over the tools used by legacy advocacy groups. Driven by a variety of "analytics" tools, MoveOn and similar Internet-mediated issue generalists simply *know more* about their online supporters than previous organizations could ever hope to. The Sierra Club, by contrast, has historically hired a survey research firm to conduct a biennial membership survey. Surveying a direct-mail-based membership is costly and slow. Surveying an e-mail-based membership can be incorporated into the daily workflow of an organization.

The transition toward a "culture of testing" has illustrative parallels in the news industry. In his landmark newsroom study, Herbert Gans (1979) noted his surprise "that [journalists] had little knowledge about the actual audience and rejected feedback from it. Although they had a vague image of the audience, they paid little attention to it; instead, they filmed and wrote for their superiors and themselves ..."[40] Recent research from Joseph Turow, Pablo Boczkowski, Philip Napoli, and C.W. Anderson examines how changes in the "industrial construction of audiences" have affected newsrooms.[41] Anderson describes how the introduction of web metrics (the number of clicks and comments per story) facilitates "management strategies that emphasized the widespread diffusion of audience metrics."[42] At one online news site, Anderson finds, "It is not an exaggeration to say that website traffic often appeared to be the *primary ingredient* in news judgment."[43] The introduction of tools that provide a rough quantitative measure of audience interest can dramatically change work routines for a news organization. Once a measure of audience feedback has been constructed, it takes on meaning within the newsroom.

Consider the parallel among advocacy groups: for Skocpol's traditional federated membership organizations, member input moved slowly up the organizational hierarchy, generally taking the form of an annual convention where local delegates could weigh in on important organizational matters. For the issue-based, professional organizations that replaced the federated civic associations, member input was even more limited, occurring through infrequent membership surveys and annual reports, if at all. (As Bimber notes, this one-way, national-scale communication was the hallmark of the broadcast information regime.) Membership surveys among these professional organizations frequently arrived as thinly disguised fundraising appeals, meant to increase supporter response rates through a veneer of grassroots participation.

MoveOn, by contrast, is capable of measuring, nearly in real-time, which issue topics, message frames, and action requests are of greatest interest to their online membership. A/B testing, in this sense, serves not only to optimize the efficiency of their action requests but also to keep them abreast of member interest. This is a particularly important point to consider in light of some of the group's more controversial tactics. MoveOn received a formal Congressional rebuke and outraged national headlines after it ran a 2007 full-page advertisement in the *New York Times* referring to General David Petraeus as "General Betray-Us." As one staffer noted to me, this tactic was overwhelmingly popular with their membership. Not only had thousands of individual small donors "chipped in" for that specific ad; the comparative open and clickthrough rates revealed that this action was more popular than more moderate frames. The supposedly radical action gave voice to the preferences of a massive, participatory membership.

Awareness of these activist preferences is a mixed blessing of sorts. It is a boon to fundraising and engagement practices—MoveOn does not need to guess whether a message frame or action request is too strident for its membership; it can run a test. But, having already attracted a polarized segment of the broader populace, it then selects tactics that appeal to the engaged minority. Much as A/B testing at *The Huffington Post* yields strident headlines even when little controversy is present,[44] A/B testing within advocacy organizations moves them further away from the passive and moderate median American voter. In the tradeoff between political participation and public deliberation, MoveOn's engagement repertoire is weighted toward improving participation.

Legacy organizations claim to speak for hundreds of thousands of "armchair activists" who support their day-to-day strategic choices through a small annual donation. By contrast, MoveOn and similar netroots groups are constantly aware of the *revealed* preferences of their activity-based, online membership. And, importantly, such results can be obtained only if an organization embraces MoveOn's definition of membership. Legacy political associations have also developed large e-mail lists, but they maintain a distinction between e-mail "supporters" and dues-paying "members." While doing so offers them some of the benefits of the new communications environment, it raises the technical challenge that these constitute two non-overlapping sets of stakeholders.[45]

MoveOn also employs a range of active democratic engagement tools. Research and Development Director Daniel Mintz describes the organization's guiding philosophy as "Strong Vision, Big Ears,"[46] and this is evidenced in three forms of member input. MoveOn sends out a weekly membership survey to a random segment of its list (screenshot in Figure 2.3). Through this active form of input, they moderate the dangers of "headline chasing" by seeking clear indications of what the organization's positive priorities ought to be. Former staffer Matt Ewing noted that input from these surveys guided the organization's decision to endorse Barack Obama on February 1, 2008—before the "Super Tuesday" primaries, when Hillary Clinton still appeared to be a strong frontrunner for the nomination. For weeks, MoveOn had monitored member interest through the weekly surveys. After John Edwards suspended his campaign, member interest in a MoveOn endorsement rose dramatically. Ewing described it as a "very scary moment" when the organization sent out a membership-wide vote, yielding 70% support for Obama over Clinton. Figure 2.4 provides the text of the organization's endorsement announcement.

In a similar vein, since the Democratic Party retook the Congressional majority in 2007, MoveOn has held a biennial voting process to establish its major priority campaigns. The multi-stage process includes online submissions of suggested priorities, local deliberation at house party events, and worldwide Internet-based voting on priority issues.[47] Membership votes serve to minimize the downsides of headline chasing. They provide digital members with greater ownership of MoveOn's campaign efforts, while also attracting media attention by signaling the results of a membership vote.

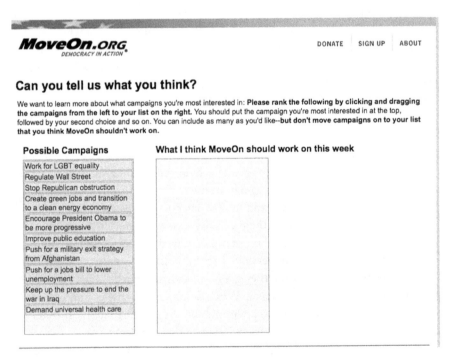

Figure 2.3 Screenshot of MoveOn Weekly Member Survey

---------- Forwarded message ----------
From: **Eli Pariser, MoveOn.org Political Action** <moveon-help@list.moveon.org>
Date: Fri, Feb 1, 2008 at 12:10 PM
Subject: [Bounce] (3,074,336; IDab8b16; 12015) MoveOn Members Endorse Obama
To: Johnny Neumann <john.von.neumann@example.com>

Dear MoveOn member,

With hundreds of thousands of ballots cast across the country, for the first time in MoveOn's history, we've voted together to endorse a presidential candidate in the primary. **That candidate is Barack Obama.**

Something big is clearly happening. A few weeks ago, MoveOn members we surveyed were split. But with John Edwards bowing out, progressives are coming together. Obama won over 70% of the vote yesterday, and he's moving up in polls nationwide.[1] As comments poured in from MoveOn members across the country, the sense of hope was inspiring. Here's how Christine Y. in New Jersey put it:

> "I've never felt so strongly about any one candidate in my entire life. He's truly an inspiration to all of us—especially the younger generation. I will stand by him 100% for as long as he's willing to stand up and fight for this country!"

MoveOn members voted to endorse Barack Obama.

By volunteering these next four days before "Super Tuesday" we can help elect a progressive president for the next four years. **Can you volunteer to help Obama win?**

I want to help.

Volunteer today!

Vote results

Obama:	197,444	70.4%
Clinton:	83,084	29.6%

What does MoveOn's endorsement mean? People-power. Together, we are 3.2 million Americans who care about our country and want change. Half of us live in states with primaries or caucuses this coming "Super Tuesday."

Figure 2.4 MoveOn's 2008 Presidential Endorsement E-mail

MoveOn's redefinition of the membership concept alleviates controversies over membership enfranchisement. A serious threat for an issue-based or identity-based membership organization is that online voting could be swamped by supporters of a candidate who has no other stake in the organization's work—another iteration of the merry prankster problem discussed in Chapter 6. The Sierra Club, for instance, has a 133-page manual devoted to the particularities of its local, state, and national endorsement process. The manual is designed specifically to prevent such attempted takeovers by "outsiders." For MoveOn, though, there is no such thing as an outsider; there is just a large swath of people who have *yet to sign up*. If supporters of a fringe candidate want to mobilize to join MoveOn and vote in favor of his or her issue positions, that just increases the size and power of MoveOn's list! Such supporters, assuming they share MoveOn's general values, can become the most active MoveOn volunteers—local campaign partisans are among the most likely to remain politically active once the campaign has ended.[48]

In theory at least, this provides an opening for conservatives to join the organization en masse in order to distort its election results and priorities. Three barriers render such a takeover unlikely. First, the sheer scale of the organization, with 5 million members, means that a conservative takeover would have to be truly breathtaking in scale. Conservative groups have yet to assemble 5 million online members for *any* joint effort. Second, such a large-scale mobilization could not happen quietly, meaning that progressives could just as easily counter-mobilize to balance out the attack. Third (and, from a structural perspective, most importantly), MoveOn's central staff decides which questions will be posed to the membership. MoveOn is participatory and democratic *in practice*, but this participation is based in philosophy rather than bylaws. In the case of a massive, malicious strategic voting effort, the staff could just stop asking the membership for their opinions.[49]

A final element of MoveOn's participatory framework is their system of roughly 200 MoveOn Councils. These Councils consist of a minimum of four active members in a given locality. The members receive increased attention and authority, and are charged with planning local actions and fostering a sense of local identity. In operation since 2004, the Council structure has been a relatively minor part of the MoveOn system, an indicator of the organization's status as a primarily e-mail-based political association. In the aftermath of Barack Obama's presidential victory, MoveOn increased staff support to the Council system, hiring 11 new field organizers to increase offline volunteer capacity. The existence of the Council system provides a cautionary note when trying to affix a single model type to any Internet-mediated organization. Just as Democracy for America is best known for its neo-federated system of strong local groups but also engages in MoveOn-style nationwide e-mail initiatives, MoveOn primarily speaks with a single voice to its national e-mail list but also includes some locally federated elements. For theoretical clarity, the role of such online-to-offline engagement tools will be relegated to Chapter 4, but it bears repeating at this point that MoveOn does not eschew such practices.

MoveOn Fundraising

There are three distinguishing features of a MoveOn fundraising appeal: *medium*, *audience breadth*, and *issue salience*. The first two have already been discussed to a certain extent: (1) MoveOn fundraising occurs via e-mail, a "push" medium that scales up near-costlessly from 500 recipients to 5 million recipients. The incremental cost of including an additional e-mail approaches zero, with the only limitation being server capacity. This allows the organization to operate as (2) an "issue generalist," reaching the broadest possible audience rather than confining itself to those members with a high propensity to give. The third feature is particularly important, however: because of their large member base and issue-generalist stance, MoveOn is capable of targeting their fundraising appeals to whatever issue dominates the current media cycle. Many controversies erupt briefly in national politics and occupy media and public attention for a single news cycle. The speed of the Internet as a medium allows groups like MoveOn to fundraise and organize public pressure around these short-run controversies. Bureaucratically organized, single-issue interest groups built for the older communications environment lack the staff structure and fundraising capacity to engage around such an issue, instead remaining focused within their issue niche. But for the duration of that short window, fundraising around the topic is particularly successful because the issue is at the "top of the head" among the politically aware masses.[50] The tremendous difference between MoveOn's online fundraising and the online fundraising of the earlier generation of political associations lies in these distinctions of audience breadth and issue salience.

Consider the following fundraising e-mails, the first from SaveOurEnvironment.org, the second from MoveOn, both of which were sent out a few days prior to December 31, 2008:

> *"We have less than 48 hours to reach our goal of raising $10,000 by 11:59PM on December 31—and we're not there yet . . .*
>
> *There are lots of reasons why you should give to* SaveOurEnvironment. org *right now:*
>
> *First, because we're counting on you. [. . .]*
>
> *Second, because the year is coming to a close. [. . .]*
>
> *And third, because there is no time like the present. The time for excuses is over: America needs strong environmental policies that support a sustainable green economy today. Help us make it happen."*

SaveOurEnvironment has, in essence, moved their traditional direct-mail-based fundraising operation online. They thus take advantage of the reduced costs of the medium, but they reach a much smaller audience than MoveOn, and their appeal lacks clear issue salience, suggesting that members should give "because there is no time like the present." Compare this to MoveOn's appeal:

> *"Dear MoveOn member, You've probably heard about how Wall Street financier Bernard Madoff scammed investors out of at least $50 billion. But you may not have heard that his victims included the foundations that support some really important progressive organizations. Groups that fight for human rights, fair elections and racial justice are getting hit hard—just in time for the holidays. We've worked side-by-side with many of them.*
>
> *If these groups can't replace the funding that came from investment accounts that Madoff stole, they may be forced to start cutting important projects or, in some cases, even lay off staff. Can you pitch in $25 or $50 for each of the four organizations we're highlighting below? Our friends at Atlantic Philanthropies*

and the Open Society Institute will each match every dollar that comes in until January 1! So, for the next three days, your donation of $25 or $50 means $75 or $150 for groups affected by Madoff. If a few thousand of us give together, it can make an enormous difference—and help repair some of the damage Madoff has done. Click here to contribute."

MoveOn then goes on to note that the year-end contribution will be 100% tax-deductible and provides a brief description of the four organizations they are supporting. The "MoveOn Effect" in fundraising regimes can be understood thusly: While direct-mail fundraising uses relatively *generic* issue appeals to solicit small *general funding* donations, MoveOn uses *targeted* e-mail fundraising to make *timely* appeals related to a *specific* fundraising purpose. MoveOn frequently will send out a newly produced television commercial, asking their members to view the commercial and then "chip in a few dollars" to help put it on the air.

The specificity of MoveOn-style targeted funding requests comes at a cost, however: legally, organizations must obey "donor intent" in their expenditures. Most of MoveOn's fundraising appeals ask for a highly targeted form of support—$25 to put a campaign commercial on the air or place a field organizer in a critical state. Targeted appeals have always had a higher rate of success, and they are routinely used by large nonprofits when approaching major donors and foundations. Anyone familiar with university administration is familiar with the challenge this presents: donors would prefer to give money toward a particular, tangible project than toward the general fund. Many nonprofits divide their fundraising efforts accordingly, with direct mail based in a "Development" office and major gifts coordinated through an "Advancement" office. Direct-mail fundraising offers the longstanding benefit that the money is unrestricted—direct-mail dollars are general fund dollars, so to speak. They can be used to pay for human resources departments, staff trainings, and physical infrastructure, whereas organizations are legally prevented from applying too large a percentage of targeted, project-specific funds to these overhead costs. For MoveOn, with its "phantom staff" and "radical decentralization" of office space, restricted online donations present little problem. But for legacy organizations forged under earlier membership and fundraising regimes, all fundraising dollars are hardly created equal. Thus, the disruptive pattern emerges.

The MoveOn Effect: Generational Displacement and Interest Group Reformation

In 2011, the Monitor Institute produced a study titled "Disruption: Evolving Models of Engagement and Support." With the backing of the Packard, Knight, and Robert Wood Johnson Foundations, Monitor Institute staff were able to conduct comprehensive interviews with membership-based advocacy group staffers.

Foundation funders wanted to know how the Internet was affecting legacy organizations, and the organizations complied. The report reveals trends that have been quietly acknowledged among advocacy professionals for years: direct mail is dying. A core revenue stream for organizations built in the past 40 years, it has now entered a steep decline. Like their analogues in the news industry, none of the longstanding organizations know quite what to do about this dilemma. Despite pedigree, reputation, and continued mass support, leading organizations face a disrupted organizational field and serious funding questions.

Two quotations from the report are particularly illuminating, colorfully illustrating trends that I witnessed during off-the-record interview sessions.[51] The first regards the state of direct mail. The second offers a comparison with online fundraising:

(1) "Over the last 15 years our direct mail fundraising has been an attempt to do more faster in order to hold on to what we have. Postage and production costs have gone up. We're like raccoons on a wheel at the zoo—going as fast as we can and not getting anywhere. Direct mail had a growth decade in the 80s. In the 90s it continued to grow but at a slower pace and, ever since 2000 it's been going downhill. But we don't yet have a proven model to replace it."[52]

(2) "We're holding on to one trapeze bar while grabbing for the next. The formula for Direct Mail membership is tried and true. It's proven. But the pitiful thing about the formula is that the percentage is so low. Money from Internet fundraising is potentially bigger and cheaper, but no one has figured out the formula and none of us is yet willing to give up what we know for what we think might work."[53]

The first quote depicts the state of direct mail. Improvements in data management and targeting have only served to slow the decline of direct-mail fundraising. A core revenue stream for longstanding membership-based interest groups is disappearing. The second quote highlights the danger that legacy organizations face. Having built stable, successful direct-mail fundraising programs, there is a strong rationale for legacy organizations to maintain them. They remain rooted in older membership and fundraising regimes, recognizing the potential of online fundraising but sensibly holding to their tried and true model. Another Monitor interviewee noted candidly that "Membership as we know it is a myth of the past." We have seen throughout this chapter that MoveOn's membership and funding models offer several opportunities for a new organization. The transition to these models is not a smooth one for legacy organizations, though. Much like the newspaper industry, whose disruptive crisis has been extensively documented, legacy groups cannot simply abandon their core capacities, but they no longer have a clear picture of how to pay for them.[54]

The newspaper industry has coined a fitting term: "analog dollars to digital dimes."[55] There is money to be made in online advertising. New online news ventures such as the *Huffington Post* and *Talking Points Memo* produce high-quality journalism, paid for through this revenue stream. But the money found online is far less, and much less reliable, than the money found in traditional revenue streams. The classified advertising market has collapsed, due not to political blogs but to competition from *CraigsList.*[56]

Competition for commercial advertisements has driven prices down. Additional data on advertising effectiveness has as well. Consider the classic advertising quote, "Half the money I spend on advertising is wasted; the trouble is I don't know which half." Traditional newspaper and television advertisements benefited from being in a data-poor environment. Advertisers had little way of knowing whether readers were skipping past their two-page spread in *The New York Times* or not. For the newspapers, that was a *beneficial inefficiency.* The lack of information on advertising effectiveness, combined with scarce advertising space, inflated prices. Digital advertising, by contrast, is data-rich. Advertisers can measure impressions and clickthroughs. They can target their advertisements toward niche markets and populations. These greater efficiencies drive advertising prices downward. Legacy media organizations then have trouble paying for their existing overhead and infrastructure.[57]

For legacy advocacy groups, the MoveOn Effect traces a parallel arc. Historically, these organizations are grounded in the 1970s-era shift "from membership to management." That generation shift was itself premised upon the emergence of novel funding mechanisms. Simply put, before there could be a large cadre of professionally managed public interest groups in DC, there had to be some way for these organizations to pay their bills. Direct mail was not the only such mechanism, but it was an important one. Jeffrey Berry has noted the role of foundations, particularly the Ford Foundation, in providing "seed money" for groups such as the Environmental Defense Fund and the Natural Resource Defense Council.[58] "Seed money" is an important turn of phrase: foundations provide only 7.3% of philanthropic contributions in America.[59] Left-wing foundations in particular have a well-known habit of providing only short-term help, offering grants to fledgling organizations to get them on their feet but expecting organizations to develop their own external funding capacity within a few years. The emergence of prospect direct mail (PDM) as a fundraising model was a primary enabling condition—necessary, though not sufficient—to the 1970s generational displacement among interest groups. It is called "prospecting" for a reason—a closer look at the functions of direct-mail fundraising reveals that it bears much in common with gold rush prospectors spending their days panning for gold by a riverside.

Kim Klein is the author of *Fundraising for Social Change*, the leading nonprofit fundraising text (now in its fifth edition). Klein details the mechanics of creating a healthy direct-mail program through a sample balance sheet, reproduced below:

Acquisition and Renewal through Direct Mail: One Organization's Results (from Klein 1994)

Income

Acquisition mailings

5 mailings of 2,000 pieces each; 1% response @ $25 = $2,500

(100 donors acquired from these mailings)

Three more mailings to those who gave asking for extra gifts

10% response from 100 donors at various amounts = $750

(30 extra gifts from the 100 acquired donors)

One renewal mailing to these 100 donors; 66% at $25 = $1,650

Total Income = $4,900

Expenses

Acquisition mailings (renting or exchanging lists, printing postage, etc.)

10,000 pieces at .35 = $3,500

Three more mailings to 100 donors

$3 \times 100 \times .40 = 120

Renewal mailings (one to everyone and a second to those who do not respond to the first)

150 letters total $\times .40 = 60

Total Expenses = $3,680

Net Gain, 66 donors, $1,670

Note that the initial fundraising appeal (costing $3,500 but raising only $2,500) comes at a net *cost* of $1,000 to the organization, and that is assuming a 1% rate of return. Klein summarizes, "The vast majority of fundraising time is spent getting people to give once and then getting them to give again."[60] Her point is that the initial mailing is meant to *prospect* for donors—individuals with a high propensity to give—so that future mailings, sent to this smaller pool, can provide a net profit and sustainable revenue stream. As Joseph Turow indicates in *Niche Envy,* "the technology that led direct marketers to revolutionize their industry was the computer . . . The computer made it easy to store, combine, and cross-tabulate many different lists. Large direct-marketing firms began to keep names, addresses, and other information on computers in the 1960s."[61]

The difference between a profitable direct-mail program and an unprofitable one is calculated through two factors: cost per member acquired and average life-time giving rate.[62] Without high-quality prospecting lists, the cost per member acquired [(acquisition mailing expenses – average initial gift)/total new donors] rises to an unaffordable rate. Chris Bosso, author of *Environment, Inc.,* notes that PDM is a "loss leader, the cost of building a base of regular contributors who in time may be convinced to go higher on the 'pyramid of support'—where the real money is."[63] This pyramid of support is central to the second factor calculated by fundraising professionals: average lifetime giving rate. Notice that this metric can be calculated only retrospectively. A longstanding organization can look back on their fundraising efforts and calculate how long and how much the average member contributed. But it is forced to assume that a member acquired in 2012 will have the same average lifetime giving rate as a member acquired in 2010. So long as this average exceeds the costs per member acquired, PDM offers a source of unrestricted organizational funding.

There is a threshold, reached when the average lifetime giving rate is too low or the cost per member acquired is too high, where PDM takes on a "shell game" quality. The initial expenditures on building a member list fail to return net revenues in the longer term. The organization keeps gaining members but finds itself in ever-worsening financial straits. Conservative direct-mail pioneer Richard Viguerie, for instance, specialized in the 1980s and early 1990s in setting up conservative public interest organizations through direct-mail operations. From 1992 through 1995, Viguerie set up *three* conservative senior organizations to combat the American Association of Retired Persons—the Seniors Coalition, the United Seniors Association, and 60/Plus. Created in quick succession, each organization prospected *from the previous Viguerie-founded organization's mailing list*. This resulted in large overlapping memberships and eventually exhausted the response rate and average lifetime gift, leaving each organization in debt despite their large member rolls (while Viguerie himself made millions in consulting fees, leading Jeffrey Berry to artfully describe him as a "one man tragedy of the commons").[64]

REACTIONS AMONG LEGACY ORGANIZATIONS

The Internet has rendered two major changes to direct-mail fundraising. The first, reflected in the initial Monitor Institute quote, is the introduction of *better databases*. Joseph Turow and Philip Howard have each covered aspects of the burgeoning "microtargeting" industry.[65] Whereas advocacy groups have historically bought and sold lists from one another in order to boost the return rate on those initial prospecting mailings (thus leading to the background noise/junk mail problem discussed in Chapter 7), a new set of vendors traffic in sophisticated consumer profiling that offers substantial increases in return rate. Microtargeting offers marginal improvements in direct-mail efficiency, lowering the cost per member acquired.

But better databases can take you only so far when faced with the broader behavioral trend. Direct-mail fundraising as a whole has "fallen off a cliff."[66] Cost per member acquired is rising steeply for nonprofits as supporters turn toward online bill payment. A 2008 study by Target Analysis Group, which aggregates data on nonprofit fundraising, indicates that donation by mail has entered a demonstrable decline, replaced by Internet-based giving.[67] Another study by the same group made note of a sharp demographic split between donors aged 65 and older, who still give through the mail, and donors younger than 65, who primarily give online.[68] One prominent progressive nonprofit noted that its cost per member acquired, which had sunk to a historic low of $7/member in 2000 in response to the Bush threat, had trended up to $21/member after September 11th and then steadily risen to over $40/member in the summer of 2008.[69]

Fundraising professionals have responded by moving their direct-mail appeals online, taking advantage of the lowered marginal costs of the new medium. This results in the gap in fundraising e-mails witnessed in the previous section. The problem is that, in direct competition with the MoveOn-style targeted appeals, such generic requests for annual donations are less successful. Legacy organizations are facing an "analog dollars to digital dimes" problem. They cannot raise enough money online to make up for the extensive overhead costs developed during the direct-mail era. As another Monitor interviewee put it, "E-mail doesn't actually give you better yield—at least not yet, but it is less expensive. And no one yet knows what to replace direct mail with."[70]

Complicating matters further, the most successful funding requests are tied to the day's headline news. But headline-chasing funding requests are restricted in nature: an organization that raises money promising to put a commercial on the air but uses it to pay the human resources department places itself in a legally risky position. Legacy groups have instead chosen to place traditional, generic requests for financial support into their online funding appeals. The yield of such requests is lower, but the money can go into the organization's general fund.

This MCP e-mail dataset offers a stark picture of how wide the gap is between netroots fundraising appeals and legacy group fundraising appeals. As an empirical test, I conducted a content analysis of all fundraising e-mails in the dataset.[71] Among the 70 organizations in the study, 350 fundraising e-mails were sent to my dummy e-mail account over the first six months of 2010. Those fundraisers fell into three categories: general funding requests (similar to the SaveOurEnvironment example), targeted fundraising requests (similar to the MoveOn example), and pass-through fundraising requests. "Pass-through" fundraising was first developed by EMILY's List in 1985 and consists of an organization fundraising directly on behalf of a candidate for office. None of this money enters the organization's coffers, but by acting as a "bundler" the group is able to strengthen its relationship with the candidate.[72] Pass-through fundraising during the first half of 2010 was mostly directed at candidates in Democratic primary elections.

Out of the 350 fundraising e-mails, 214 were general funding requests, 56 were targeted funding requests, and 80 were pass-through funding requests. As a test of generational effects, I then divided the organizational population according to the year of their founding. Organizations founded after 1996 were responsible for 185 fundraising messages, while organizations founded before 1993 were responsible for 165 fundraising messages.[73] The results are displayed graphically in Figure 2.5. While all organizations used e-mail to at least occasionally fundraise unrestricted, general donations, the targeted and pass-through fundraising came almost *entirely* from the netroots generation of organizations.[74]

Empirically, we can safely conclude that prominent legacy advocacy groups simply do not engage in the type of targeted fundraising pioneered by MoveOn. The reasoning for this becomes clear when we observe the offices and staff systems of these longstanding groups: "headline chasing" is ill-suited to large, hierarchically structured organizations with high, fixed overhead costs. The new Internet-mediated issue generalists are free to engage in such fundraising because they lack the infrastructure that professionalized political associations developed after the 1970s-era generation shift.

Thus, we arrive at the disruptive implications of the MoveOn Effect. Newly formed advocacy groups adopt variations on the membership and fundraising practices pioneered by MoveOn. Legacy organizations face declining membership rates and an "analog dollars to digital dimes" problem. From an interest group ecology standpoint, this changes the "energy" (or types of available funding) in the system, forcing changes in organizational niches and the emergence of newly dominant organization types.

Not all legacy organizations are equally threatened by these changes in membership and fundraising regimes. As Figure 2.1 indicated, prospect direct mail comprises one of three major funding sources for nonprofit advocacy groups. As Debra Minkoff and her colleagues have documented, the DC advocacy community

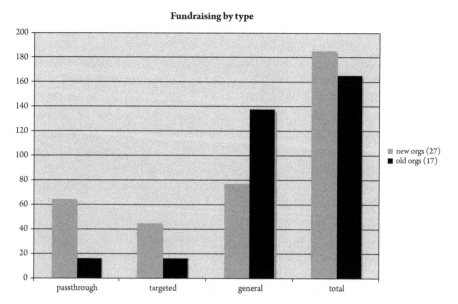

Figure 2.5 Fundraising Appeals, Pooled by Generation

was not composed of a single hegemonic organization type to begin with.[75] Variation in organization type will play a major role in determining how the MoveOn
Effect changes each individual political association. Some associations rely disproportionately on a small number of major donors, catering program development to the whims and interests of those few individuals, while others have
developed longstanding corporate, foundation, or governmental ties. The formation of the Democracy Alliance in 2005, a collaborative effort among left-wing
major donors to coordinate their giving and invest in new progressive infrastructure, produces similar tremors for large donor-reliant organizations (see Chapter 5 for further discussion), as do foundation-driven studies like the Monitor
Institute report.

Unions are a particular exception, having never relied on armchair activists
and direct-mail fundraising. While unions face their own distinct set of pressures in the early 21st century, these pressures are simply not attributable to the
MoveOn Effect. But for a wide variety of legacy nonprofit political associations,
the change in membership and fundraising regimes carries a menacing undertone. MoveOn and the other Internet-mediated issue generalists do not directly
threaten the work of legacy groups—indeed, they frequently collaborate in
their campaign efforts—but the membership and fundraising practices MoveOn
pioneered leave legacy advocacy groups in a similar position to the cross-class
membership federations of a previous era. Advances in information and
communication technology have altered membership and fundraising regimes,
and that tends to produce a generational moment at the organizational layer of
the public sphere.

For advocacy groups with high overhead costs, the general funds that used to
come from small-donor "members" are growing scarce. Advances in direct-mail
databases cannot outpace the change in how supporters give money and con-
ceive of organizational membership. As a result, those groups are forced to either
heavily downsize, cutting core staff and programs, or else become over-reliant
on alternate funding streams, putting themselves at risk. The American Civil
Liberties Union, for instance, faced an organizational crisis in December 2009
when their largest single donor announced that he would be withdrawing his
annual gift (due to stock market losses).[76] That donor was responsible for 25% of
the organization's annual budget, placing the longstanding interest group in a
financial panic. The loss of the single major donor is not caused by changes in
membership and fundraising regimes. The *over-reliance* on him is. Direct mail
was a stable, reliable, and growing funding stream throughout the 1980s and
1990s. Its decline has forced legacy organizations to search for other revenue
streams or massively cut overhead costs, placing them in an increasingly precarious position. A period of organizational crises, mass layoffs, and the eventual
collapse of at least a few longstanding advocacy groups is a likely implication of
the MoveOn Effect.[77]

VARIATIONS ON A THEME: INTERNET-MEDIATED ISSUE SPECIALISTS

Many of the newer organizations included in the Membership Communications Project differ from MoveOn and the PCCC in the area of issue generality. Groups like 350.org and 1Sky (climate), Color of Change (civil rights), Change Congress (campaign finance), and the Courage Campaign (LGBTQ issues) all focus on a single issue area. These groups still engage in a limited form of "headline chasing," tying their fundraising and action appeals to events in the news, but they send fewer mobilization messages to their member list than their issue generalist peers. They also have small, networked staff structures and limited office space. The niche specialists have adapted to the new membership and fundraising regimes—defining all e-mail recipients as members and frequently sending out targeted fundraising requests—but they have carved out specific issue niches rather than engaging in the type of "issue grazing" for which Internet-mediated generalists are occasionally criticized.

In terms of the ecology of the broader advocacy system, we should expect issue specialists to be more numerous than issue generalists, but we should expect the generalists to have larger member lists, fundraising capacity, and reputational cache than the issue specialists. The MoveOn Effect does not make all organizations into issue generalists, but it does yield additional incentives for chasing headlines that were not present in the previous information environment.

Conclusion

This chapter has highlighted three central themes. First is the historical pattern that predates the current generation of "netroots" political associations. Drawing deeply from the well of previous scholarship provides a theoretical lens for understanding the broader importance of new groups like MoveOn.org and the PCCC. Second is an evaluation of MoveOn's organizational model, including staff structure, membership philosophy, engagement practices, and fundraising strategy. Borrowing from Silicon Valley tech startups rather than standard interest group practices, MoveOn's growth has been characterized by innovative policies and practices, including headline chasing, phantom staff, radical decentralization, and passive democratic engagement. Far from sending out a constant stream of e-petitions, MoveOn seeks to engage its membership in a variety of participatory activities, both online and off. Third and finally is a full enunciation of the MoveOn Effect. Through a detailed analysis of nonprofit fundraising techniques and through content analysis of e-mail fundraising appeals, the chapter has demonstrated why the rise of "postbureaucratic" organizations is unlikely to be a smooth transition for well-known, longstanding political associations. Rather, the Internet's effect on these advocacy groups provides both the promise of new tools for engagement and the threat of radical changes to stable revenue streams.

If the entire netroots generation of advocacy groups looked and functioned like MoveOn, then the story could perhaps conclude here. All that would be left would be questions of what MoveOn-style membership and fundraising implies for American political engagement writ large. Is the transition to activity-based membership a good thing or a bad thing? What sorts of organizational functions are lost in the midst of these disappearing beneficial inefficiencies? But the Internet's effect on the organizational layer of American politics is more varied than that. New advocacy groups do not solely engage their members through nationwide e-mail campaigns. They also gather people in online participatory communities through large community blogs like DailyKos and FireDogLake. Groups like Democracy for America and Organizing for America have placed a greater emphasis on providing "online tools for offline action," attempting a near-rebirth of the federated civic associations of generations past, but with a decidedly 21st century sensibility. And there remains the puzzling partisan cast of these organizations, arising first on the American left, and only later (and with great struggle) on the American right. A full accounting of the Internet's multiple impacts on American political associations thus demands that we turn our sights beyond the Internet-mediated issue generalists, focusing instead on the networked online community that gathers annually, in person, under a banner that reads "Netroots Nation."

3

Political Blogs as Political Associations

"The most effective activism is a function of its times and is directly
related to the condition of the contemporary media."
—Markos Moulitsas, *Taking on the System*[1]

It's mid-July 2010 and over 2,000 progressive political activists are packed into the convention hall of the Rio hotel in Las Vegas, NV. The temperature outside is north of 100 degrees, but no one is particularly interested in stepping outdoors. Senate Majority Leader Harry Reid has just taken the stage, providing a lunchtime keynote address, to be followed by a moderated question-and-answer session. Reid begins with a wry aside to the assembled audience. "I'm told that I get on your nerves. And I'm here to tell you that you, at times, get on my nerves." The audience laughs in appreciation, while hundreds of fingers flash in unison across smartphone and laptop keypads, sending the witticism out over Twitter. C-SPAN cameras capture the exchange, along with several other segments of the convention, providing fodder for broadcast and online media pundits in the following week. It's the fifth annual Netroots Nation convention, and the attendees constitute an increasingly important, but often misunderstood, constituency within the Democratic Party network.

Across town, a parallel "Right Online" convention is under way, featuring half the attendees, fewer high-profile speakers, and far less media attention.[2] The progressive netroots poke occasional fun at this geographic mimicry; no one knows why, but conservative bloggers have chosen every year to trail the progressive netroots, setting up their own convention in the same city, on the same weekend. The obvious numeric comparisons, based upon conference size and speaker prominence, are never favorable to the conservatives.[3] This year in particular, they serve to emphasize that, even at the height of conservative fervor for the Internet-mediated "Tea Party" movement, the political left still holds a sizeable advantage in the blogosphere.

Reid joins over a dozen Democratic Party officials to grace the stage that weekend—House Speaker Nancy Pelosi also provides a keynote address, as do Senator Al Franken and Montana Governor Brian Schweitzer. President Barack

Obama offers a four-minute video message, an unscheduled drop-in for the attendees. The convention organizers select formats designed to push their speakers beyond simple platitudes and stump speeches. To begin the Q&A session, moderator Joan "mcjoan" McCarter—the Senior Policy Editor at DailyKos.com—hands Lt. Dan Choi's West Point ring and discharge papers to the Senate Majority Leader. Choi had been dismissed from the Army under its "Don't Ask, Don't Tell" policy—a policy that President Obama had promised to repeal. The legislation to do so was stalled at the time in Reid's Senate. McCarter informs Reid that "[Choi] says it doesn't mean what it did mean to him anymore." With cameras pointed, Reid initially demurs, stating that "he earned this ring, and I'm going to give it back to him. I don't need this ring to fulfill the promise I made to him [to repeal the policy]." As Reid hands the ring back to McCarter, calls echo from the audience, prompting her to reply, "When it's signed, Senator. When it's signed." Reid assents to this, "Okay, that's good enough with me, when the bill is signed, I'll keep it safely and give it back to him." Choi then stands up in the front row of the audience, salutes, and takes the stage to shake the senator's hand. "When we get it passed, you'll take it back, right?" asks the majority leader. "I sure will, but I'm going to hold you accountable," Choi responded.[4] This moment would receive repeat viewing several months later, when, days after the repeal of "Don't Ask, Don't Tell," Reid invited Choi to his Senate office and, posting a photo of the exchange to Twitter, exclaimed, "Five months after I promised a repeal of #DADT, I'm so happy to give back this West Point ring to @ltdanchoi."[5]

The Netroots Nation convention—titled "YearlyKos" for its initial two years—originated within the DailyKos blogging community. The primary author of the site, Markos Moulitsas, had little to do with it, though. As Moulitsas (nicknamed "Kos" during his military service in the first Gulf War) would note during his 2007 keynote speech, "Let's be honest: my chief accomplishment these past five years has been building a website. I simply provided a safe haven for progressives to meet, and then a beautiful thing happened. Without my planning or prodding, you started organizing. You started talking to each other and deciding on your own to take charge of your politics."[6] Moulitsas has gone on to write three books about American politics. He has written columns for *Time* magazine, and has become both a frequent guest on political news programs and a frequent villain in the polemics of major conservative personalities Bill O'Reilly and Rush Limbaugh. Kos's stature in elite political circles is derived less from the power of his individual online writing than through the community he has gathered on the site.

DailyKos is a blog, but it is also something more. Key modifications to the software platform allow it to act as an advocacy group. Like legacy organizations, DailyKos selects priority issue campaigns, endorses candidates for office, fundraises millions of dollars for their priority candidates and campaigns, and otherwise seeks to influence political decision-makers. Like a political association, DailyKos's goals include educating the public, influencing the political agenda, and pressuring decision-makers. The distinction between DailyKos and a traditional advocacy group is located in staff structure, tactical repertoire, and the vagaries of the tax code, rather than purpose or effectiveness. By comparison, the gulf between DailyKos and the average personal political blog is far wider. The average blog serves as a personal megaphone, echoing into geography-less cyberspace, to limited effect. DailyKos, by contrast, serves as a gathering space for an online community-of-interest. It is an online instantiation of *political association* in the purest sense of the term—like-minded individuals gather there to deliberate, converse, associate, and *take collective action* with one another.

DailyKos and other community blogs operate as an alternate organizational model to the Internet-mediated issue generalists discussed in Chapter 2. They engage their members through online participation. Rather than e-mailing a large member list, they create a venue for vibrant online conversation. Opportunities for political action appear as links in blog entries.[7] Rather than hiring field organizers or lobbyists, they hire software developers and a handful of contributing editors. Like MoveOn and PCCC, this keeps overhead costs low, while allowing the association to focus on the political news of the day. The Netroots Nation convention provides an annual, in-person focusing event—an opportunity for the community to come together, share experiences, celebrate accomplishments, and discuss future activities. DailyKos is both a major political blog and a key netroots political association. These dual roles have generally gone unrecognized by researchers and public intellectuals.

Political Blogs as Political Associations

The trouble with treating political blogs as political organizations is, of course, that most blogs *are not* political organizations. Blogging is simply a format through which content can be published on the Internet—a tremendously popular and malleable one, circa 2012. It originally arose from the Blogger.com platform, developed by Pyra Labs in 1999 and eventually acquired by Google. In the early years of blogging (1999–2003, when writers still had to explain that it was shorthand for "web logging"), there was little structural variation between one political blog and another. The software simplified digital self-publishing, eliminating the need for an online writer to learn programming languages like HTML or XML. Blog posts appeared on a site in reverse-chronological order, with the most recent post appearing at the top of the page. They tended to feature hyperlinks to other interesting content on the web, encouraging a conversational style. Older posts remained archived and easily accessible. Each author had his or her own independent blog and maintained a "blogroll" sidebar listing other bloggers and online media that he or she recommended to readers. Most blogs included a reader comment feature, also supporting interactivity between an author and his or her readers. Early blogging, even when expressly political, approximated citizen journalism more than citizen political advocacy.

To this day, the average political blog is solo-authored, hosted on a Blogger.com or WordPress.com site, infrequently updated, and sparsely visited. The immediate impact of blogging has come through this flood of self-published content. Some of the content has been excellent, giving rise to new forms of humor, discussion, social sharing, and even literature. Much of it has been amateurish, in every sense of the word. But even hastily written, inaccurate, and misspelled blog content has some virtues. Water-cooler conversation can now migrate to a format that is searchable and permanent by default rather than fleeting by default. Talk radio call-ins, presidential letter writers, and community meeting participants have long been treated as engaging in active forms of public opinion, regardless of misspeaking, misspelling, and general misinformation.[8] The great mass of political blog content can be similarly considered a more active venue for citizen political opinions. (We will return to this point in Chapter 7.) Advances in data visualization and computational social science have yielded tools for tracking and measuring these opinion sources.[9]

The sheer scope of the blogosphere (Technorati.com reports that it has grown from a mere 23 blogs in 1999 to over 100 million in 2009[10]) has led to two important modifications. First, as the practice of blogging entered the mainstream, leading media and political institutions adapted the software to their own ends. The *New York Times, Washington Post, CNN*, and *Time* magazine all host blogs on their websites. A new generation of journalists has taken to developing their writing portfolios through a hybrid approach, serving as editors of traditional high school and college newspapers while also self-publishing work at independent political blogs and larger online outlets.[11] Interest groups, think tanks, political parties, and presidential campaigns have launched blogs as well.[12] Given the malleability of the software platform, these traditional institutions naturally made stylistic and code-based modifications to the blog platforms, bringing them in line with their traditional mission statements. Newspaper-based blogs tend to provide only within-site hyperlinks, for instance.[13] Political campaigns often use their blogs to post press releases, extending the same advertising, credit-claiming, and position-taking behavior historically associated with congressional behavior.[14] This is the hallmark of the political normalization thesis—rather than offering a revolutionary challenge to political elites, we instead see major institutions adopt the new technologies and adapt novel tools toward traditional ends.[15] First blogs were used to challenge elite institutions. Then blogs were adapted to augment those same institutions.

The other secondary modification was the development of an "elite" or "a-list" blogosphere. As Matthew Hindman has demonstrated in *The Myth of Digital Democracy*, it is a mistake to equate the ability to *speak* online with the ability to *be heard*. Though new media tools such as blogs allow anyone to self-publish, removing the barrier to entry presented by the high costs of traditional printing, the resulting condition of online information abundance gives way to heavily skewed traffic patterns. Theoretically, everyone *cannot* have global reach. Hindman is one of several authors to document that web traffic displays a power law, "rich get richer" distribution, in which a handful of online hub sites receive the overwhelming majority of traffic.[16] The differences between these hub sites and a run-of-the-mill blog are manifold. Hub site traffic can rival that of mainstream publications, producing enough online advertising revenue to hire a full-time staff and invest in tailored modifications to the software platform. Among these elite blogs, we thus see further variations from the average independent blog. Karine Barzilai-Nahon has found that elite political blogs play a decisive role in disseminating viral videos, and Kevin Wallsten has found systemic differences in the content produced on elite blogs and common blogs.[17] Like any other professional organization—media, commercial, nonprofit, or political—elite blogs develop a clear mission statement, staff structure, work routines, and relationships with their readers/supporters and peer organizations.

Where I depart from Hindman is in our treatment of variation among elite political blogs. In his words, the very formation of an elite blogosphere provides evidence of political normalization—we still have an elite political system, just with "different elites."[18] By contrast, I accept this normalization process as a given, evidence of the political fundamentals that remain constant amidst a changing communications environment. At the organizational level, however, elite blogs exhibit tremendous variation. Some elite blogs function as sophisticated journalism outfits. The *Huffington Post*, founded in 2005 by Arianna Huffington, has hired several professional journalists away from the *New York Times* and the *Washington Post*. Those journalists certainly did not cease practicing journalism when they moved to an online outfit. *Talking Points Memo* has hired several professional journalists as well and won the prestigious Polk Award for investigative journalism in 2007 for its coverage of the U.S. attorney firing scandal. Treating these sites as members of a single, undifferentiated blogosphere is misleading. Rather than viewing them as elite blogs, they should be understood (and studied) as online journalism outfits.[19] Likewise, DailyKos assembles an online community-of-interest and engages in political advocacy. It is a substantial modification of existing models of organized political advocacy. By considering these particular blogs through an organizational lens, we can learn much about *how* political advocacy is changing.

DailyKos: A Political Association in Deed

DailyKos was initially launched in May 2002 as Markos Moulitsas's personal blogging home. His first post stated simply, "I am progressive. I am liberal. I make no apologies."[20] Note the pronoun, "I." For the first year and a half of its existence, DailyKos was structurally indistinguishable from any other political blog. As an individual blogger, Markos would use the novel self-publishing tool to post his thoughts, provide hyperlinks and news stories of interest to like-minded individuals, and interact with his small group of commenters. The political blogosphere was relatively unknown at that point, still being colonized by early adopters who had discovered the new software platform and were turning it to political ends. Kos was less well-known than some of his contemporaries in the progressive blogosphere—most notably Duncan "Atrios" Black and Joshua Micah Marshall—who had played a role in the first widely recognized episode in which blogging affected the broader political system—"the defenestration of Trent Lott."[21] There was no initial reason to expect his blog to become wildly more popular than those of his contemporaries.

The turning point occurred in October 2003, when Moulitsas switched his site over to a new community blogging platform offered by Scoop. Unlike the free Blogger.com software provided by Pyra labs, the Scoop platform had been developed for the Kuro5hin technology discussion boards and offered registered users the ability to create blog posts of their own ("diaries") and place them on the site. The diary feature was a key innovation. Previously, each online author maintained his or her own blog, establishing ties through in-text hyperlinks and static blogroll links. Following a networked conversation thus meant traversing multiple websites. Within the blogosphere, there was no single online space where an online community-of-interest could gather and engage in discussion, deliberation, debate, and collective action. Discussion boards like Kuro5hin, on the other hand, had a long history of fostering such online community engagement, dating back to the pre-World Wide Web years of the 1970s and 1980s.[22]

The introduction of discussion board-style community elements was a dramatic transition for the political blogosphere. By allowing readers to engage in various levels of participation—from rating a diary to posting a comment to submitting their own online essays—the new community features blurred the distinction between blogger and audience. If someone is a regular DailyKos reader who frequently comments and occasionally posts his or her own entries to the site, is he or she a "blogger"? A "diarist"? A "commenter"? The distinctions between the classifications quickly become grayscale rather than categorical, losing clear referents in the process. DailyKos community members call themselves "kossacks." Some blog actively on the site, and others comment, rate, or participate in political actions. They are primarily defined by their participation in the online political community rather than through the specific act of blogging.

Early bloggers loved the community features and flocked to DailyKos, providing the site with a first-mover advantage that continues to set it head-and-shoulders above its peers today.[23] As more participants contributed to the site, it benefited from the positive feedback loop of online *network effects*. The larger community added to both the quality and quantity of site content, giving readers additional cause to visit frequently. The greater frequency of visits meant increased online advertising revenue, which could then be invested in software upgrades and server capacity. Recognizing the untapped potential of the modified software platform, Moulitsas cofounded SB Nation, a lucrative network of sports blogs providing an online community-of-interest for rabid fans of individual sports teams.

The size of DailyKos cannot be divorced from its choice of new software platform. Richard Davis, in his 2009 book *Typing Politics*, offers a content analysis of "A-list" political blogs. Therein, Davis describes DailyKos as having hosted 429 new blog entries in September 2006, as opposed to 446 at Crooks and Liars, 529 at Eschaton, and 585 at Instapundit. In this analysis, one would believe that DailyKos produces less content than other elite blogs.[24] While accurate if one counts only postings to the front page of each site (none of those other blogs run on a community platform, thus they have no diaries), this empirical claim overlooked an *additional* 8,867 DailyKos blog entries in the course of that month.[25] Treating the community blog as though it had the same features as other elite blogs led to a twentyfold underestimation of site activity levels. Diaries that reach the recommended list routinely attract more community comments than front-page posts, an indication of high readership amongst the more engaged elements of the online community. What's more, with tens of thousands of registered users and a daily readership that fluctuates between 500,000 and 1,000,000 per day,[26] the diary feature creates a venue for thousands of online authors to reach a larger online readership than even many of the "A-list" solo-author blogs allow.

Community participation levels provide an even starker distinction. As part of the Blogosphere Authority Index (BAI) tracking system (described below), I capture the total number of reader comments posted to the top 50 progressive and conservative political blogs every month. Such comments are an excellent indicator of community activity because they demonstrate that individuals are engaging with the author and/or one another, actively inhabiting that particular online hub, rather than briefly visiting and then surfing away. In November 2007, when I first constructed the BAI, I was surprised to find that total comment activity on DailyKos was nearly equal to the comments posted to the next 24 largest progressive blogs, and roughly 50 percent greater than the *entire elite conservative blogosphere*.[27] Figure 3.1 depicts the same metric, but traced week by week over the high-traffic period of the 2008 presidential election season. Community participation on DailyKos simply overwhelms all other elite political blogs combined. The participatory engagement on DailyKos, enabled by the community features of the platform, renders it an online political community that blogs rather than a blog that attempts to affect political communities.

Features of DailyKos

DailyKos is a quasi-advocacy group whose operations are embedded in software features. The site describes itself as "at once a news organization, community, and activist hub." Technically speaking, the site is a Limited Liability Corporation

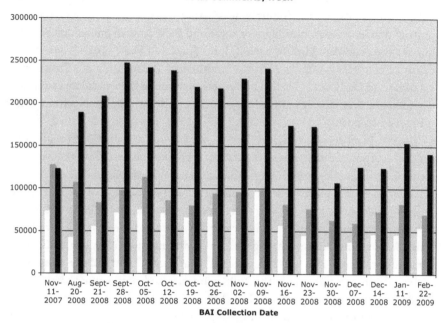

Total Comments/week

Conservative Comments ▨ Progressive Comments ■ DailyKos Comments

Figure 3.1   Comments/Week (Community Activity Score—CAS) on DailyKos, Top 24 Progressive Blogs, and Top 25 Conservative Blog

(LLC) rather than a 501c(3) or 501c(4) nonprofit. Moulitsas is listed as "Publisher/Founder" rather than Executive Director or CEO. It employs an Executive Editor, Managing Editor, and Associate Editor, along with a Political Director, a Campaign Director, and three technologists.[28] It also operates a Political Action Committee and includes a three-person DailyKos Elections team. Eleven Contributing Editors and seven Featured Writers round out the team of authors (some volunteers, some staff) with front-page privileges. Their roles and responsibilities vary, from producing political commentary and analysis to running political campaigns, supporting the "kossack" community, and developing new software support.

Similar to MoveOn's redefinition of organizational membership, "kossack" membership is defined through participation rather than financial transaction. DailyKos is a beneficiary of the MoveOn Effect, even though its organizational structure is dissimilar from the Internet-mediated issue generalists we saw in Chapters 1 and 2. The members of the DailyKos community include millions of occasional readers, hundreds of thousands of registered users, thousands of active diarists, and hundreds of "star" diarists who have built up a reputation and an active following over time. Fundraising occurs through online advertising, a small amount of merchandise sales, and voluntary donations through ActBlue.com.

In a 2008 profile, Kos described the organization's operating budget as "peanuts."[29] Most of its political fundraising is "pass-through" in nature, with kossacks posting diaries about a candidate or issue and including an embedded ActBlue link for the candidate him- or herself. John Sides and Henry Farrell have found evidence of a "Kos bump" in political fundraising. The mention of a Democratic candidate on DailyKos leads to a noticeable increase in the candidate's fundraising prowess that day, statistically significant and distinguishable from other sources of support.[30]

The site has been based upon the Scoop platform from 2003 through 2011. Scoop incorporated the "mojo" reputation system popularized on the Slashdot technology discussion board and featuring user diaries through a "recent diaries" sidebar and a more prominent "recommended diaries" section of the front page. Diaries would move to the high-traffic recommended list on the basis of community votes, rather than on the judgment of Moulitsas or the other Contributing Editors, providing a means through which community members could affect the content of the site. This led to occasional "diary wars," particularly over topics such as Clinton vs. Obama in the 2008 primaries and supporting vs. criticizing President Obama's policy stances. In February 2011, the site relaunched on a specially tailored community platform, "DK4," which added new search tools and group functionality that promote readers engaging with content beyond the front page. Moulitsas invested heavily in the relaunch, engaging a large group of kossack beta testers. In a series of front-page posts spanning several months, Kos aired key site redesign choices for community criticism, eventually backing off of a few stances after facing pushback from the community.[31]

The site includes several regular features serving the interests of the community. A regular series of mini-interviews, "Yes We're Staring at You!" profile star diarists on the front page. A daily "Abbreviated Pundit Round-Up" provides links to and summaries of op-ed pieces around the country, while a daily "Today in Congress" listing highlights the congressional agenda. A "midday open thread" offers a bulleted list of brief highlights from stories happening around the web. "Sunday Kos" features a collection of op-ed style long-form essays from the Contributing Editor corps. Regular segments also include a daily "Cheers and Jeers" comedy segment, and "Saturday Hate Mail," where Moulitsas features and ridicules some of the worst conservative hate mail he received in the previous week. In 2011, the site began syndicating political comics such as Tom Tomorrow's "This Modern World." In the 2008 election season, DailyKos also developed a partnership with the polling firm Research 2000 and sponsored its own daily tracking poll.[32] These features arise in response to reader/community enthusiasm, as do community inside jokes, such as the inclusion of "pie" as an option in most of their spot opinion polls and abbreviations such as IOKIYAR ("It's Okay if You Are Republican," a community critique of perceived mainstream media bias in favor of Republicans, invoked whenever a Republican makes a statement which, if made by a Democrat, would provoke controversy). These terms and features are included in dkospedia.com, a wiki site maintained by the DailyKos community.

Participation in DailyKos

DailyKos features a "ladder of engagement" similar to those found in traditional federated political associations.[33] Gina Cooper, for instance, started infrequently reading DailyKos in 2003. A high school science teacher in Memphis, TN, Cooper had little opportunity to meet like-minded liberals and discuss public issues. She became a regular reader and eventually signed up for an account in order to leave comments in other users' diaries. In January 2004, she posted her first diary, and the positive feedback she received from other kossacks led her to become even more engaged. In the aftermath of the 2004 election, Cooper and a few others began discussing the possibility of an in-person gathering of the DailyKos community. With Moulitsas's blessing, they launched the initial YearlyKos convention that year, drawing over 1,000 bloggers and a host of interested reporters and politicians.[34] Cooper later served as CEO of Netroots Nation before moving on to other professional political advocacy work and leaving other netroots and kossack volunteers to organize the large annual conference.[35] In Cooper's case, and in the case of hundreds of other community members, DailyKos has served as a venue for developing network connections and career skills, leading to an eventual entry into professional politics.

Like Cooper, Steve Singiser is a high school social studies teacher with a penchant for reading and analyzing political polling data. Singiser found a community-of-interest on DailyKos and, after years of posting popular comments and diaries to the site, was elevated to Contributing Editor status on May 14, 2009,[36] after Contributing Editor Arjun Jaikumar accepted a position as Blog and Netroots Outreach Manager at the Democratic Senatorial Campaign Committee.[37] Through the contributing editor system, Moulitsas is able to identify and reward the most committed and talented members of the DailyKos community, giving them an expanded platform for their political commentary. These are not fleeting relationships. Though the occasional visitor to DailyKos does not self-identify as a "kossack," the more engaged participants exhibit a much stronger relationship with the community than the passive check-writing members of legacy political associations. Here we see an echo of the rich, identity-based membership lauded by Skocpol in her research on the federated membership organizations of a bygone era, but cast within a primarily online environment.

Many diarists cross-post their work, writing pieces that appear on their own personal blogs as well as on DailyKos. They do so in order to increase traffic and visibility—DailyKos diaries receive an average of 54 comments per post, and recommended list diaries receive hundreds or thousands of comments, while the average personal blog post receives none.[38] The double-posting is indicative of an ecological phenomenon within the political blogosphere: not all blogs are created equal, or are designed toward the same ends. By navigating and participating within the large community blogs, users can develop an audience and a reputation. By hosting work at their own site, they can develop a portfolio and a niche. DailyKos benefits from strong network effects.[39] It is a hub location for a participatory community, and the members of that community use it to further their shared goals and personal perspectives.

DailyKos as Political Organization

The DailyKos community-of-interest is bound together by explicitly political interests and goals. The site endorses a slate of "netroots" congressional candidates and, utilizing the ActBlue fundraising portal, donates millions of dollars to them. In a single 48-hour period spanning October 17th–19th, 2008, after Congresswoman Michele Bachmann (R-MN06) made a colorful misstatement, the DailyKos community led the way in raising over $810,000 for Bachmann's Democratic challenger, Elwyn Tinklenberg, nearly matching Tinklenberg's total fundraising over the course of the previous *year*.[40] The site also played a central role in the noteworthy 2006 Virginia Senate election, in which incumbent Senator George Allen's "macaca moment" received wide viewership through YouTube and the senator was narrowly defeated by Democratic rival James Webb. The DailyKos community had initially "drafted" Webb into the race, supporting him over lobbyist Harris Miller in the primary. The community named the Virginia Senate race as one of their top campaign priorities, donating $193,248 to his campaign and ceaselessly raising the "macaca" issue over the course of the campaign. Webb, like a host of other elected officials, hired a "netroots coordinator" from the Kossack ranks (Lowell "lowkell" Feld) and posted several "thank you" diaries to the site. Most prominently, the DailyKos community targeted former Democratic vice presidential nominee Joe Lieberman in the 2006 primary, backing the upstart candidacy of Ned Lamont and providing hefty funding, volunteers, and media attention. The centrist Lieberman went on to lose his Connecticut primary, though he would remain in the Senate after winning the general election as an Independent.

There is an underlying tension between the bottom-up, community engagement fostered by the site's diary structure and the need for strategic decision making about whom to endorse, which issues to focus on, and how to position the site. Conservative pundits and bloggers regularly paint DailyKos as vulgar, loony, and extremist, latching onto the wildest and most offensive posts and comments they can find. After Democratic Congresswoman Gabrielle Giffords (AZ-08) was shot in January of 2011, national media attention focused on conservative icon and former vice presidential candidate Sarah Palin for her use of violent imagery and rhetoric ("Don't Retreat, Reload") on the 2010 campaign trail. Palin's Political Action Committee, SarahPAC, had released a graphic of targeted electoral districts—including Giffords's—that featured a map of the United States and gunsights over each target district. In attempting to deflect attention from Palin's rhetoric, conservative commentators highlighted a DailyKos post in which the author wrote that Gabrielle Giffords "voted against Nancy Pelosi! And is now DEAD to me!"[41] The post, by occasional diarist "BoyBlue," was wrongly attributed to Moulitsas himself in an attempt to claim that the violent rhetoric occurred equally on both sides.

Limited public understanding of the diary architecture, and the pseudonymous posting it enables, leaves DailyKos vulnerable to these reputational attacks. Individual diarists and commenters have no inherent standing in the broader online community—anyone can register for an account, and anyone can post diaries to the site. Like MoveOn's experience with the Bush in 30 Seconds contest, public misunderstanding of online content-creation practices yields fertile opportunities for opponents to aggressively mislabel the group as left-wing extremists. Moulitsas himself acts as a (semi)-benevolent dictator in this regard, with two hard-and-fast policies regarding topics that are off-limits. Any diarist or commenter who raises conspiracy theories regarding the September 11th attacks is immediately barred from the site. In the aftermath of the 2004 election, the same policy was set regarding Ohio voter fraud conspiracy theories. Moulitsas has also been a brash and outspoken critic of Ralph Nader supporters and third parties in general, and Hillary Clinton supporters in the 2008 primaries felt the site was overwhelmingly pro-Obama and announced a "strike" as they moved en masse to other elite political blogs.

The academic research community has often equated all forms of blogging with "citizen journalism."[42] The label is a shaky fit for DailyKos, however. Consider: the community engages in targeted electoral and legislative campaigns, attempts to influence media frames and corporate decision-makers, publicly thanks or criticizes public officials for their actions, advances its volunteer membership up a "ladder of engagement," and meets in-person for an annual convention. All of these activities describe the traditional actions of a membership-based political association. DailyKos has a different staff structure, tactical repertoire, tax status, and zip code than traditional DC advocacy organizations. But Markos Moulitsas has far more in common with Executive Directors Michael Brune of the Sierra Club, Justin Ruben of MoveOn, or Mary Kay Henry of the SEIU than he does with the editors, journalists, and op-ed columnists of the *Washington Post* and *New York Times*. The site also hired Chris Bowers of OpenLeft.com in August 2010 to lead their online advocacy campaigns, developing e-petitions and other Internet-mediated tactics traditionally considered under the rubric of political mobilization.

DailyKos is thus better understood as the leading example of a new variant of Internet-mediated political associations. The site is not alone in offering community features—sites like FireDogLake, OpenLeft,[43] and MyDD on the left and RedState on the right offer similar platforms and engage in similar activities. But just as these sites provide a departure from traditional advocacy associations, they also fit into a changing landscape of political blogs. The next section takes us deeper into the structural modifications that have occurred within the political blogosphere.

Understanding Blogspace

How does DailyKos fit into the larger blogging ecosystem? The previous section laid out the case for treating the community blogs as political associations. One would be hard-pressed to find another advocacy group that features "Friday Cat-blogging," though. More to the point, the site's organizational dynamics suggest a rethinking of a few core claims often made in the blog-related research literature. Matthew Hindman, for instance, has argued that the new blogging elite is demographically quite similar to the old political elite—the top political bloggers tend to be well-educated, white males. This leads him to his "just different elites" conclusion. He reaches this finding through a "blogger census," in which he surveyed the top individual at 87 major blogs.[44]

If all political blogs still displayed the one-person–one-blog architecture popularized by the original Pyra Labs software package, then the blogger census would provide an accurate representation of the elite blogosphere and would indeed be deeply troubling. Only a handful of political blogs attract readerships comparable to newspapers and newsmagazines. If each of those elite blogs provided a platform for only a single individual, then the blogosphere's influence could indeed be summarized as a mild case of venue-shifting. But the blogosphere has grown and evolved. Open authorship community blogs allow for multiple voices to be heard through hub sites like DailyKos. Hindman's "census" discounts DailyKos Executive Editor Joan McCarter and Contributing Editor Arjun Jaikumar. The list of authors with front-page posting authority includes eight women and several people of color.[45] The diversity on DailyKos's front page—the most-trafficked real estate in the political blogosphere—is obscured by the blogger census methodology. Meanwhile, a variety of *institutional blogs* have served to augment the existing web-based offerings of longstanding media, social, and political institutions. In the process, blogs have created new pathways into elite public discourse. Not all elite political blogs are created equal.

As a guiding example, consider Nate Silver's trajectory in the blogosphere. In 2007, Silver was a managing partner at Baseball Prospectus, a baseball forecasting company. He had developed a modicum of fame within fantasy-baseball circles based on his PECOTA (Player Empirical Comparison and Optimization Test Algorithm) forecasting system, but he was far from a public figure. By April 2009, thanks to his activity in the political blogosphere, he would join *Time* magazine's list of the World's 100 Most Influential People, and he has since moved to the staff of the *New York Times*—still as a blogger. To be sure, Silver's success is attributable to his particular skill set, as well as his overwhelming work ethic. But he also benefited from sophisticated navigation of the different *types* of blog now in existence.[46]

Silver's story begins in November 2007, as the Democratic presidential primary dominated political headlines. Observing the poor quality of poll analysis at that time, he speculated that a modified version of his PECOTA system could be fruitfully applied to the upcoming primaries. Registering for an account at DailyKos under the pseudonym "Poblano," Silver began posting diaries in which he thoughtfully laid out his new statistical model. The cogent analysis gained rapid popularity, and Poblano's diaries moved to the high-traffic recommended diaries list. Silver engaged with the DailyKos community, developing a reputation on the site, gaining feedback on his model, and building a collaborative relationship with Sean "pocket eights" Quinn. As the first set of primaries bore out many of his predictions, his popularity was magnified. He began to attract attention beyond the confines of DailyKos, reinforcing and expanding his sphere of influence. In March 2008, while still operating under a pseudonym, Silver launched his own independent blog, FiveThirtyEight.com (the U.S. Electoral College, which decides presidential elections, has 538 votes). Quinn joined him at the new site, posting more traditional journalistic fare, while Silver refined his algorithm and added sidebar graphics with constantly updating election predictions. FiveThirtyEight became a standard destination for "politics junkies" and began to attract attention from mainstream media reporters.

On May 30, 2008, Silver dropped his pseudonym, noting, "There are certain pleasures in writing anonymously . . . But I'm fortunate enough to have been granted the opportunity to develop some relationships with larger [news] outlets. And it just ain't very professional to keep referring to yourself as a chili pepper."[47] Silver's first national television appearance occurred two weeks later, on CNN's *American Morning*, and he would later become a frequent guest on the election news analysis circuit. Post-election, FiveThirtyEight.com attracted several additional authors, including political scientist Andrew Gelman. Silver collaborated with ESPN to develop a "Soccer Power Index" for the 2010 World Cup and developed a "Neighborhood Livability Index" for *New York Magazine*. His blog continued to attract substantial attention, ranking among the top 15 progressive political blogs according to the Blogosphere Authority Index (discussed below). Various mainstream media venues began to pursue Silver, and the *New York Times* eventually convinced him to relaunch his blog as one of their online offerings. Today, FiveThirtyEight.com has been converted to fivethirtyeight.blogs.nytimes.com.

Silver remains a blogger, but his blog now carries the *New York Times*'s imprimatur and benefits from exposure to the paper's massive online readership.

There are three distinct types of blog involved in the story: DailyKos is noteworthy for its community architecture, allowing Silver to post his content where an existing online hub of activity already exists. FiveThirtyEight is an *independent blog*,[48] in this case maintained by a pseudonymous blogger. Based on the classic, Pyra Labs-created Blogger.com software package, the site includes multiple authors, but it is closed-authorship. Readers can interact in the comments section but cannot otherwise engage in the production of the site. The site is a personal online megaphone of sorts, reachable through Google search and hyperlinks. Third is the *New York Times* iteration of FiveThirtyEight. While the site remains a venue for Silver to self-publish, it is now vested with the reputation of that longstanding newspaper. Visitors access it, and judge it, based not upon the clarity of Poblano's argument, but based upon their broader impression of the hosting news organization. Each of these features carries its own particular benefits, of which Silver took advantage sequentially.

If Nate Silver had begun by launching his own independent blog, he would have faced the wrong side of the blogosphere's power-law topography. Silver's statistical analysis could have been just as powerful, but he would have faced the tremendous hurdle posed by online anonymity.[49] Among the millions of political blogs speculating on U.S. electoral politics, pure meritocracy plays only a supporting role in determining which voices are heard. Poblano's posts would have been buried in Google search rankings, and it is exceedingly unlikely that a large readership would happen to stumble upon his statistical modeling. Likewise, if DailyKos were a closed-authorship blog, Silver would have been limited to starting from scratch. The diary function on DailyKos allowed him instead to post his content in a location where the relevant community would see it and be able to judge accordingly. The embedded recommendation system, through which popular diaries are boosted to the recommended list, gave his work greater exposure, and RSS ("Really Simple Syndication") tools allowed readers to set up a "feed" and follow his future posts.

After Poblano had gained an audience (and, importantly, after the first few primary elections had validated his algorithm), Silver was able to launch an independent blog that would not languish in obscurity. Following the "Super Tuesday" set of primary contests on February 5, Bill Kristol referenced Poblano's DailyKos posts in a *New York Times* op-ed, crediting him for beating pollsters and pundits alike in his forecast.[50] The independent blog allowed Silver to create customized features and made his content more easily accessible to his burgeoning audience—one that had swelled beyond the ranks of the DailyKos community. The audience and hyperlinks garnered by his analysis boosted the Google search ranking, and references in the blogosphere and the mainstream media further drove audience share.

An important point emerges from this set of actions: the common claim that "you can't trust what you read in blogs" is deeply flawed. Rather, the mechanisms for establishing trustworthiness are different for blogs (and new media more generally) than they are for legacy media institutions. For content to appear on television news or in a newspaper, we can assume that editors and fact-checkers have engaged in some level of review. Editors make mistakes, and some news outlets are more rigorous than others, but the fact remains that the production of old-media news carries an air of reliability not present in the new media environment. Clay Shirky has termed this a shift from "filter, then publish" to "publish, then filter."[51] In the online environment, individuals must *build* their reputation, constructing it and shepherding it over time. Silver's influence grew even while he was known only as Poblano because his claims were thoroughly documented, archived, and accessible. After strong predictions in the North Carolina and Indiana Democratic primaries, mainstream media figures actively credited "an anonymous blogger who writes under the pseudonym Poblano."[52] Poblano's reputation was based on a particular form of transparency—on the quality of his writing and the quality of his forecasts. Readers could trust what they were reading, not because blogs are innately trustworthy or untrustworthy, but because the individual blogger had a record of success.

The reputation Nate Silver built, both during the 2008 election and after it, lead to the third iteration of his blog presence. The profile he had developed—one premised upon the easy self-publishing and hyperlinks found online—made him attractive to mainstream media outlets. Being at the *Times*, in turn, augments Silver's reputation. His previous readership continues to follow him, but now other readers are exposed to his content. And new readers have no need to wonder, "Who is Poblano/Silver, anyway?" They trust it because they consider the *Times* to be a trusted source. Silver's posts are still blog entries, but they are posted to an *institutional blog*—a blog that draws upon and augments the reputation of an existing institution, rather than appearing out of Internet anonymity.

Note also that such blogs present a major problem for all studies that seek to contrast blogs against mainstream media. The *Times*—the paragon of mainstream media, enshrined in hundreds of academic studies as the standard indicator of mainstream media coverage—hosts blogs of its own and employs several individuals whose resumes were built through independent blogs. These are not two distinct populations, but rather a modified, interacting ecology of news-gathering and news-reporting institutions. And while the power-law distribution of online readership denies an upstart political blog from gaining immediate audience share, the open authorship feature of DailyKos allows new authors to reach an audience far more easily than the elite systems of old.

Figure 3.2 graphically depicts these two developments, and the varying blog types that emerge, along a two-dimensional typology I term "blogspace." The *x*-axis measures authorship—open versus closed. The defining feature that differentiates open- from closed-authorship blogs is the diary feature. Additional features can make a blog more or less open, however. Some blogs, such as Glenn Reynolds's long-influential Instapundit.com, do not allow for reader comments, leaving absolutely no room for voices other than the author's. Others, such as conservative hub blog HotAir.com, require user registration before commenting is allowed but maintain a closed registration policy so that no new users can join the commenting community. On the other end of the spectrum, some open-authorship blogs include sophisticated reputation systems that allow users to gain authority and increased community exposure, while others enable diaries but provide few tools for increasing exposure to the best diaries.

The y-axis, meanwhile, indicates the reputational basis of the blog. While the original wave of blogs were universally counter-institutional—independent sites, created by often-pseudonymous self-publishing bloggers—a second wave ported the software platform over to existing websites or added a blog feature to a broader web-based offering. Many interest groups and political campaigns, for instance, now include a blog on their websites. Such blogs are designed to augment the organization's broader mission, and their trustworthiness is based on a visitor's opinion of that institution, rather than starting from nothing. News blogs, campaign blogs, and organizational blogs all form distinct genres, categorically differing from independent blogs because they are designed to augment the broader purpose of an existing institution. Internet-mediated organizations, such as Democracy for America and the PCCC, and new online journalism organizations also fit within this category. Though such organizations do not have an existing, offline reputation, they mimic the blog practices of such organizations and seek to augment their online presence and reputation through their blogging.

A fourth blog type, called *bridge blogs*, also appears in this typology, though it rarely appears in practice. Bridge blogs combine the reputation of a large media or

	Closed Authorship/Mobility ←	→ Open Authorship/Mobility
Personal → Reputation	Independent Blogs (FiveThirtyEight.com)	Community Blogs (Dailykos.com)
Organizational Reputation ↓	Institutional Blogs (News, Campaign, or Organizational) (Fivethirtyeight.blogs.nytimes.com)	"Bridge Blogs" (HuffingtonPost.com)

Figure 3.2 The Blogspace Typology

political institution with an open-authorship platform. Such blogs are exceedingly rare because combining institutional reputation and open authorship often proves to be a challenging combination, fraught with pitfalls. The *Huffington Post* provides one example of a bridge blog. As previously noted, the *Huffington Post* has hired several reporters away from legacy media institutions like the *New York Times*. With reporters in the field, and with an online readership in the millions, it must be considered a media institution in its own right. The *Huffington Post* also features celebrity blog posts and allows registered users to post their own content to the site. A new user's content is kept far away from the front page, however, and navigation proves somewhat difficult. *Talking Points Memo* employs a similar strategy, with a front page reserved for *TPM* staff reporters and a separate "Café" where registered users can congregate and post their own material. Crowdsourcing and reputation management prove to be an awkward pairing, solved only through sophisticated institutional designs.

These four categories provide a clearer picture of prominent political blogs and their effects. Community blogs act as quasi-interest groups. Independent blogs serve as a personal, self-publishing megaphone. Institutional blogs augment a broader organizational mission statement. Bridge blogs seek to combine community user-generated content with institutional mission. While the early blogosphere was uniform in its structure—DailyKos began as a closed-authorship independent blog—the development of a "blogging elite" occurred apace with these structural modifications to the medium itself. In the context of political blogging, a particularly interesting developmental pattern emerges: as we will see in the next section, the top progressive and conservative blogs display very different structural features. In order to compare the structural features of the progressive and conservative blog networks, I developed a ranking system, the Blogosphere Authority Index (www.blogosphereauthorityindex.com), for tracking the hub political blog sites.

The Blogosphere Authority Index

My initial interest in the quasi-advocacy group structure of DailyKos led to an obvious question: how many community blogs are there in the elite blogosphere? Answering that question, it turns out, required some methodological creativity, because no reliable ranking system existed for identifying and tracking the political blogosphere. Beginning in November 2007, I developed the Blogosphere Authority Index (BAI) to provide such a ranking system. The BAI is an open data set, gathering four forms of publicly available data (network centrality, hyperlink authority, site traffic, and community activity) and converting them into a monthly updated "top 25" ranking. Network centrality refers to the frequency with which a blog shows up in the passive hyperlink lists of others' blogrolls.

Hyperlink authority refers to the total inbound hyperlinks associated with the blog, as recorded by Technorati.com. Site traffic refers to the total number of visitors the blog receives. Community activity refers to the total number of comments per week left on the blog (including diaries). Necessity was the mother of this particular invention: previous researchers had populated their studies by combing publicly available "top 100" lists, but the rapid expansion of the blogosphere had rendered most of those lists defunct, systematically flawed, or overbroad.[53] The BAI is now used by academics at several universities involved in blog-related research.[54] The methods appendix offers a summary of the BAI methodology.

Two features of the ranking system are worth emphasizing here. Firstly, the BAI tracks *clusters* of blogs, rather than ascribing political ideologies to them on the basis of text analysis. Progressive and conservative blogs are defined by the recognition of their peers, rather than imposing them through a researcher's coding decisions. This is particularly important because certain ideological subsets are excluded as a result. During the 2008 Republican primary, Ron Paul received particularly vibrant activity from his libertarian online supporters, but leading conservative bloggers derisively labeled them "paultards" and "paulbots" and excluded them from their comment threads and blogrolls. While text analysis of Ron Paul blogs would doubtless reveal conservative leanings, the evidence is clear that Paul-blogs were a separate cluster, isolated from the "rightroots" conservative network. As such, the findings presented here do not refer to *all* blog-based political activity on the left and right, but rather refer to the *clusters* of *elite* blogs that take action together.

Secondly, the BAI tracks no center blogs. The cluster-based system employed by the BAI can be applied to any subset of the blogosphere in which a large-scale "hub" blog is present. Hindman's well-established finding that online traffic follows a power-law distribution informs this methodological choice: the largest hub blogs are easy to identify because they attract an order of magnitude more traffic than other blogs in their area. Once a central hub blog of this sort has been established, the methodology can be easily deployed to map a cluster, any cluster. However, *there is no hub for "centrist" blogging.* Many attempts at establishing centrist blogs have been made over the years, but none have succeeded in attracting substantial activity. This finding has been corroborated by Yochai Benkler and Aaron Shaw in a 2010 paper on blog infrastructure.[55] Eric Lawrence, John Sides, and Henry Farrell have likewise found that blog readers are more polarized than television news consumers. The audiences of political blogs tend to gravitate toward like-minded sites.[56] In keeping with Cass Sunstein's 2001 concerns about political blogs leading to online "cyber-balkanization," it appears as though blogs as online communities-of-interest appeal only to the activist extremes. This also fits with Alan Abramowitz's research on the "engaged public," which displays stronger partisan tendencies than the disengaged, low-information center of the political spectrum.[57] Individual political centrists do blog, to be certain, and many of them find a welcome home at media blogs and think-tank blogs. But whereas the American left has the Huffington Post and DailyKos, and the American right has HotAir and BigGovernment, no hub blog has emerged as a gathering space for the American center.[58] Online collective action increases polarization through participation.

The BAI has provided monthly top-25 rankings of the American political blogosphere since August 2008. Aggregating across two years of data reveals three major trends. First, progressive blogs have remained more influential than their conservative counterparts, even during the upwelling of the Tea Party movement in 2009 and 2010. Second, the progressive blogosphere is dominated by community and bridge blogs—blogs whose open architecture allows for quasi-interest group activity. Third, the conservative blogosphere is dominated by independent and institutional blogs—conservative blogs with an open architecture fare much more poorly than their progressive equivalents.

Table 3.1 provides evidence of the ongoing dominance of progressive blogs over conservative blogs. As part of the BAI ranking system, I produce a monthly "combined BAI" top-50 list that offers an aggregate comparison of the top left- and right-wing blogs. Computing the mean rank of the average progressive and conservative blog provides a simple measure of the comparative strength of the two networks. If the left and right blog networks were at even strength (or if the rank order were randomly assigned), we would expect the mean scores to be approximately 25. The wider the gap between these two scores, the greater the conservative/progressive deficit/advantage. In the first iteration of the BAI, from November 2007, the mean progressive rank was 23.5, while the mean conservative rank was 27.48. The four-point gap between the two was indicative of a moderate lead for the progressive blogosphere. Through the course of the 2008 election cycle, that gap grew to approximately 10 points (progressive average rank 20.24, conservative average rank 30.29). The top progressive blogs were far more visited, linked to, and commented upon than their conservative equivalents.[59]

Since Barack Obama took office, online grassroots conservatism has surged, particularly in the form of Internet-mediated Tea Party organizations (covered in greater detail in Chapter 6). Many commentators have taken this to indicate a shrinking enthusiasm gap in the political blogosphere. Well-known conservative blogger/political consultant Patrick Ruffini offered boastful claims in 2009 and 2010 that conservative blogs had reached parity or even moved ahead of their progressive equivalents.[60] Chapter 6 will discuss these claims in detail, but it bears noting here that the BAI rankings do not support such claims. Over the course of the 2010 monthly rankings, progressive blogs maintained a 7.4-point advantage over their conservative analogues, fluctuating in size from 6.42 in October 2010 to 10.01 in December 2010. Though conservative blogs saw an increase in traffic and hyperlinks in 2009 and 2010, progressive blogs saw a similar increase over the same time period.

Table 3.1   **Average Site Ranks in the Combined BAI Dataset, 2008 Election Season**

Date	Prog Avg Rank	Cons Avg Rank	Difference
November 2007	23.5	27.48	P +3.98
August 24, 2008	18.72	31.96	P +13.24
Sept 21, 2008	19.6	30.96	P +11.06
Sept 28, 2008	20.48	30.32	P +9.84
Oct 5, 2008	19.28	31.36	P +12.08
Oct 12, 2008	20.08	30.56	P +10.48
Oct 19, 2008	20.28	30.16	P +9.88
Oct 26, 2008	19.92	30.68	P +10.76
Nov 2, 2008	21.52	28.92	P +7.4
Nov 9, 2008	20.72	30.12	P +9.4
Nov 16, 2008	19.72	30.84	P +11.12
Nov 23, 2008	20.24	30.4	P +10.16
Nov 30, 2008	19.64	31.04	P +11.4
Dec 7, 2008	19.96	30.72	P +10.76
Dec 14, 2008	21.4	29.32	P +7.92

The differences between the two blog networks are even more noticeable when we map the top 25 conservative and progressive political blogs onto the blogspace typology. Figures 3.3–3.5 provide such maps. Figures 3.3 and 3.4 depict the entire top-25 lists for each network. The conservative network includes a higher concentration of independent blogs (14) than the progressive network (10). The institutional blogs in the conservative network are mostly conservative attempts at building their own online newspaper equivalents, while the institutional blogs in the progressive network are mostly prominent individual bloggers who have been hired by the *Washington Post*, Salon.com, and other existing news sources.[61] The progressive network includes eight sites with community features, while the conservative network includes five (with HotAir being only partially included, as discussed below). Since blogosphere traffic approximates a power law, Figure 3.5 focuses our attention on the top 5 sites from each network. There, the picture is even clearer. All of the top progressive sites include substantial community-participation functionality. Most of the top conservative sites do not.

What should be clear from these maps is that the difference between the left and right political blogospheres is not merely one of traffic and popularity. Conservative attempts to "build their own DailyKos" have not attracted nearly the popularity

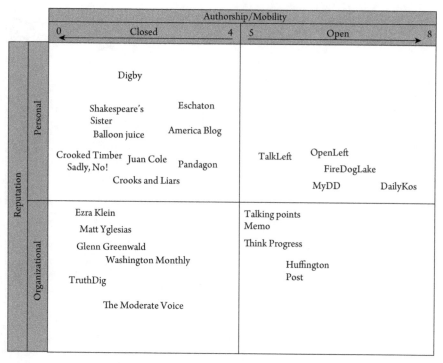

Figure 3.3 Top 25 Progressive Blogs, by Quadrant

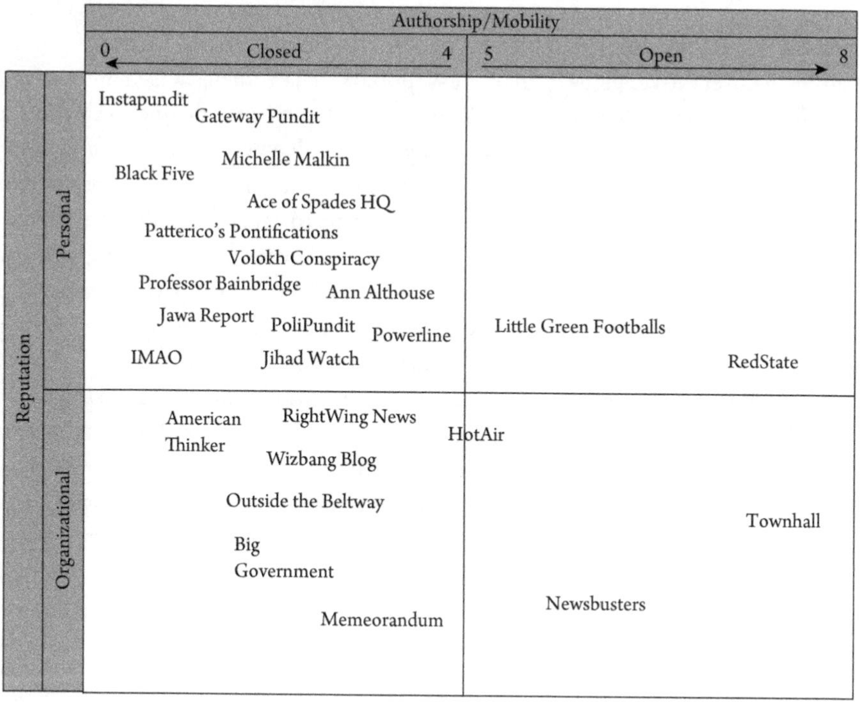

Figure 3.4 Top 25 Conservative Blogs, by Quadrant

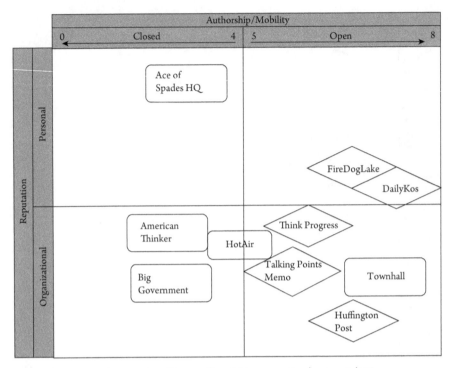

Figure 3.5 Top 5 Progressive (diamond) and Conservative (rectangle) Blogs

and engagement found among progressives. Whereas Moulitsas's site attracted tremendous participation by latching onto the open-authorship platform, open-author conservative blogs remain less popular than their closed-authorship, institutional competitors. Matthew Kerbel refers to this as a distinction between "horizontally organized" and "vertically organized" blog networks.[62] From an organizational perspective, this is a key distinction because it means that conservative blogs are at a decided disadvantage when attempting to engage in political mobilization. The architecture of DailyKos is designed to promote community engagement and foster organizational identity as members increase their participation. The architecture of HotAir relegates readers to the comments section or to e-mailing "tips" to the central authors. A small "Green Room" section of HotAir now allows registered readers to contribute content, but registration remains closed in perpetuity. In this light, it is unsurprising that the opening example from Netroots Nation included a poorly attended "Right Online" counterpart. Netroots Nation emerged from a high-functioning online political community. Right Online emerged from Americans for Prosperity's desire to compete in the same space (AFP is a deep-pocketed conservative interest group).[63] The top conservative blogs are not designed to foster such a community, instead focusing on augmentation of longstanding conservative political institutions. We will return to this pattern in Chapter 6, as evidence for a broader theory of *outparty innovation incentives.*

Conclusion: The Daily Me, or the Daily We

Cass Sunstein's Republic.com set the early tone for public inquiry into the blogo-sphere's impact on American politics. Sunstein worried about the construction of a "Daily Me," a hyper-targeted information environment in which "You need not come across topics and views that you have not sought out. Without any difficulty, you are able to see exactly what you want to see, no more and no less."[64] For Sunstein and other "cyber-skeptics," the new media environment presaged a dangerous trend for the broader public sphere, one in which targeted political information led to a situation in which neighbors would not even be exposed to the same news, and in which extreme partisanship increased under the guise of community sites.[65] Lack-ing "cross-talk" deliberation, partisans tend to reinforce their own core beliefs, leading to a deepening divide between the left and the right.[66]

The examples in this chapter add texture to Sunstein's concerns, while neither supporting nor disconfirming them. There are hub blogs on the left and on the right, but the center remains virtually empty. Active debate clearly occurs among mem-bers of the DailyKos community, but it is between varying shades of progressivism rather than between Democrats and Republicans. As Lada Adamic and Natalie Glance found in 2005, the progressive and conservative blogospheres rarely link to one another—and when they do, it is often in an effort to ridicule.[67]

But the members of the DailyKos community are just that: *community mem-bers.* They engage online with one another to talk politics (as well as talking sports, weather, science, and cats). Many of them are also members of non-political online communities—engaging with fellow sports fans through the familiar site architecture of SB Nation community blogs. Sports blogging, parent blogging, and knit blogging have all developed substantial popularity. Through venues like these, it seems that we are witnessing the rise of several "Daily We's" rather than the monolithic Daily Me feared by Sunstein. New media tools are being harnessed to allow communities-of-interest—political and otherwise—to engage with one another. Those communities act as filters for an individual's news reception, but also allow for serendipity. A kossack who knits will interact with fellow liberals on DailyKos, but also with knitters of various political stripes. The solution to the cyber-balkanization created by online political communities may be the same one James Madison's proposed in *Federalist #10* regarding the dangers of faction: the more online communities, the better.[68] From a participa-tory perspective, community blogs foster engagement in the public sphere. From a deliberative perspective, community blogs dovetail with the increasing polari-zation of American politics, but it is a *polarization through participation,* rather than the cyber-balkanization of hyper-targeted media channels. So long as active political partisans are members of other, non-political communities, we can hope that the radicalizing influences of in-group deliberation will be moderated through exposure.

This chapter has sought to distinguish a particular type of elite blog: the community blog. These play a very specific role in the broader ecology of the blogosphere, acting as a quasi-membership association. Moulitsas himself seemed well aware of this point in his 2007 address to the YearlyKos convention:

> "[The netroots] realized that our nation wasn't going to fix itself. We couldn't depend on the Democratic Party to save us. The media was AWOL. We shared a common disgust at the irrelevance of our once-proud party and its allied organizations. But what could we do? We were nobodies. And you had to be *somebody* to make a difference. . . . I was working a good, but an unremarkable job. People like me could spend hours talking about politics, but it mattered little in the greater scheme of things. Then technology changed everything. . . . while individually we were still nobodies, together we became somebody."[69]

Kos's rhetoric is of a similar type to what one might hear at the annual convention of the large membership associations of days gone by. He is appealing to a politically motivated association of volunteers—partisans who seek to play a larger role in the American public sphere. Whereas Internet-mediated issue generalists like MoveOn engage their members primarily through headline-chasing e-mail alerts, online communities-of-interest like DailyKos engage their members through voluminous online *talk*. Both represent new avenues into the broader public sphere and important modifications to the organizational layer of American politics. Both, to a limited extent, also engage people offline, using the Internet to facilitate the type of face-to-face engagement that has declined since the interest group explosion of the 1970s. A third type of organization focuses on just this type of online-to-offline participation, however. Echoing the Democratic Club movement of the 1960s, several netroots political associations have sought to provide "online tools for offline action." It is to that third model that we now turn.

4

"Online Tools for Offline Action"
Neo-Federated Political Associations

"The major difference between Philly for Change and all the other
groups is that we have a local volunteer base. The other organizations
don't have that."
—Jen Murphy, *Philly for Change chair*

The Howard Dean presidential campaign was a watershed moment for the Internet and American politics. Throughout 2003, the former Vermont governor's insurgent "Internet candidacy" attracted nationwide attention, fueled by an outpouring of volunteer support at local Meetups around the country and record-setting online fundraising. As the Dean phenomenon crashed in the cornfields of Iowa—a reminder that, as Clay Shirky put it, "support isn't votes, fervor isn't votes, effort isn't votes, money isn't votes"[1]—one thing remained clear to campaign professionals: online enthusiasm was no longer limited within the borders of cyberspace. Internet supporters, properly channeled, could be converted into valuable resources such as campaign volunteers, media coverage, and financial support.

After the candidate suspended his campaign, Dean announced that the Dean for America campaign organization would relaunch as a political association, Democracy for America (maintaining the acronym DFA). The unusual structure of the campaign operation—placing authority in the hands of a distributed volunteer apparatus—yielded two particularly valuable resources: a nationwide list of 3.5 million supporters and a host of ongoing "Meetups," with dedicated and passionate volunteer leadership already in the habit of meeting around the country. The new organization would be headquartered in Burlington, Vermont, mobilizing its national supporter list through MoveOn-style action alerts. The local Meetups would be treated as DFA groups, empowered to set their own local priorities with support from the national organization. In the aftermath of the 2004 election, Dean would be named Chairman of the Democratic National

Committee. He announced a "Fifty State Strategy" for revitalizing the Democratic Party Organization at the state and local level. DFA and its groups acted as a key constituency in moving his priorities forward and bringing new blood into the party apparatus.[2]

Democracy for America represents a third unique model of Internet-mediated political association. Internet-mediated issue generalists like MoveOn primarily seek an organization-to-member relationship, relying primarily on e-mail communication. Online communities-of-interest like DailyKos primarily offer a venue for member-to-member, online relationships. Organizations like DFA, which I term "neo-federated organizations," also provide a venue for member-to-member relationships, but it is primarily through offline engagement. Local DFA groups provide new infrastructure for self-identifying progressives to gather, discuss issues, and enact campaign strategies. In so doing, they utilize the lowered transaction costs of the new media environment to replicate many of the features common to the membership federations of old. Under the moniker of "Online Tools for Offline Action," DFA seeks to revitalize democratic participation within local communities, rather than through online communities.

To better understand this new organizational form, I engaged in eight months of participant observation with the local DFA group, Philly for Change (PFC). From June 2006 through February 2007, I attended meetings and events, interviewed the leadership, and generally sought to develop a clear picture of the operating practices of a locally grounded yet Internet-mediated organization. It bears noting that, through coincidence rather than conscious design, Philly for Change is one of the most active groups in DFA's system. Many cities lack a local DFA group, and still others saw brief activity that later disbanded. I thus consider PFC and DFA to be a "proof of existence" of sorts. The first section of this chapter provides a thick description of the local organization. The latter sections then turn to existing limitations on the model, as well as changing features of the still-evolving new media environment.

I argue that DFA should be viewed as a "proto-organizational" example of the neo-federated model. Proto-organizations, in the context of technology, emerge at a premature point in the diffusion curve, developing key institutional features before the supporting technology is ripe.[3] Such organizations serve as a guiding example for a later wave of organizational entrepreneurs, who introduce key modifications in software code or social circumstance to further effect. In particular, DFA faced two limitations at the time of its formation. First, in 2003 the Internet was still primarily accessible through desktop and laptop computing devices, providing a categorical distinction between the "online" and "offline" worlds. This distinction has since been blurred by the rise of the Mobile Web. Internet access through hip pocket devices like the iPhone has spurred a burgeoning market for location-enabled web applications, in turn expanding the opportunities for location-based political associations. Second, the size of DFA was limited to the initial

Dean Meetups—any cities that did not already have an active Meetup in February 2004 had no natural path to creating a DFA group. Compare this to the Obama for America campaign, which transitioned into Organizing for America (OFA) after the candidate won the presidency. The chapter ends with a discussion of OFA, itself an exceptional case in many ways.

Philly for Change: "Let's Take Over the Democratic Party"

Philly for Change meets once a month at the Tritone, a dimly lit bar in downtown Philadelphia. An average meeting draws between 20 and 40 Philadelphia progressives, most of them between their mid 30s and early 60s. Two volunteers sit at a table by the door, handing out meeting agendas and nametags and pointing newcomers to the sign-in sheet. The meeting is scheduled to begin at 7 p.m., but that includes around 20 minutes for people to shuffle in, order dinner and drinks, and mingle with friends. Once begun, the steering committee chair serves as emcee, introducing guest speakers, asking committee leaders to provide updates on ongoing activities, highlighting past successes, and urging the crowd to stay focused and minimize side conversations. The meeting always ends with a "take action" portion, which usually involves separating the members into small neighborhood groups where they can make plans for petition gathering or other local activities over the course of the following month. To a veteran of civic associations, the whole experience is strikingly *ordinary*. The operation of this in-person meeting is identical to those of civic associations of years past and present. "*These* are the mighty 'Deaniacs?'" one is left to wonder. Weren't they supposed to be younger, more wild-eyed, armed to the teeth with technological wizardry?

Indeed, what makes Philly for Change unique is not the introduction of novel technical marvels, but the extent to which they have converted face-to-face community engagement into political power. PFC is a testament to the value of community presence that professional advocacy groups of the direct-mail era have never been able to replicate. Jen Murphy, who served as Chair of PFC from 2005–2007, describes the organization's particular niche in Philadelphia politics as being unrelated to the Internet or the influence of Dean himself. "The major difference between Philly for Change and all the other groups is that we have a local volunteer base. The other organizations don't have that."[4] When dark-horse candidate Michael Nutter was elected Philadelphia's newest mayor in 2007—without the support of Philadelphia's powerful Democratic machine—many observers were quick to credit Philly for Change with providing the smart, savvy "boots on the ground" that proved a difference-maker. In a cover story article of the *Philadelphia City Paper*, Doron Taussig wrote, "It has been evident for some time now that something is happening in Philadelphia. Melodramatically, you could say it's a movement; more conservatively, it's the birth of a new constituency. The participants call themselves 'progressives' or, sometimes, 'reformers.' Suffice it to say that they're a new group of players in city politics, and that they're not pleased with the way things have been going."[5]

Philly for Change member Tony Payton, Jr. has been elected to the State House, and former chair Anne Dicker ran a high-profile but unsuccessful primary challenge against disgraced-but-powerful Democrat Vincent Fumo.[6] Other group members, such as Hannah Miller, have "infiltrated" the ward system of the local Democratic Party. The leaders self-describe as "party operatives" and believe fervently in Howard Dean's 50-State Strategy.[7] They canvass neighborhoods, organize petition drives, and develop sustained campaigns around issues of both local and national importance. They also create spinoff organizations, such as Ray Murphy's Philly Against Santorum, which mobilized Democrats in the 2006 Senate election.[8] Their endorsement in local races is coveted by political candidates, resulting in election-season general membership meetings crowded to the hilt with powerbrokers. The organization's membership is strongly reminiscent of the Democratic Clubs described by James Q. Wilson in his 1962 classic, *The Amateur Democrat*: "cosmopolitan, intellectually oriented amateurs," where "amateur" refers not to skill level or sophistication, but to "one who finds politics *intrinsically* interesting because it expresses a conception of the public interest," as juxtaposed against the set of professionals who are "preoccupied with the outcome of politics in terms of winning or losing."[9]

If a vibrant local volunteer base is so valuable, one is left to wonder why the membership federations and Democratic Clubs ever faded in the first place. The answer, as Skocpol notes, relates to its relative *costs* in the broadcast era: "new technologies and sources of funding created fresh opportunities and incentives for civic organizers. Suddenly, mobilizing fellow citizens into dues-paying, interactive associations that met regularly no longer made sense for ambitious elites, who could instead run professionally managed organizations able to gain immediate access to government and the national media."[10] As we stopped being a "nation of joiners," for whatever reason, it became significantly cheaper to raise funds and hire a staff of professional lobbyists than it was to build and maintain a large volunteer federation. The last few volunteer federations, including Rotary and the Sierra Club, have watched with concern for years as their volunteer base turns from salt-and-pepper to grey-haired, with no new generation filtering in behind them.[11] The day-to-day operations of PFC are not consumed with cutting-edge technology. But through the addition of a few basic structures, the costs of local association-building are mitigated to the point where groups like PFC again become surprisingly viable for a new wave of ambitious local elites. As Anne Dicker, the longtime chair of the group, put it, "The technology isn't all that visible in what we do. Mostly, it lowers the barriers to entry for getting into this sort of work. You don't need as much political experience to get started as you used to."[12]

The technology behind Philly for Change starts with Meetup.com. Meetup had its moment in the limelight during the 2004 election, as part of the wave of interest in the Dean phenomenon.[13] The logic of the site is simple enough, allowing interest-based groups to self-organize through a centralized web portal. It was chiefly developed to help hobbyists gather locally. Comic book collectors in Des Moines could find each other through the website and schedule a monthly get-together where they could debate Spider-man versus Batman to their hearts' content. The site establishes the time and location, publicizes it to other local Meetup.com visitors, sends out automated meeting RSVPs and reminders, and even solicits post-meeting feedback on how the meeting went. Howard Dean's campaign manager, Joe Trippi, famously placed a link to Meetup.com on the front page of the Dean website, driving the flood of onlooking deanforamerica.com visitors to a platform (Meetup) where they could self-organize.[14] This, in turn, generated the large and enthusiastic crowds that created the sense of inevitability around his candidacy before a single vote had been cast.[15] As Clay Shirky noted in his campaign retrospective, the media easily mistook this heightened volunteer activity for broad-based support: "Prior to Meetup, getting 300 people to turn out would have meant a huge and latent population of Dean supporters, but because Meetup makes it easier to gather the faithful, it confused us into thinking that we were seeing an increase in Dean support, rather than a decrease in the hassle of organizing groups."[16] Sociologist Seb Paquet terms this the rise of "ridiculously easy group formation."[17]

Philly for Change is best understood as a sort of *sedimentary infrastructure* left over after a heightened moment of citizen participation in politics. Anne Dicker headed the group during the Dean campaign and recalls the transition process from campaign operation to political association. "Our motto back then was 'you have a good idea, go do it!' When the campaign ended, we all gathered and started thinking about what to do next. There were committeeperson elections coming up, so we decided what we should do is take over the Democratic Party of Philadelphia."[18] Central to this story is the local decision authority vested among the volunteers. Traditional political campaigns are tightly managed by senior staff, seeking to coordinate a wider-reaching campaign "assemblage" that includes staffers, volunteers, part-timers, and allies.[19] As Rasmus Kleis Nielsen points out, at the end of the election, the staff leave town and the assemblage of volunteers, part-time staffers, and allied organizations disperse, leaving little if any residual structure in place. Indeed, this is one source of Skocpol's normative concern with the transformation of the organizational layer of American politics: cross-class membership federations provided a "laboratory of Democracy," building social ties and imparting foundational democratic skills to members. Modern campaigns, like modern interest groups, fail to provide such skills, instead focusing volunteers on simple tasks with little organizational responsibility. The Dean campaign, by contrast, placed a great deal of authority in the hands of its volunteer Meetups (arguably too much!). The 2004 primary generated a volunteer base and acclimated supporters to regularly meeting with one another and planning collective actions on a stable schedule. Unlike previous presidential primary campaigns, which have traditionally ended with the flourish of a speech declaring that the campaign ends but what it represents will live on, the "bottom up" structure of the Dean campaign operated like a wave, leaving behind a sedimentary infrastructure for future associational activity.

In fact, most of the Internet-mediated issue generalists share these sedimentary characteristics. MoveOn was initially built through the wave of citizen interest in the Clinton impeachment and substantially grew its member list through the anti-war protests. The PCCC's member base and organizational reputation are rooted in the health care reform bill. Color of Change—a MoveOn spinoff—was formed around the response to Hurricane Katrina. The finding holds less true for online communities-of-interest like DailyKos because the ebb and flow of readership leaves less "sediment" behind. DailyKos's readership surpasses 1 million unique visits per day during an election season, then falls back to 600,000–800,000 when there is less breaking political news.[20] While the Internet-mediated issue generalists harvest new e-mail addresses, thus swelling the "member rolls" during these periods of heightened interest, online communities-of-interest rely on continual visits, comments, and diaries—a "pull" medium rather than a "push" medium, in the parlance of social media professionals.[21]

Today, PFC continues to use Meetup and an in-house spinoff called DFA-Link to generate meeting reminders and manage their volunteer lists. This is the type of "back-end coordination" celebrated by Matthew Hindman in his 2005 piece, "The Real Lessons of the Howard Dean Campaign": "In the business world, the Internet's real successes have been not in retail, but at the backend: thousands of businesses have quietly used the Internet to streamline organizational logistics. Dean's example suggests that the Web may alter the infrastructure of politics in a similar fashion."[22] This "quiet use" is what separates PFC today from traditional civic associations—it allows PFC to organize locally "on the cheap." PFC fundraising consists of passing a hat around at meetings—they have debated asking for a small annual dues payment, but to date membership remains free. Their primary organizational expenses include a quarterly newsletter that they like to mail out to their membership and some small volunteer reimbursement expenses.[23] PFC chair David Sternberg explains, "Many of our members live in the city, so the biggest expense in our budget is renting cars through Philly Car Share if we want to spend the weekend canvassing."[24] Like MoveOn, PFC has no office or paid staff (DFA nationally employs a handful of staff, mostly at their Vermont headquarters), and thus it is able to operate effectively on this shoestring budget. The Southeast Pennsylvania Group of the Sierra Club, by contrast, has an office in Manayunk, PA, multiple field staffers hired to organize volunteers around the organization's "Cool Cities" campaign, an ink-and-pulp newsletter that goes out to its several thousand member list, and a five-figure annual operating budget. The lowered costs of local association-building allow PFC to build their local volunteer base at greatly reduced overhead costs.

For all of Sierra's heightened expenses, their endorsement is less coveted in local politics, and their profile in the city is much lower. The reason is that PFC serves as a *network forum* for a host of progressive Philadelphia interests (see Chapter 5 for further discussion of network forums). In their first meeting of 2007, the room is filled with presenters from allied local organizations. Each presenter is there to provide an overview of their campaign priority, pitching it to the assembled volunteers in the hopes of attracting a valued coalition partner. It is a similar scene to the electoral endorsement meeting. All members who have attended at least two meetings in the past year are invited to vote on PFC's local endorsements (with no membership dues, participation serves as the dividing line between members and non-members). Local political officials and operatives fill the room, shaking hands and handing out material, in a scene reminiscent of longstanding local politics. By contrast, few Philadelphia progressives encountered at PFC meetings or through Philadelphia Drinking Liberally (another netroots neo-federated group, detailed in Chapter 5) are aware that the national Sierra Club even includes a local volunteer presence. The organization has a multi-decade history in Philadelphia politics, but only devoted environmentalists and the public officials they target are aware of it. Sierra Club endorsements are conducted through candidate surveys and interviews with a designated local political committee. Though they are clearly valued by candidates for office, the Sierra Club endorsement process creates substantially less candidate interaction than the PFC process. PFC, as a local "issue generalist" works on elections, library funding, transit issues, health care, city recycling, and a host of national issues. Doing so attracts a larger population of volunteers and increases their prominence in the news and in local political circles.

For observers in the Skocpolian tradition, groups like Philly for Change appear to be helping to repair some of the damage wrought by a previous period of generational displacement among American political associations. A grand intellectual tradition, running through the works of Alexis de Tocqueville, John Dewey, Benjamin Barber, Jurgen Habermas, and Skocpol, among many others, posits that these well-functioning political associations play a critical role in a healthy democracy, serving as "laboratories of democracy" or "active publics."[25] From this perspective, the public sphere was weakened when organizational membership transitioned from participation to check-writing, "from membership to management." Discussions of the Internet and American politics have primarily focused on novel tools and tactics—e-petitions, Facebook, Twitter, or YouTube.[26] By contrast, technology remains in the backdrop for Philly for Change, serving primarily as an enabling condition. PFC relies on a set of "mundane mobilization tools."[27] Automated e-mail meeting reminders have replaced phone trees, drastically reducing the volunteer hours necessary for event organizing. The group requires no central office. It assembles in public spaces. It advertises through online social media, reducing a variety of local participatory costs (both financial costs and opportunity costs). If the new media environment turns out to facilitate a revival of location-based, participatory membership organizations, it would seemingly be a welcome development. The question remains, however, just how far this organizational model will spread. Is PFC a rare exception, or a sign of things to come?

Online Tools for Offline Action: The Strengths and Weakness of DFA

The tone and tenor of a Philly for Change meeting is strongly reminiscent of the federated political associations that populated the organizational layer of the American public sphere of a bygone era. Technology is mitigated to the background, enabling local participation by simplifying the tasks of local volunteer engagement. But the analogy to Skocpol's cross-class membership federations becomes less clear when we turn attention from the local affiliate to the national organization. DFA is a hybrid of sorts, with several offerings clearly designed to provide "online tools for offline action," but also operating at the national level like its Internet-mediated issue generalist peers, MoveOn and PCCC. The distribution of DFA local groups is uneven, their ties to the national organization relatively loose. Traditional features of a federated civic association, such as an annual national convention where local delegates can affect national policy, are notably absent. DFA is federation-like, but also MoveOn-like. If this is the best example of a "neo-federated" political association, then we must conclude that the federated model is itself quite limited at this juncture.

DFA's e-mail profile from the Membership Communications Project (MCP) highlights the MoveOn-like character of the national organization. DFA sent out 82 e-mails in the first six months of 2010. Fifty-one of those messages were action alerts concerning national issues, with health care, the Democratic primary elections, the Gulf oil spill, and the Don't Ask, Don't Tell repeal being the top issue topics. In 20 messages, DFA directly partnered with the PCCC, cosponsoring calls to action around health care and the Bill Halter Arkansas primary campaign in particular. Figure 4.1 provides a breakdown of their action requests. In comparison to MoveOn, DFA made a higher percentage of "pass-through" fundraising requests, likely due to their more active primary endorsement efforts that stem from the local group system. As with MoveOn, e-petitions make up a relatively small portion of DFA's tactical repertoire (17.6% of action requests).

There are two ways to interpret DFA's MCP profile. One is that the organization and its local groups maintain independent e-mail platforms. Philly for Change, for

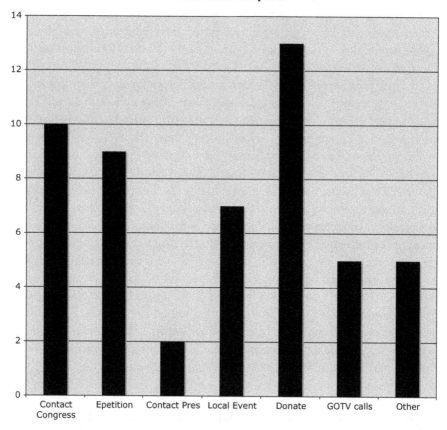

Figure 4.1 Democracy for America Action Requests

instance, is accessible through navigation of www.democracyforamerica.com but is primarily hosted through a separate domain, www.phillyforchange.com. The member lists are kept separately—not all Philadelphia-area DFA supporters receive PFC alerts, and vice versa, and while MoveOn uses its national list to plan local events, DFA may leave local events to local groups, focusing the national list on national events.

A second interpretation is that Philly for Change is an exceptional case, even within DFA's group system. The dummy account for the MCP was geographically linked to a zip code in Providence, Rhode Island.[28] Unlike Philadelphia, where PFC is a major presence among local Democratic political organizations, *there is no DFA group in Rhode Island*. Philadelphia is one of the locales where the community of Dean volunteers in 2003 possessed the right mix of size and enthusiasm to answer the "what's next" question and eventually convert themselves into an established local entity. Social network theorists refer to this as a "clustering effect"—the density of Dean volunteers (and potentially other key resources) surpassed a critical threshold necessary to support ongoing organizational activity.[29] Providence experienced no such local group formation, and DFA's selection of "online tools for offline action" is of limited utility in promoting the launch of new groups after the Dean wave had receded.

The heart of this toolset is DFA-Link, an online platform supporting local volunteer engagement available on DFA's website. DFA-Link lets users connect with a local DFA group or launch their own DFA-based affinity group.[30] It includes blog functionality, event-posting features, automated meeting reminders, and standard social networking features that link users to one another. DFA-Link is particularly useful for the organization's endorsement process. Local, state, and national candidates are invited to answer an online questionnaire, submitting themselves to an advisory vote of the membership on organization endorsement decisions. Any DFA-Link member can then recommend an endorsement of the candidate. This is meant to enable a virtuous positive feedback loop, with a natural incentive built in for candidates' supporters to join the organization and try to influence the vote. Chris Warshaw, the former Field Director of DFA who was responsible for designing this element of the system, explains that DFA intends for these miniature "takeovers" to happen, noting that "anyone actively involved in promoting a city council candidate is someone we want on our membership rolls."[31] Particularly in comparison to the Sierra Club, whose endorsement process is outlined in a 133-page manual, the DFA-Link system is exemplary in lowering the costs associated with complex volunteer tasks.

DFA-Link's potential for enabling offline action is not fulfilled by its track record. In a 2007 interview, Warshaw estimated that about two-thirds of the national member list and 80%–90% of the active members are Dean alumni.[32] The Dean campaign in 2004, like the Obama campaign in 2008, provided a wave of heightened volunteer engagement. Political volunteers flood into these presidential campaigns for the summer and fall and then disperse back to their daily routines after the election. Outside of those formative moments, there is little reason for a local progressive to stumble upon DFA-Link.

The challenge for DFA-Link, as with many other organization-based social-networking sites, can be described as a lack of "stickiness." Sticky websites are ones that users visit frequently, for extended periods of time. We can operationalize stickiness as [average visits/day × average duration/visit]. Sites like Facebook and YouTube are overwhelmingly sticky, with devoted users spending hours per day on those sites. On sites that include user-generated content, stickiness produces the network effects that allow for a power-law, "rich get richer" phenomenon—the more time users spend on the site, the more content is produced, leading that site to be increasingly valuable in comparison to sites of a similar nature. In any given hour, large quantities of new content are added to Facebook and YouTube. Dozens of posts are added to DailyKos every hour as well. DFA-Link attracts little new activity, meaning that a visitor has little reason to visit again the following day.

Indeed, one former PFC chair described the site as "inflexible," expressing a preference for the simplicity of e-mail. Of an estimated distribution list of over 4,500 PFC members, only 645 have signed up for accounts on DFA-Link, and the vast majority of those accounts are inactive. On a day-to-day basis, there is simply little reason for a PFC member to visit the site, and the same is even more the case for a DFA member in Providence or another city that lacks a standing local organization. Their progressive neighbors are online, but they are congregating elsewhere. Neither DFA-Link nor Meetup.com show signs of regular group activity beyond a core of a dozen or so groups, and the lack of activity on Philly for Change's own DFA-Link page is a clear indicator that online membership, as displayed through these portals, is a poor indicator of actual in-person group activity.

DFA's national efforts are structurally similar to an Internet-mediated issue generalist like MoveOn or PCCC. As early examples of neo-federated organizing go, DFA has been field-defining, while still being quite limited. The problem is that location-enabled search runs into a real problem with the anti-geographic nature of the World Wide Web circa 2003. DailyKos serves as the gathering place for an online community-of-interest, freed of the limitations imposed by geography. DFA, by comparison, attempts to provide a gathering place for that same community-of-interest offline, but faces some tricky constraints. What search term should an amateur Philadelphia or Providence progressive enter in order to stumble upon DemocracyforAmerica.com? Online hub sites, when divided into local entities, lose some of their transaction cost-lowering qualities. And lacking a robust nationwide system of local groups, DFA has not developed the second-order infrastructure necessary for national–local identity building. The organization has no annual convention. The small national staff offers web-based, phone-based, and in-person trainings to its local activists, and otherwise stays in touch with key local volunteer leaders. But it has not created institutions to bring together these volunteers as a national community. DFA's relationship with its groups resembles more of a confederation than a federation—the entities are loosely tied, with few formal expectations of one another.

As neo-federated organizational forms go, DFA remains only a partial example. Recent advances in how citizens access the Internet, however—in particular the rise of the Mobile Web—provide reason for us to expect the neo-federated organizational form to become increasingly salient to American politics. Indeed, as location-enabled search and utilities improve at a breakneck pace, DFA begins to look more like a "proto-" example of the new type of organization.

Proto-Organizations and the Software Ripeness: Theorizing the Drudge Report

The Internet is in a continual state of development. Barry Wellman has suggested that "an Internet year is like a dog year, changing approximately seven times faster than normal human time."[33] The medium's rapid developmental pace, with computing capacity doubling approximately once every two years, leads to a condition of ongoing disruptive innovation. New market opportunities emerge quickly, as increases in bandwidth, storage capacity, and cheap processing power render new classes of activity viable. As a guiding example, just imagine trying to launch YouTube on the dial-up connections of the mid-1990s. If DFA-Link has proven "inflexible" to its target audience and been relatively underutilized, one possibility is that the tool was similarly developed too soon. Just as YouTube required the permissive condition of high bandwidth Internet connectivity, online support for offline organizing arguably requires the permissive condition of a widely diffused Mobile Web. If that is the case, then Democracy for America falls into a category that we can best understand as "proto-organizations."

Joe Trippi, former Dean Campaign Manager and famed techno-optimist, offers the useful metaphor of "snow plowing" in his campaign retrospective, *The Revolution Will Not Be Televised*:

> "What [sites like Amazon, eBay, and Expedia] were doing was plowing snow, clearing the roads for Internet users to feel safe and comfortable enough to spend money, make reservations, and interact on the web in a million ways.... [In the 2000 election] McCain managed to pull a decent number of people, about 40,000, into his campaign via the Internet, but it was the [Apple] Newton of online political campaigns. The technology simply wasn't quite mature enough yet; enough snow hadn't been plowed."[34]

Trippi's point is twofold. First, there is "a fine but excruciating line between being the first and being the *first to succeed*."[35] The rapid development of computational equipment meant that the first PDA—the Apple Newton, in 1987—could be an abysmal failure, while a decade later the Palm Pilot proved to be a tremendous success. It is a matter of the underlying technologies ripening. Just as importantly, however, is the social learning process that occurs online. Sites like Amazon and eBay, driven by a strictly economic imperative, acclimated Americans-as-consumers to online credit card purchases. Only after that acclimation process had occurred could the Dean campaign convince large numbers of Americans-as-citizens to donate to a political campaign. "Snow plowing" refers both to the "ripening" of an underlying technology and to the social learning process driven by economic- or entertainment-driven applications of the new medium.

One result of this "snow plowing" phenomenon is that large Internet-mediated organizations and popular websites can sometimes develop as a precursor to a new wave of supportive software. For example, the DailyKos community could not have been created in 2000 because Scoop's community blogging software package hadn't been created yet. Interest in online political discussion existed but was relegated to clunkier Usenet message boards.[36] Conservatives in the 1990s gathered on one such message board, FreeRepublic.com, and that site remains active today with vibrant discussion among a devoted core of conservative activists.

We can term this type of structure the *"proto*-organizational" form. I define proto-organizations as a special class of Internet-mediated group, technically identifiable only in retrospect. They have two defining characteristics. First, they benefit from *first-mover advantage*, representing an initial major attempt at allowing Internet users to partake in some novel activity online. Second, as a result of this first-mover status, they rely upon a *bare-bones software platform* that lacks many supportive features that later become accepted as essential functions. Proto-organizations demonstrate an existing demand or market opportunity, which a later wave of entrepreneurs seek to leverage new software code or emerging trends in online participation to improve upon. The Drudge Report provides perhaps *the* classic example of the proto-organizational form.

Matt Drudge (serendipitously, his real name) launched the site in 1994, sending out a broadcast e-mail soliciting subscribers for a website that would feature "a cross section of things that the editor Matt Drudge is focusing in on . . . Already read by key players, this tip sheet will be sure to peak [*sic*] your interest."[37] The site featured a list of headlines, occasionally with brief editorial commentary, each with hyperlinks to a news story found somewhere on the web (see Figure 4.2— screenshot of DrudgeReport.com). Drudge's fame as a cutting-edge newshound was cemented in 1998, when he broke the news of the Monica Lewinsky scandal in a "world exclusive" after the major news organizations had failed to release the story. His site has had enduring power, reaching roughly 2 million unique visitors per month,[38] which gives it a larger readership than many newspapers. With a reputation for regularly breaking news of the next day's headlines, journalist Chris Cillizza (author of the Washington Post's blog, *The Fix*) describes the Drudge Report as "the single most influential source for how the presidential campaign [of 2008] is covered in the country."[39]

Is the Drudge Report a blog? Not exactly. Drudge's habit of posting hyperlinks with limited commentary is emulated by a few elite bloggers, particularly popularly early adopters such as Duncan "Atrios" Black and Glenn "Instapundit" Reynolds (see Figure 4.3, screenshot of Instapundit.com). Blogs traditionally appear in reverse-chronological order and are archived over time, whereas the Drudge Report is organized as a three-column spread of news items and includes no archives. Blogs typically include a blogroll of like-minded authors, and most of

Figure 4.2 Screen Capture of DrudgeReport.com, taken 12/15/11

them include (at minimum) the capacity for reader comments. Drudge has neither of these. In the typology of blogspace presented in Chapter 3, the Drudge
Report would appear in the farthest corner of quadrant I (independent blogs)
since it includes no community-enhancing features and draws an audience entirely on the basis of the author's individual reputation. But labeling it as a blog is
problematic. David Perlmutter, a journalism professor at the University of Kansas
and author of *Blog Wars,* instead labels the Drudge Report as a "proto-blog,"
noting, "To this day, Drudge is Drudge: one man, no interaction, no community.
The combination of independent media, hyperlinked posting, and voluntary
association that bypassed and critiqued regular media, however, was developing
at the same time, and we would soon all know its name: blog."[40]

Notice, then, how the particular chain of events unfolds. Drudge launched his
website in 1994. It burst into the public consciousness in 1998. It wasn't until
1999, when Pyra Labs created the commercial software platform Blogger.com,
that blogging became an identifiable activity even among early Internet adopters.
Compared with the latest blogging software platforms, the Drudge Report is the
very essence of "clunky" or "inflexible" software. Blogging as a form of criticism,
expression, and organization would not take off until additional software elements were added (first by Pyra Labs and later by Scoop, the platform that enabled
DailyKos's diary architecture). But thanks to the substantial reservoir of authority that he developed by virtue of his first-mover advantage, Matt Drudge has
virtually no incentive to update his site to newer software. Drudge does not need
to engage a community of participants to build an audience because he has
already established himself as a known commodity. In 1998, we would not have

Figure 4.3 Screen Capture of instapundit.com, taken 12/15/11

known to call the Drudge Report a "proto-blog" because the activity of blogging had yet to mature. In retrospect, however, it is clear that the site fills a similar niche to that of political and media blogs, while lacking many of the features later incorporated as core features of blogging software.

So what of Democracy for America, then? For local supporters in Philadelphia, PA, the organization has the *feel* of a traditional federated political association. For local supporters in Providence, RI, it feels more like MoveOn or PCCC. It includes a federation of strong local groups, but that federation is unevenly spread across the country, and no second "Dean wave" is going to provide a mass influx of new "member-sediment," so to speak. Philly for Change may be an exception— a proof of existence and nothing more—or it may be an indicator that DFA appeared before enough "snow had been plowed." At issue is the texture of the generation shift among American political associations. Will the Internet facilitate extended face-to-face engagement amongst local populations of like-minded partisans, or will it be concentrated in online tactics and brief episodes of online activity? Where will the next wave of online innovation lead us?

It is dangerous to speculate on such matters (the Internet routinely makes fools of those who boldly predict its future), but there is increasingly strong evidence for treating DFA as a proto-organizational example of a robust neo-federated model. The reason is that we are seeing a dramatic shift in the types of devices citizens use to access the Internet. In 2004, the boundary between "online" and "offline" was firm. Internet access was mitigated through desktop and laptop portals. To attend an in-person meeting, citizens had to *log off*, leaving the online world for a separate offline world. Early examples of "cyberactivism" were self-contained among "netizens," engaging in online political acts directed at *online* sources of authority.[41] The bright-line distinction between online and offline has been rendered fuzzy, however. Devices like the iPhone and other smartphones allow the Internet to be present wherever citizens can find a cell phone signal. Global Positioning System (GPS) sensors are built into these devices, leading to mass aggregation of geo-locational data and driving a new wave of economic, social, and entertainment services based upon supporting consumers in their neighborhood. Rating services like Yelp.com and foursquare.com are "plowing snow," acclimating citizens to the merger of online services into previously offline activities. In so doing, they potentially remove a few barriers that have frustrated local political associations for decades.

Meeting Notes: Information Abundance Stops at the Internet's Edge

The final half-hour of a Philly for Change meeting usually consists of breaking into small groups—neighborhood teams—to plan volunteer activities for the coming month. In the June 2007 meeting, I sit at a small table with three other West Philadelphians, but my mind is preoccupied. Earlier that day, I'd witnessed my first iPhone commercial, boasting, "This is not a watered-down version of the Internet. Or the mobile version of the Internet. Or the kinda-sorta-looks-like-the-Internet-Internet. It's just the Internet. On your phone."[42] It's brilliant marketing, and our table, in this dimly lit bar, feels palpably *offline* by contrast. My neighbors and I settle on a plan to set up a table at the Clark Park farmer's market, educating other residents about local recycling issues and gathering petition signatures. The meeting ends with neighborhood teams reporting their plans to one another, receiving encouraging applause while a group leader jots down notes on a yellow legal pad. Those notes *could* form a useful benchmark, indicating the plans we'd set, reminding us of our stated goals, and helping the organization to identify "star" volunteers. But they won't. Tracking that sort of data is about as hard in 2007 as it was in 1987 or 1967. The condition of *information abundance* that is so central to a variety of Internet-mediated organizations is not present in this bar. Data on a legal pad cannot be Googled, as it were.

Herein lies the limit of "backend coordination" tools, circa 2007. At the national level, Democracy for America is able to track many forms of member interest and engagement. Through its national e-mail list, the organization can track open rates and action rates. It can gather passive democratic input, just as MoveOn does. It can engage in A/B testing to hone its message and test out the popularity of national campaign topics. But the activity in a Philly for Change meeting remains opaque to the national organization. It doesn't know whether my neighborhood team set up that table or collected those signatures. It can't tell how the meetings are going or what interpersonal controversies are on the rise. Likewise, the DFA-Link tools aren't present with us in the meeting. To make use of it, PFC members would have to take the extra step of entering meeting notes and reminders after the fact. It is easier to just e-mail each other. Sociologist Seb Paquet has argued that the Internet enables "ridiculously easy group formation" through the lowering of transaction costs. That may well be true for online groups, but for local volunteer associations, with technology relegated to the background, many of those historic transaction costs remain unchanged—that is, unless the Mobile Web integrates online utilities into these offline circumstances.

In a 2008 interview, I spoke with Natalie Foster, former Deputy Field Network Director for MoveOn, about the potential of online–offline tracking systems.[43] "That's the Holy Grail," she replied excitedly. "We always said in MoveOn that what we needed more than anything else was a way to record feedback on which house parties and meetings went well and which ones didn't."[44] Technically, MoveOn does offer such a feedback mechanism in the form of automated post-event e-mails that are sent to participants asking that they rate and review their experience. But the response rate to such post-event questionnaires is precipitously low in comparison to other types of online feedback. Online activity like webpage visits and e-mail clicks can be passively tracked. Report-backs from offline events, by contrast, require additional, active effort on the part of the members. As a result, Internet-mediated organizations know vastly more about their members' online activity than their offline activity, and the organizations can do far less to support and cultivate that offline activity. MoveOn and DFA would *like* to invest training and organizing resources in those members who engage in the best local work—particularly in cities like Providence that have no existing local group. But the limitations presented by offline data collection heavily curtail their efforts.[45]

The Mobile Difference

The Mobile Web extends the reach and modifies the application of these tools. The iPhone has already led to an extensive (and some say threatening[46]) new field of online experimentation. With over 300,000 applications available through Apple's iTunes "app store,"[47] various economic, social, entertainment, and civic organizations are building customized applications to take advantage of geo-local tools. Organizing for America (OFA), the sedimentary offspring of the Obama for America presidential campaign (discussed below), has been at the forefront of developing these apps to support offline engagement. The Obama '08 app allows supporters to look up issue information, find local events, sign up for local groups, and use a distributed phone-banking tool. By routing supporters through the application, OFA is able to passively capture more data on the activities of their active volunteers. As Mobile Web-enabled phones gain market share, meeting augmentation and evaluation tools become a next obvious step. Rather than asking members after a meeting to fill out an online questionnaire or enter meeting notes into a backend system, those features can be built into an application that augments the in-person meeting itself. The same type of rating practices that routinely occur on sites like DailyKos—giving "kudos" to comments or recommending diary contributions—can be applied to the PFC activities that, to date, have remained strictly offline.

Sites like Yelp.com are already engaging in this sort of "snow plowing." Yelp was launched in 2005 as a sort of "Zagat ratings by the masses, for the masses," combining elements of Wikipedia, community blogs, social networks, and the Yellow Pages, all with a helping of Google Maps on the side. The site has over 53 million unique visitors per month and features over 20 million reviews.[48] Visitors to the site can browse through user-generated reviews of restaurants, shopping, nightlife, beauty and spas, or more than 15 other categories. Registered users can write their own reviews and give 1- through 5-star ratings of any location they visit. They can also rate each other's reviews, giving them credit for being "useful," "funny," or "cool," or flagging them as inappropriate content. Registered users are also invited to fill out profile information and network with each other. The most active reviewers on the site are invited to be members of the "Elite," a superuser-designation that includes invitations to local "thank-you" mixers.

Though its launch predates the iPhone's market entry, Yelp's explosive growth occurred alongside the rise of Mobile Web access. As reviews become accessible and writeable on the go, Yelp becomes an exponentially more valuable tool— restaurants can be searched without sitting down with a desktop or laptop computer, or scathing reviews about poor service can be written during a tediously long wait. Yelp's iPhone application lets users access this repository of local wisdom at all times, encouraging higher participation rates and the accumulation of more assessments. While long-established sites like YellowPages.com and City-Search.com attempt to provide top-down directories of available services, Yelp invites a growing participatory community to do the legwork behind local searches. Location awareness increases the utility of Yelp's services, in turn broadening the size and scope of the service's applicability. Yelp surpassed CitySearch as the leading local business review site in April 2009, overtaking first-mover advantage through a wave of user-generated content.[49]

Yelp is not itself a civic association, but the event- and user-rating practices it ingrains have valuable applications for DFA, MoveOn, and similar groups. As Americans-as-consumers become accustomed to using the Mobile Web to rate offline organizations and events, the learning curve required for Americans-as-citizens to take equivalent actions in the public sphere is sharply reduced. The data abundance of the Internet becomes increasingly integrated with previously offline political activities. MoveOn and DFA have not developed their own "apps" at the time of this writing, but conference panels at Netroots Nation and other netroots conferences demonstrate an increased appetite for mobile applications.

Zack Exley, former MoveOn staffer, Kerry for President Internet Coordinator, and New Organizing Institute President, offers a powerful commentary on the challenge that has traditionally faced local political associations: the "Tyranny of the Annoying":

> "The Tyranny of the Annoying stems from the fact that, except in times of extreme crisis, it is just not worth it for mature, serious people to put up with all the indignities that go along with taking and maintaining leadership of any political entity. This principle guarantees that every Elks Club, Union Local, DAR Chapter, or Democratic town committee will tend toward being controlled by annoying people—they are the ones with egos desperate to be fed by winning petty little power plays and plenty of time on their hands"[50]

Exley's hope is that the Internet can help to mitigate the "Tyranny of the Annoying"—that the same sort of tools that reward positive contributions on Wikipedia,[51] eBay,[52] and online communities like Slashdot[53] or DailyKos can be turned to local political associations, simplifying leadership tasks and rewarding "mature, serious people" for their contributions. A central limitation for neo-federated organizational models has been that online data abundance stops at the Internet's edge. You can A/B test only those topics for which you have data. The valuable contributions made by local volunteers in face-to-face meetings go unrecorded. "Online tools for offline action" remains a limited field of activity. The spread of the Mobile Web opens up new avenues for neo-federated organizational experimentation. Through novel applications, designed for iPhone and Android-based mobile devices, organizations are tinkering with what location-enabled, ever-present Internet connections can add to traditionally offline arenas of social engagement. Among netroots professionals, there is a near-consensus that mobile applications will be the "next big thing." If they provide a novel solution to the "Tyranny of the Annoying" problem, the neo-federated organizational model will become increasingly relevant.

I should pause here to note an important caveat in the spread of the Mobile Web. Among Internet scholars, there is a longstanding research program concerning the "digital divide."[54] Initially focused on the Internet diffusion gap between wealthy and poor countries, digital divide studies have also noted the gap between rich and poor citizens, as well as the skills divide between younger, urban, wealthier, and better-educated individuals and socioeconomically disadvantaged segments of society. Simply put, any benefits from the Internet disproportionately accrue to the already well-off, exacerbating existing inequalities. These concerns are equally applicable to the Mobile Web and application-based utilities. Though the Pew Internet and American Life project found in 2010 that 40% of American adults access the Internet from their cell phone, an increase from 32% in 2009,[55] there is a difference between the rich application-based ecology of the iPhone and Android phones and the limited Internet offerings provided by cheaper cellular phones.

Oddly enough, the digital divide in Mobile Web access is unlikely to limit the utility of the iPhone for political associations like DFA. The reason is that the volunteer base of such organizations has long been demographically skewed toward the very segments of the population who are most likely to afford new technology.[56] Put another way, the segment of the American public who can afford to spend their time volunteering with a political group tends to overlap with the segment that can afford an iPhone. This is a legitimate cause for concern among practitioners, particularly those who have hopes for a diversified public sphere. It is also a longstanding feature of American political life—one that new communications technology will not independently resolve.

Organizing for America—Governance Organizing and the Dilemma of Control

The savvy reader may have spent much of this chapter pondering additional cases. If Democracy for America is a proto-example of the neo-federated ideal type, what group comes next? Living Liberally, covered in Chapter 5, has a wider neo-federated network but limits its groups to social events rather than sustained collective action. The Obama for America campaign, which transitioned into Organizing for America (OFA) after his election and merged with the Democratic National Committee (DNC), is a more intriguing candidate. Indeed, OFA bears several strong similarities to DFA. The name itself is an homage of sorts—both organizations chose to adopt new names that preserved the acronym of their campaign apparatus. As Daniel Kreiss has demonstrated, the Obama campaign's New Media Team was heavily populated by Dean campaign alumni, and the Obama website and campaign tools were designed by Blue State Digital, a consultancy founded by Dean alumni (see Chapter 5).[57] Howard Dean served as Chair of the Democratic National Committee from 2004–2008 and presided over the controversial "50-State Strategy" that DFA activists supported en masse. Moreover, both organizations are the sedimentary offspring of a presidential campaign mobilization, making them distinct from groups like MoveOn and PCCC that build their lists through social movement- or issue-based sedimentary waves. Given the longstanding tradition of electoral field mobilization—what Rasmus Kleis Nielsen refers to as "personalized political communication"[58]—one might expect that the sedimentary infrastructure left behind by electoral campaigns would be particularly amenable to local volunteer association-building. The

Obama campaign volunteers were used to knocking on doors together, whereas PCCC's volunteers had mostly clicked, donated, e-mailed, or made phone calls.

OFA was first unveiled on January 17, 2009, after a stakeholder meeting in Chicago sorted through potential parameters for the group. At that time, I highlighted three key differences between OFA and DFA[59]—differences that still hold true today and that lead me to conclude that OFA should be considered as its own, exceptional organization form. First, OFA is substantially larger than DFA; indeed it is larger than any other political association in America. With a member list of over 13 million supporters, the Obama for America campaign has been referred to as the largest campaign mobilization in American history.[60] Beyond the size of OFA's e-mail list, the campaign also boasted a sophisticated field structure, including hundreds of thousands of volunteers and thousands of staff. If we postulate that groups like Philly for Change emerged in locations that were above a critical threshold of volunteer participation in the 2004 Dean campaign, then it follows that we should expect *far more* of the equivalent groups to be potentially viable after the 2008 Obama campaign.[61]

A second difference involves the bully pulpit and agenda setting. One of the major goals of American political associations involves attempts to affect the political agenda.[62] Never before has there been a political association directly and explicitly tied to a presidential administration. The Obama administration has a range of tools for setting the government's agenda, including blue ribbon commissions, press conferences, and the annual State of the Union address. At the national level, the direct agenda-setting capacity of the president's bully pulpit deeply impacts the strategic choices and operating systems his allied organization puts in place. DFA listens to its membership and coalition partners to determine its issue priorities, then attempts to raise the profile of those priorities in the media and through interactions with elected officials. OFA's issue priorities stem from the Oval Office itself. While groups like MoveOn and DFA have been labeled "hybrid organizations" that combine party-like mobilization repertoires with interest group and social movement repertoires, OFA is in fact the governing party.[63]

The third distinction follows from the second. Whereas DFA empowers its local groups to set their own issue priorities and "take over the Democratic Party," OFA already *is* the Democratic Party, placing it squarely within two orthogonal traditions: presidential party building and American political associations.[64] A substantial dilemma of control emerges as a result. After the 2008 election, OFA had active volunteer operations in every major American city. These volunteer operations were distinct from the locally elected, longstanding Democratic Party leadership. If the organization invited those volunteers to set their own agenda, it would effectively have created a rival to every local Democratic Party apparatus within the party organization. The inevitable outcome in hundreds of municipalities would have been a fractious period of party infighting, as established (and sometimes elected) local party operatives battled with "senior" OFA volunteer leaders. Recognizing this threat—which also doubtless would have proved an irresistible draw for journalists—the OFA design team curtailed all local decision authority.[65]

The lack of local decision authority renders OFA categorically distinct from the neo-federated model. DFA groups like Philly for Change make endorsements in primaries and empower their volunteers to select local issues as campaign priorities. Members can influence the organization's issue priorities and gain greater voice and authority through ongoing participation. Local OFA groups cannot make endorsements or select local priorities. Doing so would create an intra-party conflict because OFA is embedded within the DNC. Ari Melber, in a report titled "Year One of Organizing for America: The Permanent Field Campaign in a Digital Age," detailed the resulting contributions of the organization. OFA has continued to engage in heightened levels of political mobilization. Around health care reform alone, the organization reports that over 1.5 million volunteers took some action in 2009, including submission of 238,000 letters-to-the-editor of local papers, organizing of 11,906 local events, and a single day of action featuring 315,000 calls to Congress.[66] These numbers may appear small in comparison to the group's previous electoral mobilization, but they are quite large in comparison to other issue mobilization groups.

Melber coins a new term, "governance organizing," to describe the unique niche filled by this hybrid of a political organization and a formal party apparatus. I would endorse this term and add that we must consider OFA in its own unique category. An equivalent organization could conceivably be built by other successful presidential campaigns, or possibly by a governor at the state level, but the broader associational universe cannot (and in fact should not) adopt the organizational routines and mobilization strategies employed by the Obama team. OFA stands in a category of its own, apart from the netroots associational universe.

The limitations of governance organizing are apparent in two clear cases stemming from the Membership Communications Project dataset. First is the health care reform mobilization. Whereas groups like PCCC, MoveOn, DailyKos, and DFA actively called for strengthening the health care legislation as it moved through Congress, OFA remained mute on the details of the bill. There was no space for OFA volunteers to call for a public option or to pressure centrist Democrats to oppose restrictive abortion language. OFA's mobilization focused on "passing health reform now" rather than attempting to influence the contours of that legislation as it progressed.[67] Over the course of a lengthy policy battle, OFA was limited to a single, simple message, while other netroots advocacy groups stayed abreast of the latest news and engaged in a greater range of mobilization tactics.

Likewise, in the aftermath of the health care bill's passage, much of the progressive activist community was focused on supporting Lt. Governor Bill Halter's primary challenge to Senator Blanche Lincoln. Lincoln had been a vocal opponent of the public option within the Democratic caucus, and poor poll numbers indicated that she was virtually certain to lose her re-election bid against her Republican opponent. While PCCC, MoveOn, DFA, DailyKos, and several unions all devoted national attention and resources to mobilizing activist support for Halter, the local OFA volunteers had no voice in OFA's endorsement decision process. The DNC unsurprisingly supported the Democratic incumbent, and OFA quietly sought volunteers to support her primary re-election. It is possible that local OFA volunteers would have supported Lincoln anyway. But such a scenario is doubtful, given that MoveOn's, DFA's, and PCCC's member rolls are filled with Obama supporters, and the Halter campaign proved highly popular with these communities. But the larger point is that federated political associations act as "laboratories of Democracy" specifically *because* they create a venue for citizens to deliberate with one another, make decisions, and then enact those choices. The dilemma of control means that, despite OFA's tremendous size, the organization is severely handicapped in providing such a venue for its active local volunteers. OFA/DNC can mobilize mass supporter activity to "help enact the president's agenda." It cannot engage its members in discussion of local civic or political issues, though. And it cannot hand local members a democratic voice in deciding the president's agenda.

Conclusion

The neo-federated model is a work-in-progress amongst Internet-mediated political associations. In a limited set of circumstances, the Internet has usefully served to lower the costs of face-to-face engagement, invigorating local political associations like Philly for Change. From a normative perspective, this is the model that inspires the most optimism. Theorists dating back to Benjamin Barber have looked to the Internet with hopes that it could enable "strong democracy," with heightened participation in local and national affairs.[68] More recently, Skocpol has highlighted that the decline of cross-class membership federations represented a substantive loss for the American public sphere, as historic venues for citizen participation, social movement mobilization, and democratic skill-building were replaced by issue experts and professional lobbyists. My own normative preferences admittedly run in this direction as well. Many socially significant political matters are settled at the local level. If the next wave of Internet-driven innovation yields an increase in local citizen engagement, it would strike me as an unqualified social good. Local communities could use more and stronger social ties among their engaged citizenry.

Democracy for America serves as the leading example within the progressive netroots. It boasts "online tools for offline action" and leverages the lowered costs of online communication to support local affiliates like Philly for Change that are deeply reminiscent of political associations of old. But DFA is a limited example of the neo-federated model; its national activity is more in line with a MoveOn-style issue generalist. Relying on the sedimentary infrastructure built through the Dean campaign, the organization has a dozen or so strong local affiliates but few obvious opportunities for spreading that system to new cities and states.

The Internet, however, is a medium in continual development. DFA was developed years before the Mobile Web, and there is early "snow plowing" evidence that the applications and social practices supported by mobile, GPS-enabled computing devices can support major innovations in the arena of location-based activity. The wall that separated "cyberspace" from the "real world" has become a porous boundary. Internet access has come untethered from desktop and laptop devices and become an ever-present, augmenting feature of public life. The digital divide-related implications of this change are concerning but have limited impact on the potential for new political associations.

DFA, like Free Republic and the Drudge Report, seems more like a proto-organizational example of the neo-federated model. It combines first-mover advantage with a software platform that, in 2004, was far from ripe. Into this breach, the Mobile Web doubtless will have *some* impact, but it is too early to state definitively what that impact will be. The technology does not necessitate the growth of place-based netroots groups. It does, however, create a more permissive context, expanding the variety of data that can be passively gathered and rendering a digital presence in previously "offline" activities. As the Mobile Web continues to diffuse, researchers and organizers alike would be well advised to keep an eye on how the technological affordances of the Mobile Web are deployed by political organizations.

5

Netroots as Networks—Building
Progressive Infrastructure

"To respond to the challenges of elite entrenchment,
countermobilizers must develop . . . an 'alternative governing
coalition.' An alternative governing coalition is composed of
intellectual, network, and *political entrepreneurs,* and the *patrons*
that support them."
—Steven Teles, *The Rise of the Conservative Legal Movement*[1]

The organizational layer of American politics extends beyond membership associations. Along with the netroots generation of political organizations discussed
in Chapters 2, 3, and 4, a rich tapestry of non-membership advocacy organizations (NMAOs) has emerged in the past decade. These NMAOs were founded in
the midst of progressive *counter-mobilization*; the electoral and policy losses of the
2000, 2002, and 2004 elections prompted calls for new ideas, new strategies, and
new organizational arrangements within the American Left. Reacting to a perceived *infrastructure deficit* in comparison to conservative media, policy, and electoral efforts, the progressive donor community engaged in a concerted effort to
build new supporting institutions. New think tanks, training organizations, data
vendors, and backchannel communications networks were all forged in this time
period. These infrastructural endeavors drew upon the new media environment
and the changing needs of Internet-mediated advocacy organizations. The netroots' institutional capacities are shaped both by online technological affordances
and historical circumstance. This chapter extends our scope of analysis beyond
membership-based organizations, adding various types of *netroots infrastructure
organization* into the picture.

This chapter serves three purposes: first, it provides a historical backdrop to the
emergence of the political "netroots" in the first decade of the 21st century. The
new political associations among the American Left developed not only in response
to the changing communications environment, but also in response to perceived

failings of the existing institutions of the American Left. One individual—Rob Stein—was a particularly central actor in that zeitgeist, circulating a slideshow presentation on the network structure of conservative institutions among major donors and interest group leaders. Stein's slideshow directly resulted in the formation of the Democracy Alliance, a collaborative effort amongst progressive millionaire and billionaire donors to fund new infrastructure and new ideas. Given the attention paid in Chapter 2 to shifts in small-donor revenue streams ("The MoveOn Effect"), this parallel shift within the major donor community is well worth investigation. Second, the chapter seeks to round out our picture of the emerging interest group ecology of American politics. As Ed Walker, John McCarthy, and Frank Baumgartner have demonstrated, a focus on membership associations in isolation can result in a biased picture of political advocacy groups.[2] The "interest group explosion" of the 1970s changed the definition of organizational membership, but it did not change the proportions of NMAOs and membership organizations within the broader interest group population. NMAOs have long been a major component of the interest group universe, and our account of the netroots generation would be incomplete if it ignored them. Third and finally, attention to these various NMAOs highlights divergent insights about the role of online communications technologies in the (increasingly networked) public sphere. The Internet has had multiple effects on American political organizations; attention to varying types of progressive infrastructure yields a clearer picture of the changing organizational layer of American politics.

Five distinct organizational types are covered in the chapter. The New Organizing Institute convenes the annual RootsCamp "unconference" and provides training on new organizing techniques. It operates as a "West Point for Community Organizing," providing infrastructure for training political advocates in organizing skills, new and old. In so doing it serves as a *network forum*, a space where a network of professionals can meet, engage, share best practices, and formulate novel strategies.[3] ActBlue.com offers a more tangible form of infrastructure, providing an online fundraising portal for blogs, advocacy groups, and individuals alike. ActBlue fundraising pages stand in the background of the legislative and electoral campaigns conducted by DFA, PCCC, and DailyKos, among others. Whereas ActBlue is a nonprofit organization, for-profit vendors like Blue State Digital, Democracy In Action, and National Field provide technical support for e-mail, fundraising, blogs, and other new media outreach. Both legacy organizations and netroots organizations make use of their services. Populated primarily by veterans of the Dean and Obama campaign operations, these vendors provide a viable career path for members of the professional community.

NOI, ActBlue, and the vendors all provide tangible forms of infrastructure. Living Liberally, by contrast, is focused on the intangibles, building social capital among self-identifying progressive citizens. With a federation of Drinking Liberally chapters in 215 cities, Living Liberally creates a space where seasoned activists, motivated citizens, and political candidates can interact locally—a neo-federated organization whose stated goal is limited to "creating communities around progressive politics."[4] Likewise, a set of *network backchannels* stands in the backdrop of the progressive netroots. Google Group listservs like Town-House and JournoList support discussion, deliberation, and limited coordination within these burgeoning professional networks, creating a space for online discussion shielded from public view.

The five organizations profiled in this chapter do not represent a full survey of the associational landscape of the progressive netroots. A complete census would certainly include think tanks like the Center for American Progress, Center for Budget and Policy Priorities, and Campaign for America's Future. It would feature media reform operations like Media Matters for America, Free Press, and the Media Consortium. It would need to grapple with the independent cluster of organizations and conferences revolving around technology and democracy—groups like Personal Democracy Forum and the Sunlight Foundation that are decidedly nonpartisan in character. Such a study would represent a book-length endeavor in its own right. My purposes here are much narrower: it is my intention to alert the reader to the historical context in which the generation shift among political associations has occurred and to highlight a select set of additional trends among American political organizations.

Progressive Capacity-Building and the Democracy Alliance

The aftermath of the 2004 election was a nadir of sorts for the American Left. The 2000 election had been bitterly contested, devolving into the contentious *Bush v. Gore* Supreme Court decision. In the intervening four years, Republican dominance of the legislative and executive branches provided a stiff challenge, prompting a robust anti-war movement and an increasingly vocal activist base. In preparation for the 2004 election, 45 progressive advocacy groups joined together to form a "shadow party apparatus" of sorts, the America Votes Coalition. The coalition managed two interrelated efforts—the America Coming Together (ACT) voter mobilization effort and the Media Fund voter education effort. Supported by the deep pockets of billionaires George Soros and Peter Lewis (each of whom provided $20 million to the operation), along with many other wealthy donors, ACT was widely viewed as the "outsourcing" of the Democratic Party's field campaign operation (or "ground war"), replicating the election-season role traditionally played by the Democratic Party.[5] In many ways, ACT represented the collective best effort of the entire organized American Left. As George W. Bush won his second term of office, relying on a "72-hour strategy" that essentially negated ACT's large-scale coordination, all of the organizations and donors involved were left with gnawing existential questions about the effectiveness of their work.[6]

Democratic Party strategist Rob Stein had already begun circulating an existential answer of sorts several months previously. A lawyer and former Chief of Staff to Commerce Secretary Ron Brown, Stein was a minor figure among party operatives. He had developed an abiding interest in the network of conservative think tanks, media organizations, and advocacy groups, though. Years of investigation into the network of funders for conservative nonprofit organizations culminated in a PowerPoint presentation titled "The Conservative Message Machine Money Matrix." Stein's argument, as Matt Bai summarizes it, was that "the imbalance between the two parties nationally could be directly linked to this imbalance in their underlying infrastructures. The Right spent $170 million a year on national and local think tanks; the Left spent $85 million. The Right spent $35 million on legal advocacy groups; the Left spent $5 million. The Right spent $8 million to indoctrinate young conservatives at its Leadership Institute; the Left spent approximately nothing."[7] Jacob Hacker and Paul Pierson argue that these coordinated conservative expenditures arose from the 1970s—the "forgotten decade of American political history."[8] Facing the policy achievements of Lyndon Johnson's "Great Society" program and waves of social movement activism from the left, conservative interests began the work of counter-mobilization, investing in infrastructure and organizations for advancing conservative ideas and individuals across several fields of public life.

Stein presented his slideshow to over 300 advocacy organizations and influential donors.[9] Particularly in the aftermath of ACT's failure to affect the outcome of the 2004 election, his argument was enthusiastically received. At the time, chief Bush strategist Karl Rove was speaking boastfully about a "permanent Republican majority." Progressive donors were concerned that ongoing support for the same organizations would be a poor investment, failing to produce different results. Stein's explanation—that a long-term strategy of investing in think tanks, media advocacy groups, and leadership training had yielded an infrastructural advantage to conservative interests that could be productively mimicked by progressive donors—gained strong currency among major donors looking for an explanation of why ACT had failed.[10] From a historical perspective, it matters little whether Stein's network analysis of conservative intellectual, political, network entrepreneurs, and patron donors was precisely correct or not.[11] What matters is that the network of progressive advocacy leaders and major donors *believed* it to be correct and acted accordingly.

Stein's slideshow led directly to the formation of the Democracy Alliance (DA). A donor alliance of approximately 100 progressive millionaires, including billionaire financier George Soros and software entrepreneur Tim Gill, the alliance allows for strategic coordination among progressive donors and represents a substantial shift within a vital revenue stream for nonprofit advocacy efforts.

Members of the Democracy Alliance (called "Partners") pay annual dues of $30,000 and make a five-year commitment to contribute a minimum of $200,000 per year to progressive infrastructure.[12] Membership is extended by invitation only. Since their founding in 2005, DA partners have donated over $100 million to an agreed-upon "portfolio" of progressive infrastructural organizations.[13]

Recall from Figure 2.1 in Chapter 2 that the disruptive fundraising features of the MoveOn Effect are based in the transition of a *single* core revenue stream: the replacement of direct-mail fundraising with targeted online fundraising. The very existence of the DA is noteworthy by comparison simply because it represents a transition within a second core revenue stream—major or "patron" donors. The DA's impacts are shrouded in mystery, however, due to confidentiality policies that render us incapable of observing the specifics of their funding decisions. The best work on the group has come from journalists such as Matt Bai, Thomas Edsall, and Jim Vandehei and Chris Cillizza, as well as the public comments of Stein and cofounder Erica Payne.[14] As the group is not itself strictly an Internet-related phenomenon (they fund an offshoot project, New Media Ventures, that invests seed money in technology-related projects), my discussion of it here is limited to highlighting how seriously progressive advocacy leaders and donors took the "infrastructure deficit." To be clear, the Democracy Alliance is not directly responsible for the formation of the PCCC, MoveOn, DailyKos, or DFA. It did, however, play an important role in funding the netroots infrastructure that these groups often rely upon.

Markos Moulitsas offers a similar perspective in his 2008 book, indicating that counter-mobilization inspired a broad search for new ideas and new infrastructure: "Daily Kos exists because, quite simply, we had a dramatic market failure on our hands. If the gatekeepers wouldn't offer the news and viewpoints I craved, well then, I'd have to take matters into my own hands. Yet I had no template to work from. If I looked to progressive politics, all I saw was a movement splintered into 'issue silos' . . . all of them screaming that their issue was the most important, and sabotaging each other in pursuit of donor money and legislative priorities. And given the woeful state of the Democratic Party circa 2002, it was clear their approach was a failure."[15]

The various attempts to close the infrastructure gap all drew upon the new opportunities presented by online communication. Tracy Van Slyke and Jessica Clark discuss many of these newly formed institutions in their 2010 book, *Beyond the Echo Chamber*. "For many progressives, 2005 was the dawn of a new era. Multiple external factors were challenging long-held assumptions and rules for progressive media's operations, communications, and interactions with the public."[16] Likewise, Chris Bowers and Matt Stoller wrote in a 2005 white paper, "progressive Internet activists have not relied on an existing set of institutional relationships. They have instead forged a new constituency group, a new set of leaders, and a new forest of social relationships."[17] This is a pattern commonly found during periods of counter-mobilization. Facing an ascendant opposing ideological coalition, networked progressives began developing new organizational solutions. Donors and dissatisfied activists alike turn to new solutions. They seek to forge what Stephen Teles calls an "alternative governing coalition," made up of "intellectual, network, and political entrepreneurs, and the patrons that support them."[18]

The resulting netroots institutions were created to address a wide range of needs. MoveOn, DFA, PCCC, and DailyKos all seek to mobilize broad issue publics to directly affect progressive policy change, thus they organize themselves as membership-based political associations. The New Organizing Institute, Blue State Digital, and ActBlue all play complementary roles and develop as non-membership associations.[19] As such, the organizations profiled in this chapter are only loosely tied together. All provide a form of "infrastructure," and all were formed as part of the broader progressive counter-mobilization in the early 2000s. But the purposes of these organizations—the types of infrastructure that they provide and the ways they employ the Internet to provide it—are far more diverse. What follows, then, are five separate profiles of infrastructure providers. Each profile sketches their role in the broader progressive interest group ecology and explores their implications for how we should understand the multiple effects the Internet has on the American public sphere.

Thought Leadership: The New Organizing Institute

The New Organizing Institute (NOI) is meant to serve as a "West Point for Community Organizers." Its purpose and mission are devoted to refining the craft of political organizing in the digital era. Drawing upon top campaign professionals—from both electoral campaigning and netroots organizing—the organization serves as a training institute and *network forum* for the professional field. Legacy organizations send their staff to NOI trainings in order to learn data management and analytics skills. Netroots organizations attend NOI's annual RootsCamp "unconference" to discuss emerging trends. They also use NOI trainings to identify new staff members. As the tools of professional nonprofit advocacy evolve, NOI serves as an essential venue for reviewing, assessing, and disseminating best practices.

The organization was founded amidst the 2004 election. Cofounder and current Executive Director Judith Freeman describes the genesis of the organization as stemming from a 2004 retreat among "20 to 25 people who had really done a lot of innovation with how you integrate, how you link the online work and the technology with field [organizing]."[20] Cofounder and former President Zack Exley explains that "the ideal was that top people in their respective fields would agree to set aside some time from their busy careers to train the next generation—in other words, that our trainings would be driven by current practitioners who had their own stories of trial and error to personally present."[21] In a video interview, Exley further explained the perceived need:

> "A handful of [veterans from the Dean campaign and MoveOn] kept getting asked by other organizations, by people looking to hire people, 'who can we get, who can we get, who can we get?' And we didn't have anybody to recommend to them because there wasn't a whole generation of organizers who had come up doing this kind of work."[22]

Exley's perspective is focused on Internet-mediated organizing as a vocation. The set of people who have deep experience running an online activism department was miniscule in 2004. It is still quite small in 2012. Legacy organizations and netroots startups alike draw upon this limited pool when making new hires. Much like the famed Midwest Academy, founded and maintained by students of legendary community organizer Saul Alinsky, NOI seeks to expand and enrich the talent pool for membership organizations and political campaigns. NOI is the space where progressive advocacy professionals reflect upon the *craft* of 21st century political organizing. It draws together senior leaders of groups like MoveOn, OFA, DFA, and PCCC to teach online organizing to peer organizations and potential future staffers. In so doing, it serves the role of a "network forum," as defined by Fred Turner.[23] Network forums are spaces where allied but occasionally competing organizations and individuals can come together, share best practices, exchange ideas, discuss the state of their movement/community/profession, and craft new institutions.

NOI's main activities include the annual RootsCamp "unconference," an "Organizer's Toolbox," regular training events, and a clearinghouse for community organizing jobs. In the Membership Communications Project dataset, NOI was unique in that every one of its e-mails was tied to an upcoming event announcement. The group does not mobilize supporters to call their congressperson. Rather, it mobilizes supporters to attend "Dining Organizers" potlucks where they can share information and provide support to members of a shared professional community. In 2011, NOI added "Tip of the Day" e-mails, offering free tips on "organizing, new media, management, and data." Some of these tips are Internet-related ("Use Google Analytics to boost results"), while others are devoted to offline event organizing ("Communicate with attendees before events").[24] The organization functions as an Internet-enabled training academy but is not focused solely on Internet skills.

The RootsCamp unconference is a central gathering space for the political Netroots, rivaling the annual Netroots Nation convention. While Netroots Nation features major speakers and heavy media attention, RootsCamp offers an intentionally less formal atmosphere. Held annually in DC, with occasional regional summits as well, RootsCamp follows Tim O'Reilly's "BarCamp" format. Such "unconferences" rely on the attendees to fashion their own agenda, providing breakout rooms and a main convention hall and inviting attendees to propose their own panels and place them on "the Board" upon arrival (see Figure 5.1 for a photo of the Board at RootsCamp 2010). RootsCamp is a physical instantiation of the network forum concept—it literally provides a forum for the netroots professional community to interact. Unconferences succeed or fail based upon network effects—with no headlining speakers or agenda to announce, attendance is determined by who else will be attending. RootsCamp draws approximately 1,000 people annually. Organizing for America, MoveOn, DFA, PCCC, ActBlue, and alumni of the electoral campaigns all attend, and their active participation in turn attracts the rest of the professional community.

NOI's training philosophy is deeply rooted in a longstanding community organizing tradition. Judith Freeman, Zack Exley, and other NOI leaders are closely allied with Harvard professor Marshall Ganz, himself a nearly legendary figure within progressive political circles. Ganz spent decades working side by side with Cesar Chavez and the United Farm Workers. In 1991, he returned to Harvard, earned a PhD in sociology, and began teaching classes and conducting research on political organizing.[25] Ganz's imprint can be found

Figure 5.1 "The Board" at RootsCamp 2010

both in the NOI Organizer's Toolbox—a free training resource based upon the curriculum he teaches at Harvard—and on a variety of progressive political associations. His connections to Freeman, Exley, and others were forged through the "Camp Obama" trainings in 2008, which trained over 20,000 Obama campaign volunteers and staff.[26]

Ganz himself is something of an Internet skeptic. He has long maintained that online organizing is no different than traditional community organizing. Some readers may thus be surprised that NOI's training philosophy is reflective of his teachings. Ganz emphasizes the role of "public narrative," building a "culture of commitment" within organizations, developing the "ladder of engagement," and enunciating a clear "theory of change." All of these concepts are prominently featured in NOI's Organizer's Toolbox as well. For the leading practitioners of online organizing, new media offers an enhanced toolset rather than a complete departure from traditional organizing techniques.

NOI's curriculum highlights the different lenses with which academics and practitioners approach Internet-mediated collective action. Much of the academic analysis has focused on potential reformulations of Mancur Olson's classic treatise, *The Logic of Collective Action*. Arthur Lupia and Gisela Sin suggest that "historically uncontroversial assumptions" Olson made about the costs of interpersonal communication have been "invalidated" by the Internet."[27] Stu Shulman has argued that Internet-mediated political organizing is something entirely new, an "emergent form of grassroots, democratic, fire alarm activism."[28] Bruce Bimber, Andrew Flanagin, and Cynthia Stohl reconceptualize collective action from a traditional free rider problem to a phenomenon of "boundary crossing" between public and private domains.[29] These works help us sketch the *theoretical* implications of a novel communications environment for *rational* actors. The networked community that assembles through NOI trainings and events is concerned with a fundamentally different set of questions. They assemble an understanding of the *practical* implications of the novel communications environment for *overworked, underpaid* actors.[30] In so doing, NOI provides an intellectual infrastructure for disseminating actionable knowledge within a field of practice.

The Power of the Bundle: The ActBlue Fundraising Portal

ActBlue is a fundraising portal, providing the technical infrastructure necessary for the candidate-centric pass-through fundraising practiced by DailyKos, DFA, PCCC, and similar organizations. Founded in 2004 by Ben Rahn and Matt DeBergalis, the site quickly became a central component of netroots political campaigns.[31] Over the course of the following three election cycles (six years), the site has been responsible for funneling over $175,000,000 to Democratic candidates and political organizations. ActBlue stands in the background of most examples we have seen in the book thus far—from the PCCC's Wisconsin political advertisements to DailyKos's fundraising for Jim Webb (VA Senate, 2006) and DFA's national candidate endorsements. The flexibility of the site is key to its success. Rather than developing a single, centralized list of its own endorsed candidates (as do Republican sites like SlateCard and RightRoots—see Chapter 6), ActBlue provides easy-to-use tools for individuals and organizations to create their own endorsement lists. In so doing, it provides "progressive infrastructure" in the purest sense of the term. It supports the work of new political associations rather than engaging in political mobilization of its own.

Adam Green, cofounder of the PCCC, offers the following explanation of Act-Blue's niche: "At a time when we had pretty much no resources, ActBlue lowered the barrier for entry for us into the online fundraising marketplace allowing us to . . . not have to deal with the legal obstacles and technical obstacles and quickly accumulate a grassroots fundraising base . . . it's a valuable piece of progressive infrastructure. It allows groups like ours to get off the ground."[32] Indeed, during the PCCC's first two years of operation, the group raised over $2,000,000 through the site from 100,000 individual small donors. Most of that money takes the form of targeted or pass-through donations, with specific donation pages set up to fund in-district polling in Tennessee, issue accountability commercials in Montana, and direct donations to Bill Halter's Arkansas Senate primary campaign.

As Green notes, ActBlue lowers the barriers to entry for startup netroots organizations like the PCCC. Setting up a system to handle their issue- and campaign-specific fundraising needs, particularly given the speed with which their campaign actions occur, would require substantial overhead costs on the part of the PCCC. The organization would need to hire lawyers and information technology developers, either as short-term consultants or as in-house employees. ActBlue lowers that overhead cost for netroots political associations and candidate campaigns. Similar to Hindman's finding regarding web traffic, the ease of establishing an ActBlue page is hardly equivalent to the ease of raising large sums through the portal; the modal ActBlue fundraising page receives $0. But lowering the startup costs for netroots organizations is still a noteworthy phenomenon, allowing new groups to fundraise and list-build without first making their case to foundations and patron donors.

ActBlue has been a core component of DailyKos's fast-moving tactical repertoire. On Friday, October 17, 2008, Republican Congresswoman Michele Bachmann appeared on *Hardball with Chris Matthews* and, flummoxed by an interview question, suggested that "I wish the American media would take a great look at the views of the people in Congress and find out, are they pro-America or anti-America?"[33] The DailyKos community quickly seized on these remarks, noting the blatant overture to McCarthyism, and launched a "money-bomb" fundraiser for her congressional opponent, Elwyn Tinklenberg. The wave of online donations quickly crashed Tinklenberg's campaign fundraising page. DailyKos community members reacted immediately, establishing a "bloggers against new McCarthyism" donation page on ActBlue. With a ready-made Actblue "widget"—a thermometer graphic that could easily be entered into a blog post—all future netroots fundraising was funneled to the candidate through ActBlue (see Figure 5.2). Over the course of the following 48 hours, DailyKos and other blogging communities like FireDogLake would raise over $810,000 for Tinklenberg's campaign—*nearly matching the candidate's fundraising total in the previous year.* The anti-Bachmann moneybomb provides direct evidence of the resource mobilization prowess of netroots political associations like DailyKos.[34] ActBlue lurks in the background of the example, providing enabling infrastructure for the netroots tactical repertoire. Tinklenberg's small campaign was not prepared for the flood of national interest that would appear only if his opponent made an unexpected gaffe on the national stage. ActBlue provided the tools for bloggers—themselves unaffiliated with Tinklenberg's campaign—to quickly deploy a technical solution.

ActBlue is a not-for-profit organization. Registered as a federal Political Action Committee (PAC), the organization enables online small donors to engage in "bundling," a practice pioneered by networks of wealthy donors in earlier

Figure 5.2 ActBlue Fundraising Widget

presidential campaign cycles.[35] The organization is funded primarily through two sources. First, it charges a 3.95% processing fee on all gross transactions. These fees are provided to ActBlue Technical Services, a subsidiary organization launched in 2009.[36] ActBlue Technical Services designs the software platform, working to extend supported fundraising services to include state and local elections, and also develops new tools for mobile giving. The fee covers the technical and administrative costs of processing online credit card transactions. The Act-Blue PAC also includes a "tip jar," inviting donors to include an optional, incremental "tip" of 10% or 20% when making an online donation. And once an individual has donated to a candidate through ActBlue, the organization adds their address to its equivalent of a member list. ActBlue sends out a donor appeal approximately once per month.

The most noteworthy feature of ActBlue's model is that it enables the "outsourcing" of operational tasks. The largest political campaigns and organizations— Obama for America and MoveOn, for example—develop their own fundraising software internally.[37] But for smaller groups and new groups (such as the PCCC), the site removes "legal and technical obstacles." Rather than directly hiring lawyers and software developers, either as full-time staff or as short-term consultants, organizations can rely on the infrastructure provided by ActBlue. A similar trend appeared in Chapter 2, with the discussion of MoveOn's "phantom staff." Recall that MoveOn maintains a small, networked core of full-time staff. Short-term phantom staff are hired to work on major mobilizations, their salaries supported through targeted online fundraising. In both cases, what we see is an industry-wide transition, from DC-centric advocacy groups whose infrastructure is housed internally with a large staff bureaucracy to Internet-mediated advocacy groups whose supporting infrastructure is largely outsourced. Consultants, phantom staff, and netroots infrastructure organizations like ActBlue cover activities that used to be managed in-house. It is a transition in the advocacy group ecology itself. Targeted online fundraising provides less unrestricted money to cover high overhead costs. Netroots infrastructure like ActBlue fits into the new "niches" thus produced in the broader interest group ecology.

Lead-User Innovation in Practice: Changes to the Political Consultant Network

While ActBlue provides a fairly visible form of infrastructure for new advocacy groups and political candidates alike, a set of for-profit new media vendors offers a broader selection of less visible, highly technical services. Organizations like Blue State Digital, Convio, Democracy in Action/Salsa Labs, and M+R offer a range of services, including website design, e-mail writing and analytics-based testing, online fundraising support, and overall content management systems. Best known for the services they offer to electoral campaigns (as detailed by Daniel Kreiss in *Taking Our Country Back*), these organizations also provide substantial support to advocacy groups. Rather than employing in-house new media expertise, most advocacy groups turn to one of these vendors to manage their e-mail programs. In so doing, the new media consulting industry narrows the gap between legacy and Internet-mediated political associations. With the NAACP and 1Sky.org both relying upon Democracy in Action's "Salsa" e-mail platform, e-mail recipients encounter largely similar messages from organizations new and old.

The existence of this new media consulting industry is noteworthy for three reasons: convergence in practices, network-driven differences between progressive and conservative groups, and the generational implications of "lead-user innovation" in the industry.[38]

The small cadre of vendors listed above plays a mediating role for a substantial portion of progressive online mobilization. Salsa Labs/Democracy in Action, for instance, was responsible for sending 1.73 billion advocacy e-mails in 2009.[39] Within the Membership Communications Project dataset, I was able to easily identify 10 Salsa clients, including Campaign for America's Future, Catholics in Alliance for the Common Good, Center for Progressive Leadership, FairVote, Moms Rising, Progressive States Network, New Organizing Institute, 1Sky, National Organization for Women, and the NAACP. Another eight organizations just as obviously used Convio, while a few dozen used less obviously branded vendors or relied on in-house programmers. Organizations that share the same vendor offer nearly identical user experiences. As Stuart Shulman has noted, the vendors link their e-mobilization services with "Tell a Friend" and "Donate" pages, differentiating their products from one another and selling a packaged product to advocacy group clients.[40] For the reasons specified in Chapter 2, this convergence falls short of alleviating the generational differences between legacy and netroots e-mail usage—legacy organizations still have massive staff and infrastructure. E-mail programs must fit into existing work routines. But the new vendors do lower the costs facing legacy organizations that wish to move some mobilization and membership-relations functions online. Rather than creating a new department, they can develop a Request for Proposals.

Notably, this new industrial field of for-profit vendors is almost entirely partisan in nature. Jascha Franklin Hodge of Blue State Digital has articulated his company's policy that "any political work that we do will be in line with our political values."[41] Political scientists Jacob Montgomery and Brendan Nyhan similarly found that political consultants firmly align with Democrats or Republicans.[42] From an institutional perspective, this alignment acts as a mechanism for fostering cleavages between progressive and conservative Internet use patterns. Organizational learning and best practices flow smoothly within the progressive network of organizations. Associational leaders attend the same conferences and trainings (such as those convened by NOI). Organizational staffers move back and forth between nonprofits and vendor employment, facilitating the spread of shared ideas and organizational norms.[43] Those staffers then launch for-profit vendors, which in turn offer services solely to ideologically affiliated nonprofits.

Paul Dimaggio and Walter Powell coined the term "institutional isomorphism" in their classic 1983 paper, "The Iron Cage Revisited," to describe the tendency of organizations in a field to converge toward similar structures. Institutional isomorphism in Internet adoption is facilitated by professional network ties, just as it is facilitated in the corporate world through overlapping boards of directors.[44] The lack of these network ties between netroots and "rightroots" organizations is one reason why conservative advocacy groups have failed to adopt the successful organizational innovations of the netroots. Within ideological coalitions, the transfer of knowledge occurs through staff-driven, vendor-driven, and conference-driven information exchange. Between ideological coalitions, those information exchanges don't take place. Even though the Right shows a demonstrable interest in "building its own MoveOn" (as we will see in Chapter 6), MoveOn has no interest in sharing best practices with its political opponents, and the vendors that help legacy progressive associations become more MoveOn-like do not offer services to conservative political associations.

The partisan orientation of these for-profit vendors would initially appear to be something of a mystery, the incentive to increase profits by expanding the client base being presumably self-evident. A brief examination of the roots of these organizations reveals an explanation, however. Blue State Digital, Convio, and Democracy In Action were all founded by alumni of the Howard Dean campaign. M+R Strategic Services is a sole outlier, having established its new media program in 2000. Related data vendors, such as Catalist, likewise arose out of Democratic electoral operations.[45] What is noteworthy here is that the new media technical support—both for electoral organizations and issue groups—is provided almost entirely by a new wave of upstart consultancies. David Dulio has established that the political consulting industry grew by leaps and bounds over the past 50 years, developing into a robust industrial field in its own right.[46] One would expect that major consultancies would lead the way in developing new services for online engagement. Yet we instead find a clear pattern in which new waves of campaign innovation come from former campaign staffers rather than established industry leaders.

Consider the case of National Field, recipient of the "Best Campaign Technology" award at the New Organizing Institute's 2010 RootsCamp. National Field was founded by three former Obama campaign field organizers: Justin Lewis, Edward Saatchi, and Aharon Wasserman. While working in North Carolina, the organizers encountered a range of challenges in trying to satisfy day-to-day organizational reporting requirements. The three staffers bootstrapped together a modified data visualization system, creating separate programs to augment the vendor-provided software. After the campaign ended, they packaged those modifications into a new platform. They began approaching campaigns and political associations alike, touting the successes they'd experienced in the field and the tailored services that their new system could offer. Organizing for America (and thus the Democratic National Committee) hired National Field as a vendor, as did a variety of allied political organizations and electoral campaigns. After the 2010 election, the former field staffers expanded their operations internationally. A new industry leader was born. Other data vendors have followed a similar development path.

Eric von Hippel's research on commercial product development provides an apt point of comparison. One of the preeminent scholars of industrial innovation, von Hippel's work describes a pattern of "lead-user innovation," in which "users of products and services—both firms and individual consumers—are increasingly able to innovate for themselves."[47] For von Hippel, most industrial innovations originate not in the research and development laboratory, but among lead-users who refashion an existing product, eventually sharing their modification with the industry leader or launching their own product line. He contrasts this lead-user perspective against the traditional model, in which "a user's only role is to have needs, which manufacturers then identify and fill by designing and producing new products."[48] Von Hippel's work has defined an entire subfield within management and diffusion-of-innovation studies, but has rarely received attention from social scientists interested in politics or social processes. The political consulting industry provides a clear application of von Hippel's model. Consultants generally develop their reputation through direct campaign participation and then branch out to provide a specific service (yard signs, door hangers, campaign commercials, strategic development, etc.) to a wide range of clients.[49] With electoral campaign professionals working on short-term contracts that end after Election Day, the transition from "lead-user" campaign staff to new-entrant political consultant occurs at a faster rate than in more stable industrial fields. Launching a new consultancy is a standard off-year pursuit.

The end result is that new media vendors, electoral campaigns, and political associations display deep partisan network ties. The new data vendors support the diffusion of shared practices among progressives and Democratic electoral campaigns, while conservatives and Republican campaigns are cordoned off and evolve separately. Staff at Blue State Digital or National Field start out working 100 hours/week with staff at MoveOn, Organizing for America/Democratic National Committee, and American Federation of Teachers. They attend the same conferences, work in overlapping coalitions, and participate on the same backchannel listservs. New entrants to the industry emerge as an aftereffect of each campaign season, driven by the same process of lead-user innovation witnessed in more traditional economic fields. The boundaries between for-profit new media vendors, political parties, political campaigns, and advocacy groups are permeable, made up of intersecting organizations and overlapping staffs. The interest group ecology of progressive advocacy organizations is distinct from the interest group ecology of their conservative analogues.

Creating Communities around Progressive Politics: Drinking Liberally as Social Network Reservoir

While ActBlue and National Field provide a highly tangible form of infrastructure, our next example traffics in the intangible infrastructure of social ties. Every Tuesday in Philadelphia, a group of bloggers and netroots progressives gathers for drink specials and free hot wings. During my field research in 2007, the regular participants included Anne Dicker, the original chair of Philly for Change, Duncan "Atrios" Black, one of the premiere political bloggers in America,[50] and an assortment of local political operatives, lawyers, bloggers, and political partisans. Formally, it is the weekly meeting of Philadelphia's Center City chapter of Drinking Liberally—part of LivingLiberally.org's national network of social gatherings. The meeting agenda is anything but *formal*, however. A few signs and buttons differentiate the Drinking Liberally (DL) group from other bar patrons. No one keeps meeting minutes, however, and no reports are given. Local and national politics are occasional topics of conversation, but so are the Phillies and Eagles. The explicit purpose of a DL meeting is to "create communities around progressive politics."[51] An average DL meeting is a social event, a gathering space where local progressives can build social ties with one another. In so doing, DL meetings provide a reservoir of network connections for the broader progressive community.

Philadelphia Drinking Liberally is part of the broader Living Liberally network. Founded by Justin Krebs and Matt O'Neill in May 2003, the group now boasts 212 DL local chapters in 45 states.[52] It features Laughing Liberally, Screening Liberally, Eating Liberally, and Reading Liberally programs as well. The national organization is, in fact, a stronger approximation of the neo-federated ideal type than Democracy for America. It holds an annual national conference for its chapter coordinators, along with monthly conference calls and chapter check-ins, thickening the ties between the federated units and the national organization.

Though Living Liberally is neo-federated in structure, it intentionally forgoes a defining feature of other netroots membership associations: it does not engage in direct political mobilization. Rather than actively building its member list through sedimentary waves of electoral or issue-based mobilization, the organization concerns itself with informal community-building. The PCCC and DFA formally partner with one another to launch a television commercial on health care reform. Living Liberally is where their staff and volunteers can then go to refresh and socialize. The Providence, Rhode Island, chapter of DL holds monthly meetings, usually inviting a candidate for political office to meet participants, shake hands, and answer questions. Unlike Democracy for America though, the group does not make endorsements. Rather, candidates show up to these events just as they might attend a Rotary or Elks Club meeting. They do so because it is a venue for attracting committed volunteers—an Internet-mediated but locally based civic forum. Living Liberally provides the immaterial infrastructure of social ties rather than the material infrastructure of software code or organizing techniques.

The national Living Liberally organization is a Limited Liability Corporation (LLC) rather than a 501c(3) nonprofit. As such, donations to the group are not tax-deductible—a surprising design choice, since the group would certainly qualify for nonprofit status. As Justin Krebs explains it, the low operating costs of the national organization determine its tax structure.[53] Living Liberally does not need to pursue foundation funding. Instead, it holds an annual fundraiser and cobbles together limited revenue through online advertisements, merchandising efforts, voluntary chapter contributions (passing the hat), and consulting opportunities. Based in New York, the organization has never had more than three staffers and pays no overhead for formal office space. It is currently run entirely by volunteers. LLC status allows the organization greater flexibility and fewer administrative hassles with federal reporting requirements. DailyKos, HotAir, and many other political blogs are also incorporated as LLCs, a relatively new development in the nonprofit advocacy community. The benefit of incorporation as a 501c(3) nonprofit is that donations are tax-deductible—a near-necessity for organizations pursuing patron donor or foundation gifts. Several internet-mediated organizations carry low enough operating costs to forego large-scale fundraising, and this is reflected in their alternate tax status.

Living Liberally's growth occurs mostly through word of mouth and blog mentions. Duncan Black, himself a former chapter coordinator,[54] maintains a prominent link to the group's website on his blog, which receives tens of thousands of daily visitors. The group also hosts Screening Liberally and Laughing Liberally events at the annual Netroots Nation conference, further enhancing its exposure within the netroots community. Early organizational development occurred through a mix of organic, Diaspora-like growth (the second chapter was founded in San Francisco, after a New York regular moved across the country) and news coverage of the organization's events connected to the 2004 Republican National Convention protests. While the group's niche as a social gathering place for political progressives has attracted occasional media profiles,[55] the lack of political organizing results in a lower profile than other Internet-mediated political associations. The group is not in competition with any other political associations (for members, media attention, or funding). Rather, its growth occurs because it helps augment the local-level work of those groups.

Asking little of chapter coordinators—host weekly or monthly social hours and fill out a brief form to keep the national organization updated—the group provides a low-cost entry point for self-identifying progressives to form a community and build social ties.

The theoretical importance of Living Liberally to our broader narrative lies in what it tells us about the Internet and social ties. Malcolm Gladwell has become the spokesperson for the "clicktivism"-based critique, arguing that "the platforms of social media are built around weak ties."[56] High-risk social movement tactics, by contrast, are based on strong ties.[57] Ergo, he suggests, online communications tools are of relatively little use to social movements and political activism. They leverage the wrong type of social ties. Gladwell's brief foray into the literature on network ties and social movement mobilization is relatively defensible. Social movement scholars such as Doug McAdam, Gerald Marwell, and Pam Oliver have demonstrated that, while information diffuses primarily through weak-tie networks, social movement activation occurs through strong-tie networks.[58] But Gladwell's notion of Internet use is too limited. Groups like Living Liberally rely on the Internet to organize social events whose purpose is to foster strong ties between progressive activists.[59] Indeed, the *infrastructure* that Living Liberally offers to the movement can best be understood as a reservoir of strengthened social ties. It is a substrate through which advocacy organizations and network entrepreneurs can locate potential collaborators to launch future campaign actions.

Fight Club Rules: Google Groups as Network Backchannels

Along with the publicly visible social gathering spaces established by Living Liberally, the political netroots also set up publicly opaque gathering spaces through semiformal listservs—what I term *network backchannels*. Hosted through Google's free Google Groups feature, these backchannel lists knit professional communities and subcommunities together. They delineate a space for off-the-record, private conversations among self-constructed in-groups. Their off-the-record nature has made the lists an infrequent topic of analysis—only two such lists have attracted journalistic attention, and no academic researchers have ever touched upon the subject.

The backchannel lists fill a key niche for the netroots professional community—they provide a space where "internal" conversations can occur among networked political actors, much as formal offices provide a space for internal conversation among coworkers. They provide a good venue for discussion and information sharing but a poor venue for complex coordination tasks. Interestingly, the secrecy embedded in their off-the-record nature has led to clouds of media speculation about "netroots conspiracies." The reality of these lists turns out to be more mundane but also more theoretically informative. This section uses the two back-channels that have been the subject of media controversy—TownHouse and JournoList—to draw broader lessons about the intangible infrastructure provided by backchannel lists.

TownHouse's own name provides an indication of its niche. If the early netroots political community could be said to have a physical home, it would have to be the Townhouse Tavern in Washington, DC. Subterranean and grungy, the Dupont Circle bar was the favored destination for the network of DC-based bloggers and Internet-mediated political operatives after the 2004 election. They gathered every Sunday, building professional network ties through the time-honored practice of alcohol consumption. Unlike Drinking Liberally chapters, which invite all comers and openly advertise, the TownHouse sessions were invitation-only, delineating a space where they could talk informally among a self-selecting in-group. As that professional community grew, blogger Matt Stoller created a Google Group bearing the same name, inviting netroots professionals from across the nation to participate. TownHouse grew from there, apace with the rising influence of the progressive netroots.

Jason Zengerle of *The New Republic* first wrote about TownHouse in 2006, terming it a "secret society of liberal bloggers." Zengerle was speculating on progressive political bloggers' lack of interest in a mini-scandal involving blogger Jerome Armstrong's trouble with the Securities and Exchange Commission. He theorized that Markos Moulitsas had sent a message "to this secret group that plots strategy in the digital equivalent of a smoke-filled backroom."[60] Moulitsas and others countered that Zengerle's claim was overblown; Markos had simply informed a listserv that it wasn't much of a controversy (a claim borne out over time). But beltway observers relished the news of a secret blogger list. Daniel Schulman, writing in 2007 for *Mother Jones*, argued that the TownHouse backchannel discussion list "echoes the very control-the-message philosophy the blogosphere once rose up to fight.[61] One of the benefits of blogging is its interactivity and open, conversational nature. That the leading bloggers were simultaneously having conversations outside the public arena struck some as hypocritical.

A much larger controversy arose in 2010, after blogger/journalist Dave Weigel's e-mails to another backchannel, JournoList, were leaked to conservative media blogs. JournoList was created in February 2007 by Ezra Klein, himself a prominent blogger who was making the transition into more traditional publishing outlets. JournoList was designed not to support the political netroots but to provide "an insulated space where the lure of a smart, ongoing conversation would encourage journalists, policy experts and assorted other observers to share their insights with one another."[62] The list was made up of 400 or so left-leaning journalists and academics. Weigel, who covered the Tea Party beat for the *Washington Post*, had occasionally vented his frustration with sources and conservative elites to the list. (After Matt Drudge prominently linked to him twice, causing a flurry of hate mail, he wrote to the list that "This would be a vastly better world to live in if Matt Drudge decided to handle his emotional problems more responsibly, and set himself on fire.") The leak of his e-mails resulted in his forced resignation from the *Washington Post*. It also became a metaphorical "smoking gun" for online conservative media critics, proof of left-wing coordination and "liberal media conspiracy."[63] When back-channel lists enter the public dialogue, they are afforded a nefarious character. After all, why else would they be secret and off the record? In reality, they're just listservs. Their secrecy is as much a product of software design as it is practical necessity.

The Google Groups design architecture heavily influences the shroud of secrecy surrounding these network backchannels. Creating a Google Group is a three-step process, accomplished in minutes. It includes a decision between three "access levels": "public," "announcement-only," and "restricted" (see Figure 5.3). Public and announcement-only Google Groups are searchable through Google and can be accessed by anyone. Restricted Google Groups are invitation-only and cannot be found through web search. The only way to learn of such groups is to be told. For an Internet-mediated professional community that often posts commentary to public political blogs, there is no value in creating a public or announcement-only discussion list. Anything they might say to the list could just as easily be posted as a blog entry, with the added benefit of increased potential audience, exposure, and advertising revenue. Restricted lists, by contrast, provide an online space for "water cooler conversation" within the networked public.[64]

More menacing is a common list rule, often referred to as the "Fight Club rule," employed by TownHouse, JournoList, and many other such lists.[65] A common version of the Fight Club list rule, automatically appended to the bottom of all listserv messages, is "Do not mention the name or existence of the list in public or the press."[66] The Fight Club rule certainly *sounds* conspiratorial. In practice, it serves to support two goals. First, it allows backchannel conversations to remain in the background. Offline gatherings like the original TownHouse sessions limit group membership on the basis of physical co-presence. The in-group is delineated by physically *being there*. A Weigel or a Moulitsas can vent to friends or remark on a supposed scandal with tone and inflection. Their statements are made to friends and colleagues and do not remain permanently archived anywhere. By contrast, given that anyone *could* join a listserv like JournoList or TownHouse (and potentially take offense at being turned down), limiting public knowledge of a backchannel allows it to maintain some of the characteristics of a weekly dinner engagement among peer communities. Writing for *The New Republic*, Jonathan Chait offers an explanation JournoList's closed rule: ". . . Conversations consisted of requests for references—does anybody know an expert in such and such—instantaneous reactions to events, joshing around, conversations about sports and the like. Why did this have to be private? Because when you're a professional writer, even in the age of Twitter, you try to maintain some basic standard in your published work. I don't subject my readers to my thoughts on the Super Bowl as of halftime, or even (usually) the

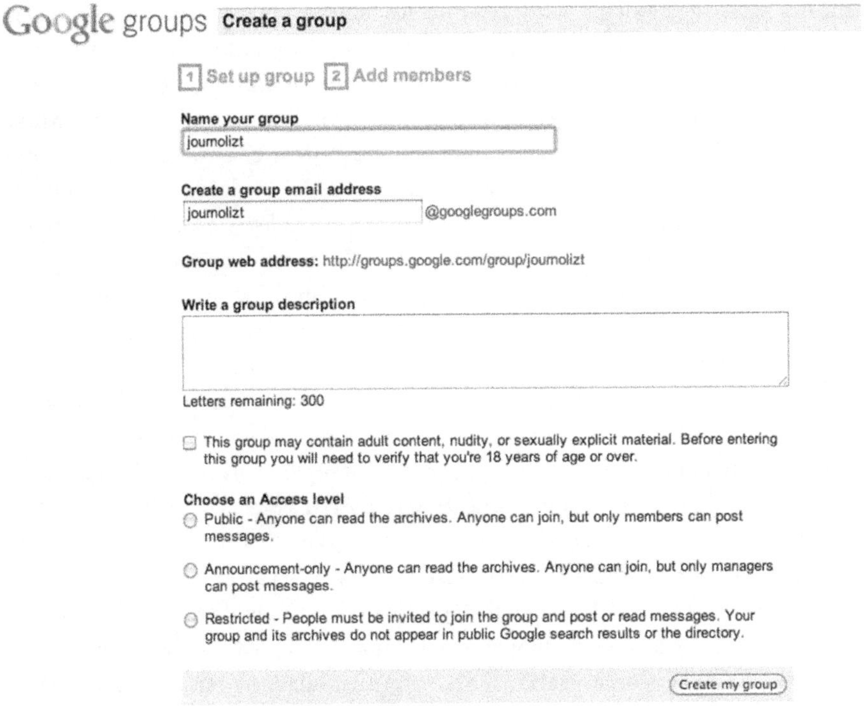

Figure 5.3 Sample Google Group Setup Page

meaning of the Pennsylvania special election two minutes after polls close. You want the ability to share your thoughts with a group to which you may not have physical proximity."[67]

The second function is to keep such lists from becoming the source of rampant conspiratorial speculation. Here the fates of both TownHouse and JournoList serve as cautionary tales of sorts. JournoList was shut down after Weigel's forced resignation, and conservative blogger Andrew Breitbart publicly offered a $100,000 bounty for the full JournoList archives.[68] TownHouse is still in existence, but interviewees commonly refer to it as irrelevant, having grown to an unmanageable size with frequent leaks. Conservative bloggers continue to invoke both lists as "proof" of liberal conspiracies, regularly claiming that Markos Moulitsas or other prominent netroots professionals issue "marching orders" through the lists.

In practice, the listserv architecture provides a terrible forum for any such Machiavellian coordination. The only sanctions available against rule-breakers are list-based shaming and removal from the list. List moderators act as "networked gatekeepers,"[69] but networked gatekeeping is a limited form of network power[70]—if a moderator is disliked, someone else can just create an alternate list. Beyond shaming and list removal, moderators possess no resources or enforcement mechanisms. Real conspiracies require some degree of enforcement or coordination; a conspiracy is, by its very nature, *difficult to manage*. The proof against claims that network backchannels distribute marching orders among net-roots leaders and journalists is that listservs are a terrible venue for such coordination. As James Fallows remarked after the JournoList controversy, "I have one question for people who are upset about an e-mail list involving 400+ mainly liberal journalists and academics: *Have you ever been on a listserv?* ... It had all of the virtues, and many of the faults, of the standard Internet e-mail list."[71] Compared to Grover Norquist's in-person weekly message coordination meetings for conservative elites, a backchannel Google Group simply does not provide effective coordination tools.

What the backchannels do provide is a resource for sharing information, telling jokes, and airing grievances among a professional community that crosses organizational boundaries. Google Groups are simple to create, and listservs are among the oldest Internet communication tools. (At a Sierra Club board meeting in 2006, one of our less tech-savvy directors remarked that he was uncomfortable with social media and "just preferred traditional listservs." Listservs, it seems, are for traditionalists now.) They can thus be created to fit a wide range of communications needs. Issue-specific bloggers participate in topical lists with the staff of legacy and netroots organizations. Short-term campaigns can launch a Google Group list to keep activists updated on breaking news and events. Former staff and volunteers of election campaigns can keep in touch after they disperse.

An unexpected result of the Fight Club rule is an epiphenomenal "Russian nesting doll" effect among these Google Groups. No one can actually know how many of these lists there are. Ruled by informality, the lists are akin to a hip new restaurant that everyone enjoys but hopes will remain secret. As information spreads over time, the crowd grows in size.[72] List growth eventually reaches two types of crowding threshold. First, more list members produce more messages, spanning wider-ranging topics irrelevant to any one individual reader. At some scale, the e-mail traffic becomes too much, leading a reader to either drop off the list or launch a separate Google Group, inviting the subset of members with which *they* wish to associate. Greg Sargent, who writes the "Plum Line" blog for the *Washington Post*, notes that he once had been a JournoList member but dropped out, "mainly because I was sick of being overwhelmed by e-mails."[73] Second, more people necessarily provide more conflicting interests. For the hundreds of progressive (or conservative) issue communities, lists-within-lists are bound to form. (Many bloggers have dismissed TownHouse to me with variations on the Yogi Berra aphorism, "Nobody goes there anymore. It's too crowded.")

The combination of the Fight Club rule and the Russian nesting doll effect leads to a peculiar research problem. Anyone can create a Google Group, and copying standard list rules and moderation policies into the e-mail footer occurs through a point and a click. As such, *the total population of backchannel lists is an unknowable quantity.* There are lists within lists, all protected by Fight Club rules. Some lists are extremely active, with dozens or even hundreds of messages per day. Others have fallen into disuse, or were created but failed to attract frequent use. Their place within the broader netroots ecosystem can be observed at conventions like Netroots Nation, though. Dozens of informal gatherings are arranged through the backchannels, setting a time and location where online watering-hole conversations can transfer back offline.

The backstage discourse on these lists is an uncomfortable fit with some long-standing viewpoints espoused by new media theorists. John Perry Barlow famously declared in his "Declaration of Independence of Cyberspace" that "information wants to be free."[74] According to this perspective, the Internet is supposed to be radically egalitarian, a space where everyone can contribute equally. Yet professional communities have always featured informal networks—dinner and cocktail parties, for instance—and the fundamental value provided by cordoning off a space for private, internal discussion remains unchanged. The netroots draw upon (not-so)-new communications technologies to establish a novel version of elite networks of influence.

What is most notable about the network backchannels is that *this privileged in-group status is now dramatically easier to obtain than in previous communications regimes.* An invitation to TownHouse or similar lists can be extended to anyone who writes smart things, meets a list moderator or influential member, and isn't a jerk (and many list participants would argue that "not a jerk" is hardly a necessary condition for group membership).[75]

Perhaps the best way to conceptualize backchannel lists like TownHouse is to compare them to formal organizational listservs. As a member of the Sierra Club Board of Directors, for instance, I was a member of the "Board-Open" and "Board-Confidential" listservs. On these lists, board members are free to speak their mind, debate issues, and vent frustrations. They are formal venues, connected to a publicly known organization. All such organizations include listservs today, listservs being a classic example of what Rasmus Kleis Nielsen terms a "mundane mobilization tool."[76] These lists are thus *public visible* and *closed.* The barrier to entry is high—I had to win a national membership election, after seven years of volunteer leadership service. Lists like TownHouse, by contrast, are *publicly opaque* but *permeable.* It is easy to join such a list, so long as you participate in the related professional community and earn some respect from your peers. Information technology does not undermine political elite networks; it changes the process by which those networks are constructed and operated.

In providing a space for private discussion and debate, the network backchannels act as a final form of immaterial infrastructure. Like Living Liberally, the infrastructure is primarily based in supporting network tie formation. Unlike Living Liberally, which provides a friendly *public welcome mat* of sorts, encouraging progressives to socialize with each other in local communities, the backchannels provide a *semiprivate, digital watering hole* where the political net-roots can discuss topics, mundane and serious, without having their conversation crawled by Google search engines.

Conclusion

The primary topic of this book concerns the Internet-driven generation shift among membership-based political associations. The political netroots extend beyond membership groups, though. This chapter has turned our attention toward a selection of non-membership advocacy organizations that provide various forms of netroots infrastructure. That infrastructure is historically embedded in self-diagnosed failures—specifically the disappointment with America Coming Together and the 2004 presidential election results. Funders and advocacy professionals alike perceived the American Left to be at an infrastructural disadvantage to the American Right, and they set about fashioning new supportive institutions as a result. Some of these institutions, like the New Organizing Institute, are concerned with developing and sharing new organizing strategies and techniques. Others, like ActBlue and Blue State Digital, are designed to provide technical infrastructure, lowering the overhead and operating costs for legacy organizations and newly founded Internet-mediated associations alike. Meanwhile, Living Liberally seeks to provide a reservoir of social ties and a welcoming entry point for self-identifying political progressives, while a host of backchannel Google Groups carve out a semiprivate space for conversation among Internet-mediated professional communities. Each of these variations on "infrastructure" plays a supporting role for the new generation of membership associations. They are elements of the new landscape of the organizational layer of American politics, and they influence the development of campaigns, strategies, organizations, and ideas alike.

This netroots infrastructure arose during a period of counter-mobilization. American progressives faced a particular set of strategic challenges at the beginning of the 21st century; they drew upon new communications technologies to craft novel solutions to those challenges. American conservatives found themselves in a very different political situation—victorious in national elections, ascendant in the broader media narrative, and proud of the organizational infrastructure they had built over the previous 30+ years. The following chapter turns attention to the partisan adoption of technological innovations, exploring the dearth of Internet-mediated conservative infrastructure. Counter-mobilization produces outparty innovation incentives, which in turn shape competition within and between party networks.

6

Don't Think of an Online Elephant

> "While the Right has been in power, defending the status quo, the Left has been storming the castle. Storming the castle is *much more fun.*"
> —Jon Henke, *Republican technology consultant*

When I began the research for this book, there was an unmistakable gap between the American Left and the American Right online. Among Internet-mediated issue generalists, MoveOn cast a long shadow over the Left. The Right boasted a string of failed attempts at building "their own MoveOn." In fundraising infrastructure, there was ActBlue on the Left and the several paltry attempts at building an ActBlue equivalent on the Right. In community blogs, the vibrant community participation on DailyKos was contrasted with the dramatically smaller RedState on the Right. In each case, the conservative startups made specific references to their left-wing equivalent, leaving no doubt as to whom they were trying to emulate and what they were trying to achieve. The progressive netroots had built online infrastructure and institutions. Conservative political entrepreneurs had taken note of these successes but—successful as they were at winning elections—proved verifiably incapable of keeping pace with the rapidly evolving netroots infrastructure.

The Internet is not the only communications technology to display a partisan bias. Political talk radio has long been dominated by conservatives. The Right features Rush Limbaugh, Sean Hannity, and Glenn Beck (among many others).[1] These hosts reach millions of daily listeners, and talk radio serves as a "farm system" of sorts for conservative pundits and television hosts. The Left attempted to build comparable infrastructure a decade later with the ill-fated launch of Air America radio in 2002. While Air America enjoyed some limited success as a farm system—Rachel Maddow and Cenk Uygur both earned hour-long television programs at *MSNBC* after building exposure through Air America—the network never developed financial stability and went through multiple bankruptcies before formally shutting down in January 2010.

We know surprisingly little about these partisan technology adoption trends. It is clear that talk radio is a "conservative" medium. It was equally clear, from 2004 through 2010 at least, that many areas of the Internet—the political blogosphere, Internet-mediated advocacy organizing, online small-donor fundraising—were "progressive" media. But *why* is that the case? And will the Internet, which is really a suite of continually evolving communications technologies, display a talk radio-sized gap in progressive and conservative infrastructure? Or will the gap prove more fleeting in nature? What are the underlying mechanisms that drive the partisan adoption of technology?

This chapter provides an initial exploration of these questions through an analysis of the dearth of online conservative infrastructure. While previous chapters have drawn lessons about the Internet and American politics from careful analysis of progressive netroots organizations, this chapter advances related lessons through analysis of conservative attempts to build parallel organizations. The chapter begins by detailing these failed attempts. They are numerous and public, yet they often go overlooked in the academic literature.[2] As I have emphasized throughout the book, the progressive and conservative political networks have substantively different internal mechanics. They have different legacy organizations, fundraising traditions, revenue streams, think tanks, staff structures, trainings, conferences, and media institutions. Institutional isomorphism—the process through which organizations within a given field adopt similar institutional structures—occurs *within* these two networks much more than it does *between* them. The network ties that enable information flows between organizations are densely concentrated within ideological coalitions and are infrequently found between them.[3] The profiles of conservative organizations are more limited (a thorough analysis would make this a multivolume affair) but serve to sketch the parameters of the broader theoretical puzzle.

The Tea Party movement, launched immediately after Barack Obama assumed the presidency, further complicates our picture. The Tea Party has achieved a few substantial successes, to be sure. But they must be evaluated cautiously. The Tea Party is a "meta-brand," providing an umbrella for assorted conservative interests—Ron Paul libertarians, traditional social conservatives, and the Club for Growth have all rebranded themselves under the Tea Party's mantle.[4] Some of the Tea Party is a new, Internet-mediated phenomenon. Some of it is a repackaging of existing activity. In the area of online infrastructure, it has done surprisingly little to erase the conservative deficit.

The chapter then evaluates three competing explanations for the partisan adoption of Internet technologies. The first, *ideological congruence*, is the most frequently offered in practitioner and layperson accounts of the new media environment. According to this perspective, the Internet's "bottom-up" nature is simply better suited to anti-hierarchical progressive ideology. The second, *outparty innovation incentives*, builds upon the counter-mobilization perspective and social movement research on "opportunity structures" in the policy process.[5] Outparty innovation suggests that technology is neither fundamentally progressive nor conservative, but rather that well-known incentives driving social movement mobilization and interest group formation have novel applications in technological adoption. A third explanation, *merry pranksters*, argues that the lowered transaction costs of the Internet create a problematic trend for later-adopting partisan organizations. Groups like DailyKos, DFA, and MoveOn developed under the radar, building robust participatory communities over time. Nascent conservative analogues face the threat of progressive "trolls" outnumbering their genuine supporters in the early development stages, and this influences them toward self-limiting, closed design choices.

The three explanatory theses are not mutually exclusive, but they do lead to competing expectations about the future of online political organizations in America. I argue that outparty innovation incentives exert the strongest force. Rather than an inherent, ideologically driven advantage, progressives have been advantaged online because the technology happened to ripen while they were engaging in counter-mobilization. It stands to reason that, as the Internet continues to evolve, conservatives will assume the lead in embracing the next waves of online innovation (at least as long as they remain the outparty in American politics). They face a particular challenge in matching the online community-building accomplished by progressives, however, due to the novel affordances of the new medium. The sheer size of progressive communities makes it easy for the Left to short-circuit conservative attempts at building open, parallel infrastructure, and the Right has responded to this perceived threat by relying on closed systems that limit their capacity for building vibrant citizen associations.

But first, let's consider the recent history of online conservative infrastructure-building.

"All the Dogs That Didn't Bark"

It is worth recalling that the Left did not always hold an advantage in online infrastructure. The John McCain presidential primary campaign raised $3 million online in the 10 days following the New Hampshire primary in 2000, establishing the cutting edge of the time.[6] The "Web 1.0" era clearly benefited Republicans, as sites like the Drudge Report and FreeRepublic.com offered an outlet for Republican critiques of the liberal media. Chris Bowers and Matt Stoller estimated that, as of 2003, "the conservative blogosphere was between two and three times as large as the progressive blogosphere."[7] As recently as 2005, it appeared to many observers as though there was no strong partisan advantage on the web, at least when viewed through the lens of the political blogosphere. Lada Adamic and Natalie Glance's 2005 paper, "The Political Blogosphere and the 2004 Election: Divided They Blog," used hyperlink maps to demonstrate that left-wing and right-wing blogs operated as largely independent neighborhoods. Noting that conservatives linked to one another with greater frequency, Adamic and Glance suggested that the Right was, if anything, leading in the blogosphere. Robert Ackland conducted a follow-up study with the same dataset and found that conservative bloggers were indeed more "prominent" online.[8]

At that time, conservative law professor Glenn "Instapundit" Reynolds was the most popular political blogger, Matt Drudge's "Drudge Report" proto-blog stood unrivaled in its effectiveness, and the multi-author conservative blog PowerLine had been named *Time* magazine's "Blog of the Year."[9] In the public eye, progressive bloggers had made headlines by taking down Trent Lott after his Strom Thurmond speech, but conservative bloggers had countered by taking down Dan Rather after debunking the "Rathergate" memo as a forgery. The Howard Dean campaign had turned heads as an example of the Internet's potential impact, but his campaign's collapse left plenty of fuel for skeptics' arguments. MoveOn had developed an impressive size and scope, but their efforts at combating the war and the Bush agenda had produced much noise and few tangible results.

As detailed in Chapter 5, it was in the aftermath of the 2004 election that new progressive infrastructure-building began in earnest. The extended period of counter-mobilization gave rise to new organizational designs. New Internet-mediated organizations began to form. Top political blogs began to develop large communities and, adapting the novel features of the community blogging platform (Chapter 3), increasingly began operating as quasi-interest groups. Through this time period, the gap between the online Left and Right grew. Over the course of 2009 and 2010, as demonstrated by the comparative feature of the Blogosphere Authority Index, that gap has remained largely unchanged.

COMPARING BLOG NETWORKS

As a measure of comparative strength, the monthly updates to the Blogosphere Authority Index (BAI) include a combined "top 50" ranking. Dating back to November 2007, this metric provides a window into the overall amount of site traffic, hyperlinks, and comment activity among the elite political blogs of the American Left and Right. In the first iteration of the BAI, the average rank for progressive blogs was 23.5, while the average rank for conservative blogs was 27.48. The four-point difference in rank order indicates that the top half of the rankings was slightly weighted in favor of progressive blogs.[10] Over the course of the 2008 election season, which featured a highly motivated progressive netroots and low conservative enthusiasm, that gap grew from 4 points to approximately

10 points (displayed in Table 3.1). All political blogs experienced surges in traffic during the election season, but the surges were much larger for the elite progressive blogs.[11]

Since the 2008 election, a general media narrative has focused on the rising tide of conservative online enthusiasm. Conservative blogger and political consultant Patrick Ruffini has attracted substantial attention for his claims that the conservative blogosphere reached "parity or better" with the progressive netroots.[12] *Time* magazine included DailyKos in its list of "most overrated blogs" in both 2009 and 2010, including the rationale that "with the Bush years now just a memory, Kos's blog has lost its mission, and its increasingly rudderless posts read like talking points from the Democratic National Committee."[13] If nothing else, one would expect that the rising tide of Tea Party activism would increase traffic to elite conservative blogs, producing an approximate equivalence with the "overrated" progressive blogosphere.

The data from the BAI tells a very different story, however. As revealed in Table 6.1, the gap between progressive and conservative blogs has shrunk only slightly through 2009 and 2010. In summation, the gap between elite progressive blogs and elite conservative blogs has shrunk from 10 points to 9 points and remains substantially larger than the 4-point gap that existed in 2007.

Table 6.1 **Average Site Ranks in the Combined BAI dataset, 2010[1]**

Date	Prog Avg Rank	Cons Avg Rank	Difference
January 2010	20.04	30.52	+10.48
February 2010	20.36	30.24	+9.88
March 2010	20.64	29.88	+9.24
April 2010	19.72	30.96	+11.24
May 2010	20.72	29.92	+9.20
June 2010	21.68	28.8	+7.12
July 2010	20.4	30.32	+9.92
August 2010	20.72	29.96	+9.24
September 2010	21.56	28.96	+7.40
October 2010	21.72	28.96	+7.24
November 2010	21.2	29.8	+8.6
December 2010	20.6	30.00	+9.40
2010 Average	20.78	29.86	+9.08

[1]Wilcoxan Mann-Whitney Rank Sum Test produces a z-score of −5.4773, significant at the 0.0001 level.

What appears to be occurring here is that, even as conservative blogs have increased in traffic, progressive blogs *also* continue to build a larger audience. *Time* magazine's blog criticism notwithstanding, the community activity on DailyKos, FireDogLake, Huffington Post, and other top progressive sites remains vibrant, as political progressives engage in spirited debate over how and when they should critique President Obama from the Left. The conservative blogosphere has grown, as Ruffini and others claim, but it still trails far behind the large quasi-political associations of the progressive netroots. RedState.com increased from 50,000 page visits/day to 150,000 page visits/day, but that pales in comparison to the 500,000 to 1,200,000 visits/day experienced by DailyKos. Andrew Breitbart's collection of sites—BigGovernment.com, BigJournalism.com, BigHollywood.com, and BigPeace.com (collectively known as "the bigs")—are designed to be a conservative response to the Huffington Post, but their traffic is minimal by comparison. The heightened conservative activism embodied by the Tea Party has not translated into equivalent Internet-mediated communities-of-interest in the blogosphere.

A CONSERVATIVE MOVEON?

As with RedState's limited success in offering a "conservative DailyKos," there have been several right-wing attempts at launching a "MoveOn for conservatives." Justin Rubin, MoveOn Executive Director since 2009, has noted, "If I had a dime for all the 'right-wing MoveOns' that had announced themselves and then faded into obscurity, I'd be eligible for top-end tax cuts . . ."[14] RightMarch was the first such attempt, founded in 2003. By that time, MoveOn was transitioning from its small online petition niche into a 3-million-strong progressive behemoth. Heralded in mass media coverage and promoted by wealthy Republican backers, RightMarch promised to be "the 'Rapid Response Force' against the ongoing liberal onslaught."[15] It never lived up to this billing, though, failing to do much of anything with the large e-mail list they claimed to develop.[16] In an interview with *Mother Jones* magazine, Bill Greene of RightMarch defended their lack of tactical innovation, stating, "Well I don't think that our members are as interested in [podcasting and social networking] because they've got families and they're working people and they don't have time to meet at someone's house and watch a webcast."[17] In terms of fundraising capacity, RightMarch has been similarly underwhelming. According to data collected by the Center for Responsive Politics, RightMarch spent $60,750 in the 2004 election cycle versus MoveOn's $31.8 million.[18] In 2006, RightMarch raised $102,699, while MoveOn brought in $28.1 million. They improved against their own standard in 2008, raising $646,089, but that hardly compares to the $38.4 million raised by MoveOn in the cycle (and by that point, MoveOn had demonstrated the capacity to raise six-figure sums in a single day).[19]

A promising competitor to RightMarch, TheVanguard.org, was founded in March 2006 by a group of tech-savvy conservative leaders. With a strong base of sophisticated Internet entrepreneurs who had previously built the popular online financial transaction site PayPal.com, The Vanguard seemed better positioned to keep pace with MoveOn's breakneck pace of technological innovation.[20] Despite heavy promotion from the outset and a collection of conservative activist heavyweights on their board and staff, the organization never fully coalesced. Five years later, it continues to claim to be in "beta" and "launching soon," but the mantle of a conservative answer to MoveOn has been passed to other startups.

Freedom's Watch was launched by a collection of former Bush administration appointees and staffers with an initial wave of ads that countered MoveOn's controversial "Betray-Us" newspaper ad in the summer of 2007. In a January 20, 2008, feature story about the group in the *Washington Post*, titled "A Conservative Answer to MoveOn," Executive Director Joe Eule announced the group to be "a permanent political operation here in town. We're not going to be Johnny One Note."[21] Aided by a reported budget of $200 million, this group was heralded as, finally, a successful conservative response.

That excitement lasted all of three months, as a *New York Times* story in April, 2008, titled "Great Expectations for a Conservative Group Seem All but Dashed" described the organization as "plagued by gridlock and infighting, leaving it struggling for direction" and coming up well short of its supposedly gigantic budget figures. The organization was almost solely funded by conservative casino mogul Sheldon Adelson—at the time the third-richest person in the country.[22] After Adelson's company, Las Vegas Sands Corp., lost 95% of its stock value in the fall 2008 market decline, he withdrew his funding and the group announced that it would permanently shut its doors.[23] As with community blogs, conservatives have recognized the value of novel organizations like MoveOn, but their attempts to build an equivalent force have sputtered and failed.

In the midst of the swelling Tea Party movement, another new organization attempted to fill this gap. Liberty.com launched in the summer of 2010, led by conservative political organizer Eric Odom. Boasting a list of 70,000 supporters and an initial funding base of $700,000, the group boisterously claimed, "We're looking to compete directly with MoveOn.org. We're looking to be a player for a long time. No one else on the right is doing what we're doing."[24] Occurring in the midst of the electoral season, with the potential to create the same type of sedimentary infrastructure that benefited Internet-mediated organizations like MoveOn, DFA, and OFA on the left, the potential was certainly there. I signed up for the group's e-mail distribution list and applied the same content analysis scheme to Liberty.com that I use in the Membership Communications Project. Figure 6.1 provides a summary of the action requests made by Liberty.com in their first six months.

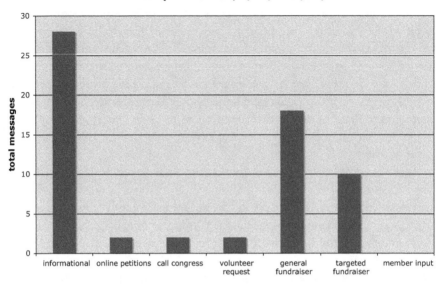

Figure 6.1 Liberty.com E-mail Breakdown

What becomes immediately clear is that the organization bears absolutely no structural resemblance to MoveOn and other Internet-mediated issue generalists. Odom sent an average of one e-mail every 3.5 days. Nearly all messages consisted of blog-like position-taking, with links to blog posts or video reports. Targeted fundraising consisted mostly of requests to fund issue advertisements in Nevada. Many e-mails requested that supporters "become a member" by donating $5 a month to the group,[25] indicating that the group has not adapted to the MoveOn Effect in membership regimes. Action alerts almost never occurred, and there was not a single call for membership input. The group's grassroots fundraising capacity also proved miniscule. A February 8, 2011, message to their list announced, "We raised just under $5,000 in our first week, so we're on track to hit our goal by the end of the month."[26] A week later, a follow-up message announced that they had raised only $1,000 more from their membership.[27]

These institutional failures should not be taken as proof that the Tea Party is, itself, an "Astroturf" or fake-grassroots phenomenon. As I will discuss below, there is every reason to believe that hundreds, if not thousands, of local Tea Party organizations operate throughout the nation. Fox News-supported rallies such as Glenn Beck's 9/12 event have drawn large crowds. But the lack of parallel infrastructure remains a mystery. Conservative advocacy group leaders have devoted considerable resources to building large Internet-mediated issue generalists. They have repeatedly met with failure.

COMPETING FUNDRAISING PORTALS: A CONSERVATIVE ACTBLUE?

In the online fundraising arena, we see the same chasm developing with a few interesting wrinkles. The malleable approach that ActBlue has applied to fundraising has proven outstandingly effective, allowing the PCCC to raise $2 million in its first two years and the DailyKos community to raise $310,000 for Elwyn Tinklenberg in a weekend despite the crash of his fundraising site. As discussed in Chapter 5, ActBlue is a classic example of netroots infrastructure—it makes online fundraising easier for a variety of progressive interest groups, lowering the startup costs for new political associations.

The same cannot be said for ActBlue's right-wing equivalents. Launched in 2006, the "RightRoots" fundraising site was meant to be a Republican counter to ActBlue. RightRoots included one crucial limitation, however: it set out its own list of endorsees, developed by a small circle of prominent conservative bloggers and insiders, and chose not to give users the ability to develop their own lists. Micah Sifry of Personal Democracy Forum pointed out that this lack of malleable functionality meant that "It's probably fairer to see RightRoots as a mirror of the 'Netroots' fundraising pages on ActBlue, which focus attention on a handful of 'netroots-endorsed' candidates that have been hand-picked by a few key bloggers."[28] Indeed, if compared to that single ActBlue fundraising page, RightRoots performed acceptably, raising one-fifth of the amount raised through a joint DailyKos/MyDD/Swing State Project fundraising page.

RightRoots essentially fell into disuse in the 2008 election cycle, replaced by SlateCard.com, which suffered from similar top-down management challenges. SlateCard raised "nearly $650,000 for Republican candidates and committees" in the 2008 election cycle,[29] setting the combined fundraising totals of the two Republican answers to ActBlue at around $1 million in two cycles (less than 1% of ActBlue's total in that time period). SlateCard then disappeared in the 2010 election, no longer reserving the URL, while the RightRoots homepage circa 2011 still boasted, "We're updating our website for the 2010 election, so check back soon!"[30] For some reason, despite seeing the obvious value of this type of site, Republican strategists have proven unable or unwilling to invest in the set-your-own-endorsement-list system that has made ActBlue so valuable to online progressives and political candidates. This is particularly perplexing given that (a) the software code involved is not terribly complicated and (b) the progressive advantage in this arena is so easily quantified in terms of dollars raised.

Conservatives throughout the 2010 election cycle did succeed in raising large online amounts for their candidates. Some of this money came through revised corporate expenditure rules, dictated by the *Citizens United* ruling that removed limitations on independent expenditures by corporate entities. Much of it came from the grassroots, however. The lack of an ActBlue equivalent on the Right cannot be explained by a lack of conservative small-donor fundraising. Rather, the Right has failed to turn that small-donor enthusiasm into the type of infrastructure that can easily be used to support the work of a new generation of Internet-mediated political associations. Instead, conservative technology vendors have focused on building proprietary systems for their client organizations and campaigns.

There is one noteworthy exception to this story of conservative online fundraising, however: the Ron Paul "revolution" primary campaign. The "Paulites" are best known for their single-day "moneybomb" on November 5th, 2007, which raised somewhere between $3.75 and $5 million. They also used the Meetup-style tools pioneered by the Dean campaign to promote local actions throughout the country. Though Paul never experienced Howard Dean's meteoric rise and fall, his devoted base of supporters has remained active, playing at least some formative role in the Tea Party movement and helping to elect his son, Rand Paul, to victory in the 2010 Kentucky senate race. What is particularly remarkable in this case is that the segment of the conservative party coalition that appears to have most successfully emulated the development of netroots online infrastructure has been the upstart Paulites. Positively ridiculed by the elite conservative blogosphere, banished from comment threads wherever they popped up during the 2008 primary season, Ron Paul supporters have functioned as an outparty of sorts *within* the conservative coalition. And while the network of elite conservative consultants, party operatives, and politicians has consistently tried and failed to build web-based participatory communities, the biggest organizational success has come from the vocal minority.

SLAYING THE WRONG DRAGONS—CONSERVAPEDIA AND QUBETV

Media criticism appears to be the one area where online conservatives have proven highly engaged and participatory. The "Rathergate" scandal remains the often-cited example of conservative blogosphere efficacy,[31] while top conservative blogs Newsbusters, BigGovernment, and HotAir.com have all focused heavy attention on "exposing liberal media bias." Building on this strength, online conservatives appear to have frequently attempted to "slay the wrong dragons" in developing online communities-of-interest. Conservapedia.com, for instance, offers a conservative alternative to Wikipedia's "Neutral Point of View" standard, which conservative activists view as nonetheless displaying a liberal bias. QubeTV.tv, meanwhile, is set up as a conservative alternative to YouTube. Neither of these sites attracts substantial traffic, which is not surprising because both Wikipedia and YouTube benefit from overwhelming network externalities, leaving them undisputable power-law hubs. What incentive would an online conservative have for posting content to QubeTV rather than YouTube?

The overwhelming number of online video viewers—be they conservative, liberal, or politically apathetic—turn to YouTube to view video content. Why, given the lack of restrictions on ideologically related content posting to YouTube and Wikipedia, would users en masse choose to switch to a site with smaller traffic and fewer network externalities?

The presence of sites like Conservapedia and QubeTV suggests that many conservative elites fundamentally misunderstand the nature of the new media environment.[32] That alone is not noteworthy—many progressive elites misunderstand the new medium environment as well—but it does factor into the counter-mobilization trend. From 2000–2010, the progressive netroots focused their critique on all elements of the Democratic Party network. Markos Moulitsas, Duncan "Atrios" Black, Jerome Armstrong, Jane Hamsher, and other netroots leaders forcefully argued for new leadership, new institutions, and new ideas within the progressive community and the Democratic Party alike. Online conservative activists during those years instead focused criticisms on the liberal media and thus devoted energy to building conservative-branded new media channels. The Tea Party as a meta-brand has likewise served as a vehicle for many existing components of the Republican Party network. The movement has produced fewer intra-party institutional challenges than the progressive netroots did.

THE TEA PARTY COUNTER-MOBILIZATION: META-BRAND OR MOVEMENT?

The Tea Party movement is still an evolving phenomenon. More than any other topic in this book, I can state with confidence that this passage will seem outdated by the time it reaches the reader. Some brief commentary is nonetheless appropriate. The genesis of the movement is rooted in conservative counter-mobilization. The Tea Party movement appeared on April 15, 2010, using a website to organize tax-day rallies across the country. The object of their ire was high taxes that had not, in point of fact, been raised from their 2008 levels. The governing party had changed and spurred an upwelling of grassroots conservatism in response. Entering the summer of 2009, conservative activists would show up at health care town hall meetings across the country, organizing vocal demonstrations and altering the dominant media narrative on the legislation. Conservative activist James O'Keefe, armed with a hidden camera and selective editing skills, created a firestorm of controversy that eventually destroyed ACORN (Association of Community Organizations for Reform Now), America's premier welfare rights organization. Conservatives also jumped onto Twitter, using the hashtag #tcot (top conservatives on twitter) to share messages with one another.[33]

To its credit, the Tea Party has achieved some noteworthy victories. In 2010, conservatives united under the Tea Party banner helped elect Republican Scott Brown in a special election to fill the late Ted Kennedy's Massachusetts senate seat. Throughout the spring and summer of 2010, an energized conservative base unseated several sitting incumbents through bruising primary battles. High turnout by the motivated base, along with a horrendous economy, produced steep congressional gains in the 2010 election. Republicans won 63 House seats and 6 Senate seats, regaining the House majority and severely reducing the Democratic Senate majority from an 18-seat advantage to a 6-seat advantage.

But, unlike the political netroots, it is particularly hard to distinguish Tea Party organizations from legacy conservative organizations. The Tea Party is best understood as a conservative "meta-brand" rather than as a more analytically concise social movement. The large crowds gathering at 2010 rallies were mobilized both through Twitter and through ample glowing coverage on Fox News Channel. The aggressive primary challenges were an extension of tactics employed for a decade by the Club for Growth. "Tea Party" refers to (1) a neo-federated network of conservative citizen's groups, (2) the audiences of media elites like Fox News television host Glenn Beck, and (3) a variety of conservative Political Action Committees newly empowered through the 2010 *Citizens United* decision. The three occasionally overlap and occasionally clash. They are not a single movement, though. Anyone is free to invoke the Tea Party brand, and (particularly during the 2009–2010 height of its popularity) all conservative interests had a strong incentive to do so.

To be clear, there *is* a strong grassroots component to the Tea Party, with hundreds, if not thousands, of local groups assembling in libraries and coffeehouses around the country.[34] Tensions crop up between these movement participants and national mobilizing organizations such as the Tea Party Express. In her book-length study, *Boiling Mad*, *New York Times* journalist Kate Zernike notes, "Some Tea Partiers disdained the Tea Party Express as 'The Astroturf Express.'"[35] Organized by FreedomWorks, a conservative advocacy group founded in 2004 with funding from the Koch brothers[36] and led by former House Majority Leader Dick Armey, the Tea Party Express is one of several national organizations branded with the Tea Party label that display far more of an "Astroturf" character. The Tea Party Express tours the country, financing rallies and bus tours in an attempt to generate media attention and cultivate a narrative of citizen outrage against the Obama administration.[37]

Fox News has likewise heavily covered and promoted national Tea Party days of action, including Glenn Beck's own 9/12 rally.[38] There has never before been such a close link between a national media organization and a "grassroots" movement. Leading up to the April 15th rallies, Fox News created a website where citizens could find their local Tea Party rally and actively urged viewers to attend.[39] Fox News contributors Glenn Beck, Sarah Palin, and Sean Hannity have all been prominent speakers at national Tea Party events.[40] To the extent that some members of the public will show up to *any* televised event (the crowds who gather behind *Good Morning America* television hosts, for instance), such active promotion plays an inflationary role in the size of Tea Party events. Without a mass-media channel actively supporting it and encouraging viewers to turn out, there would still be a Tea Party movement, but it would be smaller and less of a public spectacle.

The media spectacle accompanying the Tea Party characterizes a substantial difference between the Tea Party of 2008–2010 and the progressive netroots of 2004–2008. The popularity of the term (and the intense curiosity shown by media observers on the left and right alike) led existing conservative leaders to relabel themselves as members of the Tea Party movement. The term "netroots" never attracted such a degree of popularity. The only rationale for claiming to be part of the progressive netroots was to gain support from a *specific cluster* of individual actors or to appear broadly tech-savvy. The rationales for claiming membership in the Tea Party movement are much wider, including increased media attention and fundraising prowess. Any conservative political entrepreneur seeking to raise money in 2009 would have good reason to claim the mantle of the Tea Party. And, importantly, there is no central coordinating institution charged with determining who is and is not part of the movement. As a result, multiple competing clusters of the Republican Party network have an incentive to relabel themselves as the Tea Party.

Discussion of the Tea Party often devolves into an anecdotal shouting match of sorts. Liberal commentators argue that it is "Astroturf" corporate groups and racially motivated protestors. Libertarian supporters point to the Tea Party's roots in Ron Paul's insurgent 2008 presidential primary campaign. Movement conservatives claim that it is a social movement made up of political Independents, driven by public disgust with government spending and high taxes.[41] Those debates become mired in an endless loop because all of them are, in a sense, correct. Astroturf corporate groups and racially motivated protestors can all label themselves the Tea Party. So can Ron Paul libertarians and more traditional movement conservatives.

The Tea Party movement represents the latest wave of counter-mobilization-based grassroots conservatism. As Lisa McGirr, Mark Rozell, and Clyde Wilcox have all demonstrated, Democratic presidential administrations frequently are accompanied by an upwelling of grassroots conservative engagement.[42] Both the Jimmy Carter and Bill Clinton administrations saw waves of grassroots conservative political engagement. The Tea Party provides new garb to the same forces that motivated the Christian Coalition and the New Right in earlier decades.

At the organizational layer of American politics, what matters most is not the existence of grassroots conservatism waves, but the new political organizations that form as a result. McGirr notes that John Birch Society conservatives in the 1960s seized control of the California Republican Party, setting the stage for both Barry Goldwater's 1964 presidential campaign and Ronald Reagan's 1966 gubernatorial run.[43] 1990s-era conservatism led to the formation of the Christian

Coalition, which mobilized voters for several electoral cycles and altered the distribution of power within the Republican Party network.[44]

The Tea Party has mostly served to augment the authority of existing conservative elements within the Republican Party network. Leading Tea Party voices include existing conservative leaders—Sarah Palin, Senator Jim DeMint, and former House Majority Leader Dick Armey, for instance. The Tea Party is credited with defeating several moderate Senate candidates and incumbents in the 2010 primaries, but the strategy of active right-wing primary challenges was established a decade earlier by the Club for Growth.[45] While the progressive netroots created their own new infrastructure as a challenge to the various institutions of authority within the Democratic Party network, the conservative Tea Party has largely incorporated existing infrastructure and organizations; the Club for Growth and Americans for Tax Reform are longstanding players in the Republican Party network, and the Tea Party has augmented their efforts rather than displacing them. As a result, we have seen polarization through participation on the conservative side, but little generation shift among conservative political advocacy organizations. The Tea Party has not produced a MoveOn or DailyKos or ActBlue equivalent. The online spaces where the Right holds an advantage over the Left are social media sites like Twitter, which was still in the early adoption phase in 2008. Where they have tried to counter the online organizational advantages of the netroots, they have continued to stumble.

Ideology, Outparty Incentives, or Merry Pranksters? Three Explanatory Theses

Why does the online infrastructure gap exist? Political progressives and conservatives use the same Internet. They seek the same electoral ends—raising money, disseminating policy ideas, turning out votes, influencing decision makers, etc. The growth of MoveOn, ActBlue, DFA, and DailyKos have hardly been a secret, and indeed conservatives have continually attempted to build equivalent organizations and infrastructure. How can we explain the partisan character of the new generation of Internet-mediated political associations? In conversations with political bloggers, netroots activists, and fellow researchers, three broad classes of explanation emerge. First is what I will term "ideological congruence" or, in its strongest form, "ideological determinism." This asserts that the Left is advantaged online because the bottom-up nature of the medium is better attuned to progressive ideology. Thus particularities of *ideological fit* lead to differential adoption. The second, "outparty innovation incentives," asserts that technological innovations are generally adopted by the party out of power. For a host of reasons, the "team" that is losing in the political arena will look to change the rules of the game. Thus path-dependent particularities of timing and institutional control lead to differential adoption. The third thesis, "merry pranksters," focuses on the ability of large communities-of-interest to disrupt nascent opposing communities in their early developmental stage, an activity that is uniquely possible in an online environment of "ridiculously low transaction costs."[46] Thus particularities of *group formation in a new media environment* lead to differential adoption. These explanations are not mutually exclusive; we can think of them as three variables contributing to the outcome, with each thesis suggesting primary importance for one over the other two:

> Ideological Congruence + Outparty Incentives + Late-Forming Community Disruption = Differential Adoption Rates

This section will discuss each explanation in turn, as they lead to very different predictions about the likely future for conservative online institutions.

Thesis 1: Ideological Congruence

Discussions of the partisan adoption of technology invariably begin with an initial assertion that the Internet is, at some underlying level, a liberal medium. Progressives value community organizing, while conservatives (memorably Rudy Giuliani in his 2008 Republican National Convention keynote address) treat it as a subject for ridicule. SlateCard and RightRoots, RightMarch, and The Vanguard have all failed to give their users the sort of participatory toolset offered by their successful progressive counterparts. This may be because they are ideologically more attuned to a business culture that features clearly defined, hierarchical roles. Likewise, the argument goes, talk radio is dominated by conservatives because it attracts blue-collar, rural audiences during their drive to work. City-dwelling, creative-class liberals listen to National Public Radio rather than call-in shows. Democratic attempts at breaking into the medium were doomed to failure due to ideological fit. Radio and television are top-down, broadcast tools, the thinking goes. The Internet is bottom-up, yielding an advantage to the party steeped in a community organizing tradition. As Howard Dean put it in an interview, "Our tendency in the Democratic Party . . . is decentralizing democratization. The Internet is fundamentally a democratizing tool . . . The Republicans are inherently not interested in (small *d*) democratic organization; they tend toward top-down centralization and organization."[47]

There is a certain intuitive appeal to this argument. As Clay Shirky and others have argued, the lowered transaction costs of the Internet encourage "ridiculously easy group formation."[48] Rasmus Kleis Nielsen notes in a 2009 article that the ease of online communications can nonetheless lead to "overcommunication, miscommunication and communication overload."[49] If the American Left's populist ethos encourages its members to take advantage of online community-formation op-portunities at higher rates than their right-wing counterparts, and if a devotion to the craft of community organizing leads the Left to better manage the challenges created by social coordination tools, then one would certainly expect the Internet to be a boon for the liberal end of the political spectrum.

Likewise, conservatives themselves often argue that they have a more "top-down" ideology—rooted in the hierarchy of business culture—that is perhaps better suited to media like talk radio. Thus, purportedly, they refuse to offer the malleable functionality of an ActBlue or the agenda-setting responsiveness of a MoveOn because they fundamentally place greater value in hierarchical decision-making. As former MoveOn Executive Director Eli Pariser put it when inter-viewed about his upstart conservative competitors, "The Vanguard folks are spending a lot of time thinking about what they want, and then figuring out how to spin it to their members."[50] Adam Green from the PCCC (formerly of MoveOn) noted in response to the launch of Liberty.com that "The reason these right-wing groups all fail is because they think the power of progressive groups is money. So a bunch of millionaires chip in from the top down. But it's not about money. It's about people—people-powered activism generated from the bottom up."[51]

One of MoveOn's key innovations, by contrast, has been their "culture of testing." MoveOn has crafted novel passive democratic feedback mechanisms that keep abreast of membership preferences. One MoveOn staffer noted to me that the chief mistake made by scholars and journalists when studying the organi-zation is in suggesting that MoveOn adopts radical tactics *in order to* gain an audi-ence: "Radical tactics don't go viral. If you want to build a large audience and have an impact, you need to listen to your membership."[52] There is a strong populism here, a notion that the lowering of online transaction costs can free the pent-up energies of the (progressive) masses and give them a larger and more powerful voice in the political system. Not surprisingly, this explanation is particularly ap-pealing to social movement activists who have long contended that theirs is a battle of "the people versus the powerful."

The conservative version of the thesis likewise begins from an assumption that they themselves are part of a "silent majority." But conservative mobilizers voice a sentiment that the Internet favors the lifestyle preferences of the "professional ac-tivist" Left. Bill Greene, founder of RightMarch, suggests that "most of [his orga-nization's members] are just hardworking everyday patriotic Americans that have families and kids and dogs and cats and jobs."[53] Likewise, grassroots conservatism has long been based in offline institutions such as churches, providing a substrate for conservative grassroots mobilization efforts that progressives needed to repli-cate online. If "everyday patriotic Americans" are too busy for blogging or MoveOn-style house parties, then we should see the "activist class" among the political left develop more vibrant online community infrastructure because they are the ones who primarily have the time for such activities.

The limits of the ideological congruence thesis are manifold, however. Firstly, it does not provide a robust explanation for previous eras of grassroots conservatism in American history. Both the Goldwater-era conservatives in the 1960s and 1970s and Ralph Reed's Christian Coalition in the 1990s engaged in substantial grassroots community organizing.[54] Were these conservatives less "hardworking"? Did they have fewer "kids and dogs and cats and jobs"?[55] Community organizing is not an activity solely appreciated by the left—indeed, Zernike details Tea Party training sessions that include selected readings from Saul Alinsky and active attention to community organizing principles.[56] Likewise, MoveOn's substantial message-testing framework has much in common with the types of focus group activities that business managers are well familiar with, and "networked organizations" have been a popular and growing field within the business community for decades.[57] MoveOn and other Internet-mediated groups call for membership input and voting on those issues that the staff feels are appropriate—hardly an ideal of bottom-up decision making. Blogger and political consultant Jon Henke of TheNextRight.com offers a counterargument: "While the Right has been in power, defending the status quo, the Left has been storming the castle. Storming the castle is *much* more fun."[58]

Henke points to a second concern: if the Internet is ideologically attuned to the political Left, then we ought to see a left-wing online advantage in other countries. Yet, in the United Kingdom, it is British online conservatives (who had the "castle-storming" task of criticizing the liberal majority party) that developed an online advantage. The largest blog in the UK is Iain Dale's Diary, named "Political Blog of the Year" by *The Guardian* in 2005. One could of course argue that British Conservatism and American conservatism are distinct ideologies, but such an argument only serves to further undermine the ideological congruence thesis! The Democratic and Republican coalitions have changed over time. In the process they have emphasized various ideological arguments to a greater or lesser degree.[59] If this particular brand of American conservatism is a poor fit for the online information regime, would that not presage an ideological shift in the conservative coalition itself? (One might argue that is exactly what is happening with the present-day Tea Party.) If there are various brands of conservatism, then the Internet is not a particularly "progressive" medium; it is just a medium poorly suited to the particular Republican Party leaders who held power circa 2004–2009. Netroots progressives such as Markos Moulitsas and Jerome Armstrong make the very same criticism of the Democratic Party leadership of that time period.[60]

The third (and deepest) concern with the thesis is its teleological nature, simply formed as, "Progressives dominate online, therefore the Internet is a progressive medium." Such an argument also maintains that talk radio is an inherently conservative medium because conservatives dominate those airwaves. Data from 2008 from the Pew Internet and American Life Project finds only marginal partisan differences in Internet usage, with 55% of Republicans, 61% of Democrats, and 48% of Independents turning to the Internet for political news, and 49% of Republicans, 50% of Democrats, and 48% of Independents using the Internet, e-mail, or texting to "learn about the campaign and engage in the political process."[61] Given that Republicans and Democrats are similarly logging onto the web, it is unclear why the political Left gravitates toward one type of site while the political Right gravitates toward another. Ideological congruence is hard to disprove, but for this same reason it proves to be almost *too easy* of an explanation. While ideology must have *some* impact on the development of online infrastructure today, the historical and cross-national evidence cautions us against placing too much causal impact on this, the simplest explanation.

Thesis 2: Outparty Innovation Incentives

These very critiques of the ideological congruence thesis point to an alternative argument. History and cross-national comparison both suggest a set of *structural* mechanisms, embedded in the condition of counter-mobilization. At the organizational, candidate, and party network levels, there are several incentives that lead us to expect the party out of power to more aggressively adopt novel communications platforms and campaign tactics. For new organizations, as Henke puts it, "Storming the castle is *much* more fun." It also yields better membership and fundraising trends. For candidates, innovative campaign strategies offer an opportunity to "change the rules of the game." Dark-horse candidates—those who expect to have only an outside chance under the existing "rules"—are more likely to take risks on these innovative tools. Within party networks, novel campaign technologies are introduced by a new set of elite actors displacing the previous set of established actors. That displacement is more likely to happen when a party has been losing elections and is searching for new ideas and new leadership.

These three levels of analysis combine to form the outparty innovation incentives thesis, or the "opportunity structure" thesis. The study of political opportunity structures has a firm tradition within social movement studies. Sidney Tarrow highlights a pattern of "innovation and counter-innovation," as contentious political movements develop new tactical repertoires in response to the established reactions of existing elites.[62] The actions of the governing elite shape the space within which social movement actors operate. Political scientists ranging from David Truman to Gerald Rosenberg have noted how the actions of a governing elite prompt reactions from counter-mobilizing elites.[63] Within the context of American politics, the partisan makeup of each branch of government plays a powerful role in determining which issues will rise on the public agenda, and what the terms of the debate will be.

Technological adoption patterns have not historically been treated within an opportunity structure or counter-mobilization lens. The partisan adoption of technology has been woefully understudied, and so the implications of social movement theories have not been explored in regards to the Internet and politics. Note that the outparty innovation incentives thesis mutes not only the role of ideology but also the particularities of the medium itself. Rather, this thesis is concerned with political innovations in general, treating the new generation of Internet-mediated organizations and online campaign tools as the latest example of a recurring pattern.

OUTPARTY INNOVATION INCENTIVES IN THE INTEREST GROUP COMMUNITY

Henke's colorful suggestion about "storming the castle" finds additional support from the history of interest group mobilization. Recall, for instance, that MoveOn's substantial membership and reputational growth occurred only after it became the central outlet for the anti-war movement. For several years, the organization was able to unite its membership under the banner of opposing the Bush administration's latest initiative, a strategy that became a central element of their fundraising model. Likewise, the Sierra Club's membership rolls more than doubled after Ronald Reagan assumed the presidency, as the organization was able to cast Secretary of the Interior James Watt as an identifiable villain attacking status quo environmental protections.[64] Bill Clinton's election led to a membership decrease among various left-wing interest groups—a decrease that was mitigated when Newt Gingrich was elected Speaker of the House behind the Contract with America. Steven Teles has likewise charted the conservative Federalist Society's membership growth, finding that it skyrocketed during the Clinton administration.[65] "Storming the castle" isn't just more fun—it is also a better business model.

What's true historically for membership associations is even more important for Internet-mediated issue generalists. The issue-based sedimentary waves that provide the foundation of new Internet-mediated organizations occur more frequently for the opponents of government policy proposals. The American policy process is agonizingly slow by design. It is far easier to mobilize in opposition to changes to the status quo than to mobilize in favor of the variable permutations of a complex policy proposal as it moves through several stages of congressional negotiation.

It appears as though the flow of resources (both money and potential volunteers) into the interest group population fluctuates based on the party in power. During periods of counter-mobilization, when advocacy groups can serve as an outlet for political discontent, they receive more donations and greater volunteer interest.[66] If so, then if equally skilled political entrepreneurs on both sides of the ideological spectrum sought to launch novel political associations at a given moment in time, we would expect the side that is out of power to experience greater success. Indeed, the early history of Tea Party activism accords with this pattern. The first round of "tax-day tea parties" occurred even though President Obama had not raised taxes. Groups like FreedomWorks and Americans for Prosperity had attempted to rally grassroots conservative activism for decades. Suddenly, they found a more receptive audience and deftly converted that base of support into increased media attention. What had changed was neither public policy nor information technology, but party governance.

OUTPARTY INNOVATION INCENTIVES AT THE CANDIDATE LEVEL

Writing in 1974, David Mayhew offered the following observation in his classic work, *Congress: The Electoral Connection*: ". . . for members in great electoral danger it may on balance be wise to resort to ostentatious innovation."[67] For individual electoral candidates, there exists a set of official rules and informal norms regarding the campaign process. The rules (campaign law) are well established and change only through legislative or judicial decision-making.[68] The norms, however, are a set of shared understandings among political consultants, party elites, large donors, interest group leaders, and journalists. The value of yard signs and robocalls, for instance, has only recently begun to be measured through Donald Green and Alan Gerber's field experiments.[69] Despite their demonstrably limited impact on vote share, yard signs are used almost universally in campaigns because of the shared understanding among campaign elites that successful campaigns are *supposed* to have them. Mayhew's point is that, at the candidate level, those individuals perceived as long-shot or "dark-horse" candidates have an incentive in adopting novel strategies that fall outside the existing norms. If the widely shared expectation is that you are going to lose, try to alter the rules of the game. And since formal campaign *rules* (established in law) are not easily alterable, they fiddle with strategic *norms* and supporting technologies instead.

We find particularly strong evidence for this instinct in presidential campaigns. It bears recall that, in the 2000 primaries, the McCain campaign was viewed as *the* trailblazer in online fundraising. Given the candidate's 2008 admission that he himself used neither e-mail nor the Internet, we can safely assume this was not borne of a personal predisposition in favor of new campaign technologies.[70] Rather, George W. Bush was the established frontrunner, and the McCain campaign embraced new technologies ("ostentatious innovations") in an effort to alter the campaign dynamics. Likewise, the Howard Dean campaign's meteoric rise occurred entirely before a single caucus vote had been cast in Iowa. Dean chose a strident tone ("I'm here to represent the

Democratic Wing of the Democratic Party") and a novel communications platform that let his supporters self-organize through Meetup.com. The Meetups and the online fundraising, more than his anti-war stance, were what attracted such heavy media attention. Without the technological innovations, there would have been little to separate Dean from perennial fringe primary candidates like Dennis Kucinich. And whereas McCain's and Dean's technological innovations failed to secure them the nomination, Obama's narrow margin among 2008 Democratic convention delegates was primarily based on his overwhelming support in caucus states. In those caucuses, his Internet-mediated field program overwhelmed presumed frontrunner Hillary Clinton, taking her campaign staff completely by surprise.

Each of these cases features a "dark-horse" candidate in a highly contested, high-profile presidential race. The Ron Paul presidential campaign exhibits the same qualities. A case could be made that the Ned Lamont and Jim Webb Senate primary campaigns, with their heavy inclusion and outreach to the "netroots" blogosphere, provide similar examples of such innovation.[71] I would posit that substantial campaign innovations—understood as alterations to the presiding "norms" among the network of campaign actors—will primarily be found in races that are (1) highly contested and (2) competing for high enough office to attract substantial campaign funding, staffing, volunteers, and media interest. The long-shot candidate for state senate and the challenger to a congressperson with 70% approval ratings may have the same interest in "ostentatious innovation" as the dark-horse presidential candidate, but campaign innovations alter the presiding rules of the political system only when they are (a) widely noticed and (b) credited as "successful." If the proverbial tree falls in the forest, but no one hears it, then the norms governing political campaigns remain unaffected. Such notice and success can occur only when the stakes are high enough to attract media attention and substantial financing, and when the contest is close enough to affect shared expectations. Put another way, if a new communications strategy allows a challenger to win 40% of the vote on Election Day rather than 35%, journalists and campaign elites will categorize the campaign as a "blowout loss" regardless.

Dark-horse candidates, particularly in presidential primaries, can be found in either party; the Democratic Party enjoyed a Senate majority heading into the 2008 election, but Al Franken (D-MN) and Kay Hagan (D-NC) were nonetheless challengers in their individual races. But if we aggregate across the subset of races that are both high-profile and closely contested, the outparty will feature substantially more challengers. More challengers provide an increased incidence of high-profile races where a strategic or technological innovation may be attempted. At the candidate level, then, the outparty has more chances to experience one of these successes, in turn generating a wave of adoption into the party network's normative understandings of "effective campaigning."[72]

REGARDING OLD DOGS AND NEW TRICKS: OUTPARTY INNOVATION INCENTIVES AT THE PARTY NETWORK LEVEL

Power within party networks can be understood as a zero-sum game. Policy priorities, strategic choices, and leadership positions are all matters of internal competition. The increase in netroots power came at the direct expense of the Democratic Leadership Council (DLC), which dominated Democratic politics in the 1990s. Markos Moultisas and other top bloggers leveled frequent criticism at the DLC.[73] When the netroots endorsed primary candidates like James Webb (2006 Virginia senate), it was in opposition to DLC-backed opponents. Moulitsas and DLC chair Harold Ford agreed to a two-part debate in 2008, occurring at the DLC convention and at Netroots Nation. When the DLC disbanded in February 2011, Moulitsas publicly crowed, "Where is the grave, so I can dance on it?"[74]

The zero-sum characteristic is even clearer among campaign consultants, where it can be assigned dollar amounts. David Dulio notes that campaign consultants tend to specialize in particular campaign tools, with some consultants focusing on direct mail and others specializing in robocalls.[75] Individual campaign budgets are finite. Dollars awarded to a new media consultant come at the expense of dollars awarded to an old media consultant.

Consider what this means for the partisan adoption of new campaign technologies at the party network level: if (1) new technologies and strategies tend to be attached to a new set of consultants, *displacing* an older set of established consultants (if within consulting, we only rarely observe the "old dogs" mastering the "new tricks"), and (2) the party that has sustained a string of recent election losses is more likely to seek out new consultant advice, then outparty innovation becomes a logical consequent.[76] Regardless of whether the communications medium consists of the Internet, television, radio, or direct mail, so long as we have a professional consultant-class devoted to managing elections, and so long as those consultants tend to specialize, we should see the party out of power leading the way in mastering new technologies.

As evidence, consider Amy Sullivan's widely read call to arms following the 2004 election, evocatively titled "Fire the Consultants!" Sullivan's essay raised the central question, "Why do Democrats promote campaign advisors who lose races?" She went on to provide an exposé of sorts into the elite network of Democratic campaign consultants and strategists: "Every sports fan knows that if a team boasts a losing record several seasons in a row, the coach has to be replaced with someone who can win. Yet when it comes to political consultants, Democrats seem incapable of taking this basic managerial step."[77] Echoing Sullivan's words, the netroots organized a nationwide campaign to name Howard Dean as the new chair of the Democratic National Committee, an effort premised on Dean's controversial "50-State Strategy," which massively reallocated resources through the state party affiliate system.[78] Two years later, one of the largest campaign consulting firms behind the wave of Democratic congressional victories was Blue State Digital, founded by alumni of the Dean campaign. One of the founders, Joe Rospars, went on to serve as New Media Director for the Obama campaign. Democratic campaign consulting dollars shifted from old consultants to new consultants. As discussed in Chapter 5, Dean and Obama campaign alumni are responsible for founding most Democratic new media vendors. Where legacy political consultants have entered the field of campaign technology, they have done so through mergers and acquisitions, buying up organizations founded by these Dean and Obama campaign alumni. The campaign technology contracts have flowed to a new generation of left-wing party operatives *at the expense of* a previous generation.

The contrast with the Republican Party network is stark. It is not the case that no Republicans "get it" with regards to new media technologies and campaign techniques. Patrick Ruffini, Michael Turk, Jon Henke, Mindy Finn, and other Republican strategists are held in high regard within the technology consulting community and are often called upon by the media as authoritative sources on the subject. Ruffini is the former head of the Republican National Committee's Internet Department. Turk was the RNC's e-campaign director until 2005. Henke was hired by George Allen in the Virginia 2006 senate race to coordinate counter-strategy against netroots Jim Webb supporters. All of these individuals regularly appear on panels with their Democratic equivalents at conferences like Politics Online and Personal Democracy Forum. The key difference between these individuals and their Democratic counterparts is their "soft power" within the party network and the amount of consulting contracts they receive. Simply put, the "Internet people" within elite Democratic circles have become key players, while in Republican circles they are still relegated to the periphery. Republican technology consultant David All remarked in a 2007 interview that "The RNC has never called me. They don't call any of the tech and politics crowd. They're just going it alone, which is fine if you want to be a failure. We've never needed the Internet before . . ."[79]

A few days after losing the 2008 presidential election, a group of longtime Republican elites—including Grover Norquist of Americans for Tax Reform and Tony Perkins of the Family Research Council—gathered at the home of conservative scion Brent Bozell, President of the Media Research Center.[80] Ruffini, Turk, Henke, Finn, and All were not invited. Writing about the meeting on TheNextRight.com, Ruffini suggested, "Whatever happened at the country estate will be irrelevant to the future of the movement. I'll bet not a single person under 40 was even at the table . . . The future will be shaped digitally . . . on blogs like this one, RedState, Save the GOP, American Scene, and the dozens I have a feeling will be created in the wake of Tuesday's wake-up call."[81] Ruffini and company instead launched a website, RebuildtheParty.com, that featured an online petition urging the candidates for RNC chair to embrace and fund online infrastructure. Henke has likewise noted that one major difference between the progressive and conservative netroots today is that many top progressive bloggers hold their position full-time, as opposed to top conservative bloggers who are also political consultants, media figures, or lawyers[82]

Outparty status appears to have provided a boon to Ruffini and company through the 2010 election season. His consultancy, Engage DC, was involved in several prominent electoral campaigns. More contracts, and more resources, flowed to the new wave of Republican consultants. They in turn invigorated candidate engagement on Twitter and Facebook, producing a Republican advantage in these social media spaces. At the consultant layer of the Republican Party network, 2010 did produce some change among the "coaches." Yet the "meta-brand" effect complicates this matter: with existing components of the Republican Party network embracing the mantle of the new movement, and with fewer consecutive electoral defeats, the Republican Party has experienced fewer calls to "fire the coaches." Many of the new leaders of the conservative resurgence, at least at the time of this writing, are longstanding party leaders. The zero-sum conflict over power within the Republican Party network will continue to play out over time, aided and abetted by technological innovation.

The parallels between conservative technological adoption in 2008 and netroots activity in 2004 are illustrative. Along with the advantages that accrue to interest groups when mobilizing opposition, and the stochastic increase in opportunities for innovative campaign strategies among high-profile "dark-horse" campaigns, the longer a party coalition endures electoral defeat, the greater the calls for "firing the coaches." Innovative campaign strategies and campaign technologies are introduced by a new set of elite actors within the party network. The success of those actors comes at the expense of existing partisan elites—it is a zero-sum, internal struggle for power. Given enough electoral losses, Democratic Party elites called publicly for "firing the consultants." That was driven neither by ideology nor by the particularities of online communication platforms, but rather by the shifting opportunity structure provided to challenging members within the party network.

The outparty innovation incentives thesis does a good job of explaining many of the historical drivers behind the progressive–conservative online infrastructure gap. It also helps to explain why British Conservatives, as the outparty, developed their advantage in the UK blogosphere. It even intuitively fits with the partisan adoption of talk radio. That said, the Internet has often been described as the "largest advance in communications technology since the invention of the printing press." Leaving the nature of the medium itself muted in our explanation is limiting—it presumes that there is nothing special about this new media environment. After arguing for five chapters that the Internet alters the organizational layer of political engagement, can we now retreat to the stance that there is *nothing* special about the Internet? In particular, outparty innovation incentives do not adequately explain why conservative bloggers and other online elites continually make certain basic mistakes. Why do the top conservative blogs all close their user registration, stifling the growth of their attendant communities? Why has the sedimentary wave of Tea Party activity produced no conservative MoveOn? Why do SlateCard and RightRoots fail to give registered users the ability to create their own endorsement lists? The ideological congruence thesis may explain this—conservatives might at base simply prefer hierarchy and limited interaction. But another possibility deserves serious consideration.

Thesis 3: Those Wacky Saboteurs

There was an urban legend of sorts at my undergraduate institution, Oberlin College. Oberlin is a small liberal arts college, with a proud history of left-wing activism.[83] During my time there, the campus boasted five socialist organizations to its single Student Democrats chapter. The story goes that there had once been a campus Republicans chapter, until the end of one school year when the socialists decided to have a little fun. A few of the campus socialists learned that the campus Republicans would be electing the following year's officers at their next meeting. Anyone in attendance could vote. So they swarmed the meeting, elected themselves, and disbanded the group. Dispirited, Oberlin Republicans receded into disorganization.

The campus socialists *could* take such an action because it was easy, and because the open rules permitted it. They *would* take such an action because it was fun. In comparing the vibrant left-wing netroots to the less-organized right-wing attempts to build parallel institutions, a similar pattern emerges. Internet-enabled "ridiculously easy group formation" makes prankful "trolling" commonplace. And that, in turn, yields a substantial benefit to the initial wave of online political organizations. Groups like DailyKos, Dean for America, and ActBlue all benefited from a cloak of relative Internet anonymity in their early development stages. Anyone could join these groups, but conservative trolls had no reason to target them en masse. Netroots organizations designed an array of open community-engagement tools as they grew in size and sophistication. When conservatives try to build equivalent spaces, however, they essentially announce themselves as "valuable online real estate," thus attracting *Merry Pranksters and their Digitized Wooden Shoes.*[84]

To be clear, the merry prankster thesis does not contend that progressives are breaking any laws. There are no organized mobs nefariously attempting to undermine upstart conservative political associations. There are no progressive plants at Tea Party gatherings. The leading netroots organizations do not coordinate such acts (DailyKos being an occasional exception—Moulitsas revels in aggressive partisanship from time to time). Rather, the lowered transaction costs of the web make it easy for large, partisan communities-of-interest to disrupt the activities of opposing communities-of-interest. The *threat* of such disruption affects the design choices of conservative organizational leaders. There is strong evidence that progressive bloggers, particularly those who populate the humor-oriented blogs Wonkette.com and SadlyNo.com, find pleasure in acting as "merry pranksters," harassing online conservatives. Conservatives display similar preferences but are at a tremendous size disadvantage. Dealing with 10 trolls in a standing community of 1,000 is easy. Dealing with 1,000 trolls in a standing community of 10 requires modifications to software architecture.

The contention of this thesis is that, in the presence of mature communities-of-interest from the opposite end of the political spectrum, developers of conservative online infrastructure adopt "closed" design rules. Such structural decisions leave their sites less vulnerable to attack but also less capable of promoting community participation. This presents a novel community-formation puzzle in the current technological environment, one that had not been present in previous information regimes. It suggests that duplicating online infrastructural success is particularly difficult because community formation is highly vulnerable in the early stages. I offer three such examples below.

WONKETTE HELPS TO "REBUILD THE PARTY"

As previously mentioned, in the immediate aftermath of the 2008 election, a group of "ideologically diverse young Republicans" launched a website urging the RNC chairman candidates to support a 10-point action plan to strengthen and modernize the Republican Party.[85] Along with an e-petition, an "action network," and a blog, the website also featured a platform for user-generated content: ideas.rebuildtheparty.com. This is exactly the type of community engagement that progressives often criticize online conservatives for ignoring. Like Democracy for America's "endorsement" tool or MoveOn's campaign priority process, it invites users to register with the site and then submit their own ideas for rebuilding the party, cast votes in favor of one another's ideas, and comment on each idea individually.

When the liberal comedy blog Wonkette.com got wind of the effort, their active community saw an opportunity for some light entertainment. Within hours, the most popular suggestions on the site included "Hire more ninjas" and several references to crass inside-Wonkette jokes. Their top suggestion received 4,344 votes and 1,608 comments before being closed down by the site administrators.[86] So many of the suggestions came from left-wing pranksters that genuine suggestions disappeared from the list. Site administrators eventually countered with a distributed moderation tool that made such antics easier to identify and remove, but by then the community-building opportunity had ended. The Wonkette pranksters had greater numbers and greater motivation than the nascent conservative community. RebuildtheParty failed to produce a lasting infrastructure. The Wonkette community themselves referred to the action as "juvenile harassment" and "puerile antics."[87] In discussing the action on their site, one regular poster wrote, "Look, in the end who cares? We pulled a stupid, very fun prank . . . Wonkette is for the cynics who'd like a better world, but know how the game is rigged."[88]

Wonkette is a politically oriented community-of-interest, albeit one that primarily exists to make fun of politicians. Interestingly, Wonkette is not considered part of the elite liberal blogging community in the BAI methodology because other elite blogs in the cluster do not link to it in their blogrolls. Wonkette is more of a gossip blog than a forum for political discussion and mobilization. It creates a substantial problem for conservative Internet-mediated organizations attempting to adopt the community-engaging tactics of a DFA or a MoveOn. MoveOn and DFA are able to treat all e-mail recipients as members and hold open voting processes because of their existing size advantage. Online conservatives could attempt to rig such votes—indeed, the Internet term for coordinated online poll attacks of this type is "freeping" because the action was pioneered by the conservative forum FreeRepublic.com—but such attacks face a size disadvantage. There are over 5 million MoveOn e-mail recipients. There is no such hub for conservatives to coordinate an online voting attack (sarcastic or otherwise). And while the "serious" political hubs such as MoveOn and DFA do not engage in such juvenile antics, the threat from hubs like Wonkette nonetheless prevents conservative sites from adopting the same tools that make the progressive Internet-mediated organizations successful.

THE "SADLYNAUTS" AND CLOSED REGISTRATION ON CONSERVATIVE BLOGS

SadlyNo.com is among the top 25 blogs in the progressive community, routinely receiving about 100 comments per post and attracting roughly 10,000 page views/day. The site self-describes as a "liberal progressive humor site" and describes its niche as follows:

> "The site's main running joke is in finding embarrassing slips or untrue statements by conservatives and linking to a refutation, saying, "Sadly, No!" Other running gags include posting pictures of conservative columnists on Internet dating sites, battling with a "singing troll" who sends homemade songs deriding the site's contributors and commenters, and doing line-by-line putdowns of columns by Christian evangelists and other right-wingers. Sadly, No! also occasionally publishes phony columns at right-wing sites, and engages in other pranks."[89]

When SadlyNo links to a conservative blogger, that individual's blog incurs a spike in traffic and a flood of argumentative replies in the post's comments section. The "SadlyNaughts" engage with conservatives as a band of merry pranksters, attempting to egg their ideological opponents on into fits of rage. This is the very essence of throwing "digitized wooden shoes," with the dramatic reduction in online transaction costs allowing a few hundred progressives to have fun at the expense of nascent conservative bloggers. Again, this activity of "Internet trolling" is hardly limited to the left end of the ideological spectrum.[90] But the size advantage enjoyed by progressive communities-of-interest means that the 20th largest progressive political blog can easily derail the comment threads of all but a few conservative counterparts.

In a March 30th, 2009, article for the *Washington Times*, conservative blog proprietor Andrew Breitbart complained about these tactics. He argued that "Hugh Hewitt's popular site shut off its comments section because of the success of these obnoxious invaders . . . Other right-leaning sites such as Instapundit and National Review Online refuse to allow comments, knowing better than to flirt with the online activist left."[91] It is difficult to feel much sympathy for Breitbart himself, given his prominent role in doctoring, distorting, and leveraging video clips to smear ACORN, Shirley Sherrod, and Planned Parenthood.[92] The puzzle he outlines is quite real, however. The top conservative blogs—sites like Hotair.com— have a closed registration policy that serves as a barrier to new Internet-mediated grassroots participation. You cannot build a large online participatory community if new members cannot register. The prankster antics of the "SadlyNaughts" offer an explanation to this puzzle: in the early stages of a blog's community development, a little coordinated harassment from left-wing pranksters can go a long way.

DAILYKOS URGES, "MITT FOR MICHIGAN"

In his 2008 book, *Taking on the System*, Markos Moulitsas describes the "Mitt for Michigan" campaign that he launched on DailyKos on January 10, 2008:

> "Without a real Democratic contest on the ballot, and a lack of party registration in Michigan, this is an open primary. Anyone can pick up a Republican ballot. So Michigan Democrats and independents who want to see the Republican battle royale continue should just take a few minutes on Tuesday, January 15th to cast a ballot for Mitt Romney in the Republican primary."
>
> ". . . If we can help push Mitt over the line, not only do we help keep their field fragmented, but we also pollute Romney's victory. How 'legitimate' will the Mittster's victory look if liberals provide the margin of victory? Think of the hilarity that will ensue. We'll simply be adding fuel to their civil war, never a bad thing from our vantage point."[93]

"Kos" does not speak for the entire progressive blogosphere, but he certainly speaks *to* much of it. In response to commenters' replies that progressives should be above such dirty tricks, he offered the following rejoinder:

"There are some concerned that this is 'dirty tricks' and that we shouldn't 'stoop to their level.' This is perhaps the key difference between traditional liberals and movement progressives. The former believe that politics is a high-minded debate about ideas, the latter have seen movement conservatives use every tool at their disposal to steal power and cling to it."

He notes that the campaign was a "big PR success for *Daily Kos*" and uses the example to punctuate his general stance that "If the cause is just, then the goal should be victory. All reasonable options should be on the table."[94] Rush Limbaugh advocated that his listeners pursue a similar strategy in the Indiana Democratic primary, furthering the lengthy contest between Hilary Clinton and Barack Obama.[95] The benefits of being an established, interactive community are manifold. And while Kos himself faced relatively few conservative trolls in the early days of his site, prospective conservative analogues risk an outsized threat from the robust progressive community sites. One reason The Vanguard, RightMarch, and Freedom's Watch may have failed to engage with their member base in the same style as MoveOn is out of a *legitimate* fear that progressives will swarm the sites and game the system.[96]

It would then seem that, for reasons of strategy or sport, the size advantage enjoyed by progressive Internet-mediated organizations creates substantial hurdles for conservatives seeking to create parallel online infrastructures. These progressives are breaking no laws, nor are they engaging in activities foresworn by the Right—Internet trolling displays no partisan persuasion. But the size of existing progressive online communities, which were allowed to form unencumbered from mass partisan harassment, alters the development path for their conservative counterparts. Apart from ideology or outparty innovation incentives, the dramatic reduction of online transaction costs creates substantial problems for new conservative attempts to replicate Internet-mediated organizational successes. Perhaps for this reason, the biggest successes of online conservatives post-2008 have come in newly emerging Internet-mediated fields. Conservatives have out-organized progressives on Twitter, while experiencing continual failure in building their own DailyKos. Internet-mediated infrastructure-building on the right seems to occur mostly through adaptation to the next wave of online innovations rather than through the creation of parallel online infrastructure.

Conclusion: Whither Online Conservatism, or Online Conservatism Withers?

The argument presented in this chapter is threefold. First, at the organizational layer of American politics, innovations diffuse *within* ideological networks rather than between such networks. The adoption of information technology by political associations has been decidedly partisan in nature, with progressives demonstrably leading their conservative equivalents throughout the early years of the 21st century. Second, partisan technological adoption is largely driven by outparty innovation incentives created through periods of counter-mobilization. The Internet is not a fundamentally liberal-friendly medium. The success of MoveOn and DailyKos tells us more about the Left's infrastructural and electoral deficits in the 2000s than it does about the natural "bottom-up" inclinations of progressive activists. Third, developments in the organizational layer of politics are path-dependent in nature and mediate a set of intra-network battles over power and authority within the party coalition.

I will hasten to remind the reader that the three theses presented in this chapter are not mutually exclusive. There is *some* role played by all three factors. As the Tea Party phenomenon matures and conservative counter-mobilization continues, social science researchers will enjoy an unprecedented opportunity to test these developmental theories. The three theses should be understood as follows:

Ideological Congruence + Outparty Incentives + Late-Forming Community Disruption = Differential Adoption Rates

The strongest form of the ideological congruence thesis (which I would term ideological determinism) is unsupportable. It leaves no room for past periods of grassroots conservatism and little room for the success of online conservatives in, for instance, the United Kingdom. That said, these very exceptions, along with the early success of Ron Paul Libertarians and online Tea Party activity, all point to a central prediction about the future of online conservatism. Both UK Conservatives and Ron Paul Libertarians are a different *type* of ideological conservative than currently dominates the Republican Party. Parties, viewed over time, represent changing ideological coalitions. The Republican Party of 1954 was a different ideological beast than the Republican Party of 2004. And we have already seen that the success of the progressive netroots came at the expense of central actors within the Democratic Party coalition—actors who themselves preferred a more "top-down" approach. To the extent that the Internet advantages "bottom-up" organizing, then, what we can predict is that the development of parallel online institutions in the Republican Party will be accompanied by a shift in the party coalition itself. The Tea Party represents a continuing trend toward polarization-through-participation, for good or for ill.

Such a prediction blends well with the predictions emerging from the outparty innovation incentives thesis. The incentives occur on three levels—organizational, candidate, and party coalition. The organizational benefits of "storming the castle" have already become apparent through events like the tax-day Tea Party protests. They have invigorated a limited set of new conservative political associations—limited specifically because the meta-brand has let many existing party elements reposition themselves and avoid direct competition. Groups like Liberty.com and TheVanguard.com continue to pale in comparison to MoveOn.org, but this is largely because their support from existing conservative funders leaves them with fewer incentives to embrace the "MoveOn Effect." They are not challenging the Club for Growth or Americans for Tax Reform the way that the netroots challenged legacy progressive interest groups.

Then there are the merry pranksters to consider. Conservatives' greatest successes online have come not in building parallel infrastructure to netroots successes, but in building activity around the next wave of Internet-mediated innovations. When trying to replicate progressive success, conservatives face the threat (perceived or realized) that existing communities of online progressives will disrupt their open architecture, either for fun or strategic gain. When trying to develop new efforts in the next wave of technological advancement, they benefit from the same sort of relative anonymity that DailyKos, MoveOn, and ActBlue enjoyed in their early developmental phases—the first examples of such organizations become widely known only after they have achieved some surprising public success.

Online conservatism is unlikely to wither, therefore. Rather, we should expect to see ongoing, differential development at the organizational layer of American politics. Progressives and conservatives will continue to adopt new technological innovations in response to changes in the electoral landscape, shepherding newly ripened technological opportunities into novel organizational forms. The longer one side endures counter-mobilization, the deeper the intra-party tensions and the more substantial the new infrastructural developments. Conservatives may never develop their own MoveOn or DailyKos, but they will find other ways to utilize the Internet to communicate with and mobilize their partisan supporters.

7

Innovation Edges, Advocacy Inflation, and Sedimentary Organizations

> "Technology is neither good nor bad, nor is it neutral."
> —Kranzberg's First Law of Technology[1]

What then are we to conclude about the MoveOn Effect? A new generation of netroots organizations has emerged. Those groups take a variety of forms, but all share similar membership and fundraising practices. They tend to be issue generalists, mobilizing citizen support around the pressing issues of the day. They are sedimentary organizations, developing their member lists by riding waves of public interest and offering an outlet for citizen action. They have developed a culture of testing that yields passive democratic feedback, keeping them abreast of membership sentiments. Their advocacy work extends well beyond "clicktivism," engaging supporters in large-scale, sustained collective action. Their work routines and campaign strategies are built around the Internet—these organizations would be impossible without e-mail and the World Wide Web—but they are far different from the "organizing without organizations" often heralded in public discourse.

The skeptical reader might venture a challenge: "Is that really all?" The field of political advocacy is changing, but the new groups are not necessarily more effective than their legacy peers. MoveOn did not stop the Iraq War. The PCCC pressed hard for the public option, but the Affordable Care Act was passed without it. Most of DailyKos's legislative and policy goals remain unfulfilled. What's more, the organizational layer of American politics is a relatively small patch of real estate. A small number of major organizations make up the bulk of the political netroots' force. Compared to the national electorate, MoveOn's 5 million members are less than 2% of the population. From the perspective of the average American citizen, a shift from ignoring direct mail to ignoring e-mail may appear to be little change at all. And from the perspective of elected officials, e-petitions are as easy to ignore as faxed petitions. The hopes of early Internet optimists—that the new medium would "push power to the edges" and lead to a massive upwelling in deliberative, "people-powered politics"—are left unfulfilled.[2] Barack Obama may have relied on an Internet-mediated campaign apparatus to win the presidency, but he has hardly governed as a "netroots president." The new organizations have instead become (to borrow a term from Richard Davis) "agenda seekers," facing the same structural constraints that have long defined American political life.[3] Many readers likely hoped for more of a revolution from such a "revolutionary" technology as the Internet.

This final chapter places the generation shift among political advocacy groups into the broader context of changing communications technology and unchanging "fundamentals" of American politics. It then provides four closing observations about emerging dynamics in the new media environment. As I have sought to emphasize throughout the book, the Internet is not finished developing. These closing observations—regarding *advocacy inflation*, new forms of *activated public opinion*, the dangers posed by the loss of *beneficial inefficiencies*, and some subtle benefits and positive incentives emerging from *sedimentary organizations*—provide a roadmap of key issues for future reflection and discussion amongst political practitioners and academic analysts alike.

Political Normalization and Organizational Change

The Internet "revolution" has been limited in character because of fundamental attributes of the American political system. Here I stand in complete agreement with my colleagues from the normalization tradition. Elections are still conducted biennially, decided by a plurality of voters in a particular geographic boundary. Congressional bills still require the support of 60 senators to overcome a filibuster. Those are structural constraints. They have a greater impact on individual policy proposals than even the most radical of changes in communications media. Likewise, it is still primarily the wealthy, the well-educated, and the white who are mobilized to contribute money, contact their congresspersons, and otherwise engage in the public sphere.[4] Those with excess wealth, free time, and privilege remain advantaged. Matthew Hindman has remarked that the average elite political blogger is an Ivy League-educated, white male—. . . hardly a subset of the population that has gone historically underrepresented.[5] Eszter Hargattai has likewise found that a digital "skills" divide has replaced the digital access divide.[6] For the poor, the elderly, and the poorly educated, digital tools only create further distance between themselves and the trappings of wealth and privilege. The new medium has not been a panacea for the ills of society, nor will it be anytime soon.

Relative citizen preferences also act as a political fundamental. Politics remains far less popular than sports and entertainment.[7] Faced with a dizzying array of media choices, the "knowledge gap" between political information-seekers and the rest of society is only exacerbated further.[8] Those who enjoy the spectacle of politics can revel in it; those who dislike it can modify their news and entertainment sources accordingly.[9] Even if the new organizational hubs of citizen political engagement were to completely replace the old organizational bases of citizen political involvement, the great mass of the American public would remain poorly informed, unmotivated, and uninvolved. DailyKos receives between 500,000 and 1.5 million visits per day. Perez Hilton receives approximately 3 million visits per day. MoveOn's 5 million members pale in comparison to the video game World of Warcraft, played by 11.5 million worldwide. Politics as profession, vocation, or hobby will simply never be more entertaining than entertainment. Lowering the transaction costs of political engagement may (to paraphrase Chris Anderson and Clay Shirky) more fully reveal the "demand curve" of the American public.[10] But if the average citizen was not thirsting for political information, they will not develop a taste for it simply because it has been rendered more easily available.

Changes in communications media—even major changes that could be labeled revolutionary in character—do not alter the fundamentals of an electoral system. The United States remains a single-member, simple-plurality (first past the post) system, with a bicameral legislature designed to make substantial policy change frustratingly slow and difficult. As Michael Schudson has admirably demonstrated, the American citizenry has *never* displayed the highly active, highly informed characteristics that political theorists and lay historians wish upon them.[11] To state that the Internet has not rendered us a nation of politically informed, politically involved citizens is simply to grant that there are limits to the power embedded in communications technology. The Internet has *also* not made us all fabulously wealthy (although it has made *some* individuals wealthy, and they are not the captains of industry of old). No serious observers ever believed that the web would make us all rich; no serious observer should claim that communications technology will seamlessly change political interest levels or render inert the forces imposed by the electoral system, legislative system, or historic patterns of structurally induced inequality. Information technology mediates and modifies power relationships; it does not overthrow them.

Incidentally, it is for this very reason that this study has been limited to American political associations rather than looking at transnational or international advocacy groups. Political associations develop on the basis of a variety of factors, of which party strength and electoral system are two of the most important. The United States has particularly strong interest groups because it has traditionally weak parties.[12] Italian, Canadian, British, German, or Australian political associations have distinct histories, embedded both in local culture, path-dependent historical events, and electoral system design. I would venture the prediction that each of these countries will experience *some* form of disruptive innovation among their advocacy groups and political parties, but we should not expect it to be the *same* form in each.[13]

That said, we should recall Melvin Kranzberg's First Law of Technology: "Technology is neither good nor bad, nor is it neutral." Scholars in the "organizing without organizations" or "theory 2.0" tradition have largely held that the Internet is good for American politics. Some of the costs of collective action have been reduced by the new medium, resulting in novel forms of political expression. Researchers in the "clicktivism" camp argue the opposite. They suggest that the new medium creates perverse incentives that degrade political action, pollute the public sphere, and create "echo chambers" of information cascades of rumor and falsehood. Researchers in the "normalization" tradition, meanwhile, tend toward the view that this is essentially much ado about nothing. Political behavior and governing political institutions remain unchanged in important ways. It is still a nation of elites; they're "just different elites." To each of these camps, I would invoke Kranzberg and reply that changes at the organizational layer of politics are neither good nor bad, but they most certainly are not neutral.

We should not confuse the ongoing importance of political fundamentals with a neutral technological impact. In point of fact, the change in information technology has engendered *multiple effects*. This book has represented an inquiry into one particular set of effects, located specifically at the organizational layer of American politics. It has done so both because those changes have gone largely unexplored, and because of my own personal research interests, rooted in a lifetime of participation among such organizations. The new media environment has had other effects, though. It has benefited large corporate entities that have created a market for disturbing amounts of information on our consumer preferences.[14] It has spurred a practice of "political redlining," in which electoral campaigns make use of this consumer data for sophisticated microtargeting.[15] It has supported dissident groups in non-Democratic countries,[16] and cross-national social movements.[17] It has also yielded dangerous tools of control and surveillance to powerful actors, including the governments that seek to suppress dissident groups and social movements.[18] It has supported echo chambers of public opinion, proving just as useful to neo-Nazis as it has to knitting circles.[19] The new medium is changing how we produce the news, even as it aids the spread of disinformation.[20] These effects work at cross purposes with one another. They occur at several layers of global, national, and local politics, and even at different layers of the Internet itself. They cannot and should not be lumped into a single framework. The final tally as to whether the new media environment is a boon or a pox upon our polity depends as much upon one's values and social standing as it does upon data collection and research design.

The MoveOn Effect operates within the confines of existing political funda-mentals.[21] It changes how organizations form, communicate, fundraise, and mobilize. It affects the scope of issue engagement and strategic decisions. It mod-ifies the interest group ecology of American politics. It alters intra-party competi-tion within party coalitions and furthers a trend toward "polarization through participation." These are neither neutral nor minor items. They are complex tra-jectories. So while the skeptical reader would be correct to conclude that the MoveOn Effect leaves mass political behavior and elite political institutions largely unaltered, I would counter that change in the organizational layer is none-theless of dramatic importance to democratic participation. "Political mobiliza-tion is seldom spontaneous," and the bases of such mobilization have changed.

The Limited Scale of the Engaged Public

Famed anthropologist Margaret Mead is best known for the eloquent phrase, "Never doubt that a small group of thoughtful, committed citizens can change the world. Indeed, it is the only thing that ever has."[22] Among voluntary political as-sociations, Mead's statement is canonical. (In my college organizing years, I could go a full week wearing conference t-shirts with that dictum.) Although its accu-racy is debatable—*large* armies of *armed* citizens have changed the world a time or two as well—the sentiment illustrates an important point: given the approxi-mate size of the public sphere, most citizen participation occurs among segments of the populace small enough to fit within the margin of error of a nationally rep-resentative opinion poll.

Consider as one example the "Environmental Bill of Rights." In 1995, Newt Gingrich and his Republican House majority began enacting their "Contract with America" legislative agenda, including rollbacks of several foundational environmental laws. The nation's environmental organizations, dismissed as fading and irrelevant by major media outlets, came together and settled upon a collaborative mass mobilization campaign. The central tactic—the Environmen-tal Bill of Rights—was a petition that enumerated four core environmental values and called upon Congress to stand up for existing environmental laws. Over the course of several months, the collective organizing capacity of the entire national environmental movement was directed toward distributing these petitions, gath-ering signatures, and educating the public about the threat to bedrock environ-mental laws. The Environmental Bill of Rights served as my personal introduction to the movement—I was one of thousands who helped gather over 1,000,000 pe-tition signatures across the country. At least within the environmental commu-nity, the collaborative campaign was viewed as a major organizing success. The effort publicized Republican legislative overreach, demonstrated the strength of public opinion in favor of environmental values, and successfully moved

President Clinton and other governmental officials to take a more aggressive stance against the rollback of the Endangered Species Act, Clean Water Act, Clean Air Act, National Environmental Policy Act, and other major laws established in the 1970s.

As a high school student at the time, I was inspired by the sheer size of the effort—an outpouring of grassroots support, demonstrating the depth and breadth of mass support for the values I myself held. Yet years later, the relative magnitude of those numbers give me pause. The American population in 1995 was approximately 262,800,000. Our 1,000,000 petition signatures represented the vocal opinion of 0.38% of the U.S. population. By the standards of issue-based political engagement, in an essentially pre-Internet information environment, that 0.38% was *in fact* a large outpouring of public support. Compared to a baseline of everyday citizen participation, the Environmental Bill of Rights *was* massive. What's more, those 1,000,000 people had not themselves attended a march or a rally. They hadn't contacted their elected official directly or deliberated at length with their neighbor. Several dozen of them had signed the petition solely because I was bugging them about it during our high school lunch period! And this was against the backdrop of an issue area that routinely polled with 70% or greater support among the American public.

The subset of the American populace that actively participates in traditional political activities beyond voting has simply never been all that large.

That subset is, however, important. A longstanding tradition within the field of public opinion research is concerned with the role that "active" or "activated" public opinion plays in politics. Herbert Blumer lambasted an audience of early pollsters in his 1947 American Sociological Association Presidential Address, scolding them by noting that "current public opinion polling has not succeeded in isolating public opinion as a generic object of study."[23] He goes on to propose that the passive opinions obtained through polling—what we now term "mass opinion"[24]—cannot be equated with public opinion because "*in any realistic sense* public opinion consists of the pattern of the diverse views and positions on the issue *that come to the individuals who have to act in response to public opinion.*"[25] E. E. Schattschneider, writing in 1960, places a similar emphasis on the role of the activated, participatory subset of the American public in his field-defining book, *The Semi-Sovereign People*: "Political conflict is not like an intercollegiate debate in which the opponents agree in advance on the definition of the issues. . . . He who determines what politics is about runs the country."[26]

Among contemporary scholars, Taeku Lee and Susan Herbst offer two modern equivalents of the Blumerian/Schattschneiderian tradition. Lee's *Mobilizing Public Opinion* treats presidential letter-writing as a form of "activated mass opinion." He argues that "'Public opinion' as gauged through survey responses may differ crucially from 'public opinion' as revealed through political action."[27] Herbst's *Reading Public Opinion* follows Blumer's early advice, interviewing the very individuals—media and government elites—who have to act in response to public opinion. She finds that "the construction of public opinion happens also in the minds of citizens: People tend to define public opinion as part of an *argument* they make—to themselves and, at times, to others—about political life more generally."[28] If the public sphere is to have a real-world instantiation, if it is to be anything more than a Habermasian ideal, then it must include the citizens' associations that support small groups of thoughtful, committed citizens as they go about attempting to change the world.

Theda Skocpol's *Diminished Democracy* provides a parallel argument for taking the organizational layer of politics seriously. Skocpol's work began as a rejoinder to her colleague Robert Putnam's study of the decline of American social capital, *Bowling Alone*. It is an argument that many of the mass behavioral trends identified by Putnam can be understood as an impact of change amongst mediating organizations. The decline of federated, cross-class civic associations and the accompanying primacy of single-issue, professional advocacy groups played a causal role in the subsequent decline of American social capital. Americans were united through these civic associations. They learned democratic skills through civic associations. When they engaged in mass social movements, they did so through civic associations. Those civic federations are long since gone. (The neo-federated netroots organizational model is an attempt to recreate some of their features, but it is still present only in proto-organizational form.) The organizations that replaced them are now "legacy" groups, facing disrupted revenue streams and changing public conceptions of organizational membership. If we retrospectively accept that the previous "generation shift" had major impacts on civic life, then the current generation shift likewise deserves thoughtful attention.

Not all single-issue, professional advocacy groups will disappear, and they will not disappear overnight. But there is strong reason to believe that the adoption of new technology, particularly in areas of membership and fundraising, will be driven by new organizations. Indeed, the Membership Communications Project dataset provides empirical support for this expectation—legacy political associations engage in less "headline chasing" and less targeted fundraising, and contact their membership around a narrower range of issues. Outparty innovation incentives explain why these changes have been concentrated on the left, among progressive advocacy groups and the Democratic Party network. Conservatives are not ideologically disadvantaged in the new media environment. Rather, the technology has ripened at a time when Republican officials dominated all three branches of government, providing far more organizing opportunities and "sedimentary waves" for their left-wing opponents. The three models of Internet-mediated organizations indicate that the organizational ecology of American politics is in a critical formation phase. The lowered overhead costs for new political organizations allow for more niches, and the continual changes to computational technologies and devices allow for ongoing waves of social and political innovation. The story of organizational formation and competition within party networks is far from complete.

Looking to the future, I would offer four closing observations to guide our understanding of the interplay between new media technologies and the public sphere. First, the political system moves faster and becomes noisier as a result of the ongoing incentive to innovate. This results in a phenomenon I term *advocacy inflation*. Second, social media platforms allow for alternate measures of activated public opinion, many of which are unmediated (or at least less mediated) by traditional parties, interest groups, and media institutions. The opinion on such platforms is neither representative of the nation as a whole nor actively directed toward swaying decision-makers. Rather, it is best understood as a novel form of *activated public opinion*, much like the presidential letters of an earlier era, as studied by Taeku Lee. Third, the largest threat posed by the rise of Internet-mediated organizations can be understood as the loss of *beneficial inefficiencies*. Many important organizational functions may be both costly and not particularly exciting to supporters. Whereas the older, less efficient information environment allowed organizational managers to direct resources where they were needed, the newer, more efficient information environment may give them less freedom, reducing an indirect subsidy for a public good. Fourth and finally, there are some underlying benefits to *sedimentary organizational forms* that leave reason for hope. The new organizations have more capacity for responding to membership sentiment than their legacy peers. They have some new incentives to approximate meritocracy in their work routines, rendering the boundary between elite networks and motivated citizens a bit more permeable. Normatively, that strikes me as a positive development.

Advocacy Inflation and the Half-Life of Political Tactics

In his classic 1925 field experiment, Harold Gosnell determined that the simple act of mailing a reminder to voters before Election Day produced a 9% increase in municipal election voter turnout.[29] Seventy-five years later, Donald Green and Alan Gerber led a revival of the field experiment research tradition and reexamined the utility of political mailers. Unsurprisingly, mailings had lost much of their effectiveness.[30] Green and Gerber's findings, of course, did not disprove Gosnell's earlier findings. Generations had passed. Campaigns, elections, and society itself had changed substantially. The efficacy of the political tactic was embedded in a system of political competition, and that system had evolved in the intervening years.

Leaders of the netroots organizations featured in this book have called attention to a parallel phenomenon occurring online. Occasionally termed "the tragedy of political advocacy" or "advocacy inflation," it is the recognition that specific tools of digital organizing—e-mails, videos, e-petitions, and Meetups, to name a few—decline in effectiveness over time.[31] Indeed, I would argue that this is a generalizable phenomenon: the efficacy of any popular political tactic decays over time. The field of political competition is continually *thickening*. Once a novel tactic is deemed effective, it diffuses into wider adoption. Opponents then develop response tactics, and decision-makers learn to tune out the increasing "noise." (Sidney Tarrow calls this process "innovation and counter-innovation."[32]) As Markos Moulitsas put it in his criticism of 1960s-era protest tactics as deployed in the 21st century, "The most effective activism is a function of its times. . . . The traditional media won't cover the mundane, routine, predictable, or familiar. Forty years of organized protests and marches for every conceivable cause . . . have desensitized not just the press but the broader public to the street spectacle."[33]

Three mechanisms facilitate this "half-life" among popular tactics. First, and operating near immediately, is the *novelty effect*. Innovative campaign tactics attract added public attention *specifically because* they are new. Political and technology beat writers are attracted to the new angle or "hook" in the phenomenon. Thought leaders and technological entrepreneurs likewise lend their support—attracted both by the technology and by the candidate or issue.[34] The first time a candidate launches a blog, it is newsworthy. The third time, it is commonplace. Daniel Kreiss has studied this feature of the Howard Dean and Barack Obama presidential campaigns at length.[35] He argues that a central element of the Obama campaign's new media strategy was to convert the online presence into positive mainstream media coverage. Obama's Facebook support was more valuable for the long-form, glowing stories it generated in the mainstream press than for the "likes" and wall posts it generated.

A second mechanism is the rise in *background noise*, also known as the "junk-mail problem." Consider again the case of direct mail. The volume of unsolicited mail appearing in people's mailboxes increased substantially in the decades between Gosnell's and Green & Gerber's studies. Mail recipients became accustomed to tuning out the barrage of unwanted solicitations, reducing the likelihood that they would open any particular message. The field of direct-mail marketing has developed a variety of tricks to combat these falling open rates: scrawling "urgent message" or a faux-handwritten note on the front envelope, for example. The industry leaders in this field have been commercial interests (credit card companies in particular). Political and nonprofit organizations engage in less direct experimentation, instead adapting proven commercial techniques to their particular needs. The same phenomenon has clearly occurred in the digital communications environment. The rise of e-mail "spam," broadly defined as unsolicited e-mail messages, has made communication through that medium increasingly challenging. Though the marginal costs of sending an e-mail to 100 or 10,000 people approach zero, the probability that any one individual will read the message and respond falls over time. New tools, such as Gmail's "priority inbox" feature, help recipients to filter out background noise, while conferences and trainings run by groups like the New Organizing Institute help digital organizers to share techniques that help distinguish the "signal" of their action alerts from the broader background noise of e-mail communication. The general progression of any mass communication medium will tilt toward increased noise.

The third mechanism is *decreasing marginal returns*, a change in efficacy that emerges through overuse. When political mailers were rare, each had a more substantial effect on voter behavior. As entrepreneurial members of the political mobilizing profession came to identify this effect, the tactic spread. Today, voters are awash in political mail and electoral messages. Increasing the number of election-reminder postcards from 20 to 21 has far less effect than an increase from 0 to 1. In a similar vein, Green & Gerber's finding about the efficacy of door-to-door canvassing—an underutilized tactic in 1998—led to an explosion in door-to-door mobilization attempts by America Coming Together and many allied organizations.[36] Each incremental door-knock is only marginally useful, and at *some* crowding threshold ceases to have any impact whatsoever.[37] As an industry arises surrounding the tactic, its utility in any individual case decreases. Put another way, Green & Gerber's modern-day randomized field experiment cannot actually test the condition of "receives political mail" against the condition of "receives no political mail." Rather, they can test only "receives one additional piece of mail" against "receives no additional pieces of mail." Similarly, advocacy groups, political parties, and electoral campaigns rely on largely overlapping tactical repertoires, meaning that any individual mobilization effort is occurring in an environment where many other groups are trying something similar. (For this reason, unpopular or ineffective tactics do not suffer the same half-life, since they do not face the same overuse hurdles.)

The half-life of political tactics substantially complicates empirical studies of the Internet and political engagement. In particular, it suggests that initial case examples of digital success may be of limited relevance to the longer-term role of new media in political campaigns. The first well-publicized use of a new tool will receive novelty attention and active participation from technology enthusiasts who are themselves well-off, highly educated, and well-connected within elite circles. Barack Obama's campaign website, My.BarackObama.com, received an influx of positive media attention in 2008. In 2012, it is unlikely that the site will receive such novelty attention. After an initial win, the following wave of copycat efforts can, like a film or television show seeking to mimic a new genre ("It's *Lost* meets *Survivor*, with a twist!"), bear little resemblance to the original despite relying upon many of the same elements.

Additionally, the "innovation edge" that comes from successive waves of strategic or technological advances helps to determine the path-dependent course of

American political development.[38] As Chapters 4, 5, and 6 have demonstrated, the alumni of the Dean and Obama campaigns have altered the makeup of the Democratic Party network. The individuals who fashioned new campaign tools gained influence within the party. Even when candidates like Dean lost, the practice of political campaigning, and the people hired to conduct such campaigns, changed substantially as a result. Dean himself went on to become chair of the Democratic National Committee, and to reinvigorate much of the party apparatus with his "50-State Strategy," against the protestations of longstanding party leaders. The incentive to attempt something new, to overcome the decay in tactical effectiveness through modification or wholesale transformation of tactics, results in changes to the party network. It plays a role in determining who holds power in our political system.

In his 1993 classic, *The Politics Presidents Make*, Stephen Skowronek coined the term "political thickening" to describe the increasing size and complexity of the executive branch over time.[39] Presidents in different centuries are comparable based upon the political moment in which they find themselves, but they also hold substantially different forms of authority based upon the expansion of the state apparatus. Advocacy inflation, or the half-life of political tactics, operates as a parallel institutional feature. The innovation edge that leads actors to develop new tools, set new records, and produce greater results drives the political system to move *faster*. Along with a thicker, more complex bureaucracy, we develop a denser, noisier communications environment as entrepreneurial groups and individuals seek the incremental advantage of a fresh tactic whose effectiveness has not yet begun to decay. While many of the fundamentals of the American political system remain fixed and unchanging, this is one area in which change is a constant.

Social Media as New Venues for Activated Public Opinion

Much of the political content appearing on social media platforms like Facebook, YouTube, and Twitter can rightly be understood as "organizing without organizations." When millions tune in to the State of the Union address, typing and retweeting comments and jokes across Twitter, no coordinating organization is pushing that activity. Much of it, likewise, can be dismissed as unlikely to have a substantial impact on contested political outcomes. The Facebook group "100,000 in support of gay marriage" is not going to convince any senators to vote for the repeal of the Defense of Marriage Act. An auto-tuned remix poking fun at Democratic spending priorities will not affect entitlement spending. One of the central goals of this book has been to distinguish between this political *activity* in the new media environment and the political *organizing* that occurs through netroots organizations. Scholars and observers who fail to make such a distinction—who fail to differentiate between sustained, organized efforts and momentary tactics—are likely to arrive at mistaken "clicktivist" conclusions.

Though my own focus has been on the organizational layer of American politics, these disorganized forms of political speech are independently relevant in their own right. I would suggest that we should view these new types of speech as a novel form of "activated public opinion." Just as Taeku Lee treats presidential letter-writing as a form of political voice, and uses them to identify a specific form of public opinion, Facebook groups and Twitter hashtags provide an insight into the views of attentive segments of the American public. Such activated opinion does not provide a representative sample of the nation as a whole, but it does provide a meaningful signal in its own right.[40]

Consider for instance, 2010 Delaware Senate candidate Christine O'Donnell. After an upset victory in the Republican primary, O'Donnell's past career came under public scrutiny. O'Donnell had been a frequent guest on comedian Bill Maher's television program, *Politically Incorrect*, in the 1990s, and had made several colorful statements. One such statement was that she had "dabbled in witchcraft" in high school.[41] Comedy shows like *The Daily Show with Jon Stewart* and *Saturday Night Live* riffed on this comment, leading O'Donnell to begin her first general election campaign advertisement with the statement "I'm not a witch."[42] The YouTube community seized upon this, with username "schmoyoho" producing an auto-tuned remix of the commercial that received over 2,870,000 views.

What are we to make of this YouTube activity? It is not representative of mass opinion. It is not specifically political in nature—many of these viewers are surely watching the video because it is funny rather than because of their interest in the Delaware Senate campaign. What's more, unless the viewers themselves live in Delaware, forward the video to someone they know in Delaware, or donate money to O'Donnell or her opponent, Chris Coons, those views will have no discernable impact on the election results. Many of my students at Rutgers had seen the video. Their watching had more to do with what Lawrence Lessig calls "remix culture" and Henry Jenkins calls "convergence culture" than it does with traditional forms of political power.[43] It is a form of speech, but it does not fit neatly into our traditional understanding of political participation or communication.

Recent research by Lance Bennett points to some substantial effects associated with remix culture online. Younger Americans appear to be re-imagining ideals of citizenship, rejecting the "dutiful citizenship" model of previous generations and instead adopting an "actualizing citizenship" model. They turn their attention to participatory or consumptive activities rather than traditional governmental forums.[44] They share public sentiments through tweets and Facebook likes, and view this as a legitimate form of expression. We should treat these new trends seriously while also remaining clear about where they occur. Citizenship models hold long-term implication for civic life. A change in public notions of citizenship responsibilities is what I would term an "Internet effect" located at the mass behavioral rather than the organizational level. It demands a different set of analytic tools and affects different elements of our political system.

YouTube also featured heavily in Virginia Senator George Allen's famed 2006 "macaca moment." Allen narrowly lost his re-election bid to netroots-supported Jim Webb that year, delivering a Senate majority to the Democrats. He had been heavily favored until an August 11 campaign event where he referred to an audience member—a video camera-wielding opposition "tracker" from the Webb campaign—as "macaca." The tracker, S. R. Siddarth, was of Indian descent, and macaca is an obscure racial slur. The video received coverage by the *Washington Post* and received over 400,000 views on YouTube. Allen was plagued by questions of his racially checkered past throughout the rest of the campaign, leading many observers to attribute his loss to the power of YouTube.[45]

YouTube did play a role in Senator Allen's loss, but it was hardly the central cause. Allen's history of racial commentary had previously been covered by journalist Ryan Lizza in an article for *The New Republic* several months earlier.[46] The video itself was not placed on YouTube until after *The Washington Post* had agreed to run a story on the matter. As with the Christine O'Donnell matter, many of the YouTube viewers lived out of state and thus had no vote in the matter. What made this case distinctive was the way an Internet-mediated political group (DailyKos, to be specific) tactically deployed the YouTube video. They effectively framed the issue, raised nearly $193,248 for candidate Webb through ActBlue, and continually hounded Allen over his ongoing racial misstatements. This was not activated public opinion or actualized citizenship, but well-organized political resource mobilization.[47]

YouTube and other social media channels thus play a dual role. They serve both as a venue for disorganized political "mashup culture" and as a novel toolset for organized political tactics. We should avoid equating the activated public opinion on such "web 2.0" platforms either with representative mass opinion surveys or with the resource mobilization attempts of political associations. Social media platforms provide a new set of tools for political associations to engage their communities and convert resources into political power. They also provide a venue for citizens to speak out, sharing opinions and spreading news (true or false). Developing an understanding of how these new media tools are affecting the broader public arena requires a nuanced understanding of their operation. The first step toward such an understanding lies in acknowledging their dual role. They are both a novel venue for activated public opinion, equivalent to spontaneous letter-writing of previous eras (but more versatile and publicly accessible), and a toolset for coordinated citizen mobilization efforts.

Cause for Concern: The Loss of Beneficial Inefficiencies

The new generation of Internet-mediated political associations is optimized for the new media environment. In a world of 24-hour news cycles and trending Twitter topics, the large bureaucratic structures of legacy membership associations act as ballast, weighing groups down and keeping them slow in a quickened political system. While A/B testing originated with the direct-mail programs of legacy organizations, groups like the PCCC, MoveOn, and DFA can run multiple tests in a single day, identifying member interest through passive democratic engagement tools and seizing the news cycle while older groups are busy arranging staff meetings and setting up conference calls.

Ballast can be valuable, though. There are some critical capacities to which the nimble staff and rapid tactics of Internet-mediated organizations are poorly suited. MoveOn will never sit down across the table from management to negotiate a new collective bargaining agreement. Democracy for America has no policy experts or research scientists on staff. DailyKos isn't going to employ a field staffer or lobbyist in every state capital. And each of these functions adds substantive value to long-term efforts at building political power and supporting an alternative governing coalition. Some valuable functions require substantial overhead costs, regardless of the changing information landscape. A few of these tasks have migrated, covered by "phantom staff" or by netroots infrastructure organizations and vendors. Others, however, represent a troubling net loss for American political associations and the interests they represent.

The concern here is that targeted online fundraising appears to work much better for funding television advertisements than volunteer trainings. It is much easier to fundraise for a specific, time-limited issue outcome than it is for field offices. The advantage of the new revenue stream is that it is more efficient than its direct-mail predecessor. Online funding appeals are cheaper, timelier, and allow for greater topical specialization. Direct-mail appeals are costly, slow, and generic in nature. But it is entirely possible that the inefficiency of the previous fundraising regime included a type of *beneficial inefficiency*.

Beneficial inefficiencies provide a solution to a subset of public goods problems.[48] They are perhaps best understood through an aphorism Clay Shirky uses when discussing changes to the journalism industry: "For a long time . . . The expense of printing created an environment where Wal-Mart was willing to subsidize the Baghdad bureau. This wasn't because of any deep link between advertising and reporting . . . It was just an accident. Advertisers had little choice other than to have their money used that way, since they didn't really have any other vehicle for display ads."[49] Some forms of journalism—particularly local and international public affairs reporting and investigative journalism—are widely considered to be a public good.[50] They are also among the more expensive forms of journalism, and some of the types that are hardest to replicate through online-only outlets.[51] The news crisis has not left us with a dearth of sports and entertainment reporting. For those popular topics, we have entered an age of overwhelming abundance. Your local zoning board meeting is another matter.

Legacy media institutions provided for that public good through the old, inefficient revenue streams like subscriptions and classified advertisements. Newspapers for decades had been able to "monetize eyeballs" twice, charging readers for the paper and charging advertisers for the readership. A fraction of the resulting revenue streams were invested into these costlier forms of journalism that attracted more accolades and prestige than they did readership. News operations have long been characterized more by the traditional logic of the marketplace than the idealized logic of the "marketplace of ideas."[52] Yet the inefficiencies of the old revenue streams left enough funding for the costlier, public-interest types of journalism.

As news revenue streams changed, driven by online advertising, free CraigsList classified ads, and free online news content, the news industry as a whole has entered a period of disruption. Major newspapers have entered bankruptcy, laid off reporters en masse, or shut down entirely. The standard business model of the news industry is now unclear. This has prompted a broad intellectual debate: "How can we provide for expensive but socially valuable forms of journalism?" At the time of this writing, there exists a plethora of proposed solutions, but we have little confidence as to which, if any, will work. Public interest journalism was provided in limited amounts through the beneficial efficiencies of the old financial system. The new, more efficient signals provided to digital journalism outlets leave less revenue floating around. For all the benefits of the digital media environment for news and opinion-sharing, a few key functions of the journalism industry are now endangered.

An analogous phenomenon is emerging at the organizational layer of American politics. Legacy advocacy groups developed substantial overhead and infrastructure over the previous 40 years. These are not profit-driven enterprises, but they are nonetheless premised upon stable revenue streams. And online fundraising is not a direct replacement for the unrestricted funding that flowed through direct mail. It is unclear, as of yet, whether the new membership and fundraising regimes can support valuable organizational overhead—training departments, full-time lobbyists, and field organizers. Even with the lowered transaction costs of digital media, sustained collective action still requires professional organizers. The craft of organizing still requires training and support. Lobbying relationships and policy expertise must be cultivated even when an issue is far from the media spotlight.

New media tools have reduced the costs of many individual actions and altered the political economy of political associations. But many valuable tasks remain costly and difficult. It is unclear at this juncture how these costs will be covered in the new funding environment. Major donors and foundations (particularly on the left) have never been a reliable source of long-term overhead support. They tend to provide seed money and to target specific projects rather than funding general overhead costs. Unless alternate revenue streams emerge, or the large-donor community develops a new taste for funding overhead and infrastructure, the emerging ecology of American political associations may be devoid of some essential niches.

This is a complicated matter, left opaque because the relevant data is held behind proprietary firewalls. But it is one that should alarm political practitioners. A subset of public goods problems—specifically, providing for training, expertise, and field capacity among social movement participants—has long been solved through the subsidies provided by generic organizational membership dues. Direct-mail fundraising was beneficially inefficient. Advocacy practitioners and major donors would be well advised to think through the vital functions that, previously funded through direct mail, are now at risk of dramatic decline. The disruptive transition of the political advocacy system will carry some unfortunate and unintentional costs.

Cause for Hope: The Benefits of Sedimentary Organizations

The sedimentary aspects of Internet-mediated political associations carry some subtle benefits for American political engagement. Membership in legacy organizations is a coarse, marketing-based relationship. Direct-mail-based members are acquired through the same techniques used to sell credit cards. Door-to-door canvasses sell advocacy group membership as though it were a set of steak knives. Legacy advocacy groups "hear" very little from these members. The membership relationship is little more than a financial transaction. As a veteran of one of those organizations, I have always found the direct-mail membership regime to be an awkward arrangement. Our "members" were not the people attending rallies or writing letters, but the people with the free backpacks and calendars. Legacy advocacy organizations can claim to speak *for* their membership, but they can rarely speak *with* those members.

Membership in netroots organizations is more ephemeral but also more interactive. The large organizations in this study all built their membership lists by providing an outlet for waves of citizen activity. MoveOn was a venue for expressing liberal outrage at the Clinton impeachment hearings, and later for anti-war organizing. Democracy for America is the sedimentary remains of the Dean campaign. The PCCC provided an outlet for progressive mobilization around the public option. DailyKos provided a hub space for like-minded political bloggers. Membership in these groups is defined through a minimal threshold of participation—clicking a link, signing a petition—rather than through a financial transaction. And through the "culture of testing" embedded in their organizational work routines, the new generation of organizations can identify member sentiment in ways that their legacy counterparts never could. When they speak for their membership, it is after passive democratic feedback tools have constructed an image of member opinion. Netroots groups know more about their members than legacy political associations, though "membership" means even less than it used to.

The result is both a more polarized and a more participatory advocacy group system. The "engaged public" tends to gravitate toward the poles of public opinion surveys.[53] The Internet is much better for partisan communities-of-interest than for cross-talk deliberation.[54] There is neither a vibrant centrist blogosphere nor a centrist equivalent to MoveOn. Internet-mediated advocacy organizations have not caused America's polarized political discourse, but neither will they be its solution. Rather, netroots advocacy groups have a strong incentive to galvanize public action around the issues that motivated partisans care the most about. They also have novel tools for identifying member sentiment and exercising political power. Active segments of the American public have new venues for expressing their will and engaging in sustained collective action. This is a more modest "Internet revolution" than readers may have once hoped for, but it is a positive development in the organizational layer nonetheless. The field of organized political advocacy has become more interactive. The Internet will not save the world, but it does add something of value to the work of world-saving.

Research Appendix—Method Notes for Studying Internet-Mediated Organizations

The social scientific enterprise includes both theory building and theory testing. This study was designed for the former. Given the "unexpected" nature of the generation shift within the interest group ecology of American politics, I chose to rely primarily upon elite interview, process tracing, and other qualitative observational techniques. The purpose has been largely descriptive: "How do the new advocacy organizations operate?" "How do they differ from traditional advocacy groups?" As a devoted methodological pluralist, the choices I made in designing the study were based upon three factors: (1) assessment of the existing state of academic research, (2) professional skepticism about the limitations of publicly available data, and (3) leveraged opportunities from my own dual roles. This methodological appendix will discuss these core research design choices and then offer a more detailed explanation of the two quantitative datasets created for this study: the Blogosphere Authority Index and the Membership Communications Project.

The research is rooted in a thorough review of the various, non-overlapping literatures on the Internet and politics. This is a topic area that has received attention from the fields of political science, sociology, anthropology, communication, social movement studies, science and technology studies, and law. Lawyers and authors of popular nonfiction have been particularly influential in the emerging field. Due to longstanding disciplinary boundaries, these studies are rarely placed in conversation with one another. Internet politics is not a stable subfield, but rather a cluster of subdisciplines, spread across journals and rarely interacting with one another. Or, to paraphrase computer scientist Jim Hendler, "Web science is not a single new discipline, but rather a space where various disciplines can talk to each other."[1]

One key finding from the existing literature concerned the power-law topology of online communities. A.L. Barabasi, Matthew Hindman, Clay Shirky, and Azi Lev-On & Russell Hardin had all produced studies demonstrating that online traffic produces a heavily skewed "short head" of hub sites and a "long tail" of low-traffic outlets.[2] The difference in traffic and activity between hub sites and the long-tail sites can be several orders of magnitude. Lacking from the literature was any organizational analysis of how these hub sites operate in the political realm. Studies of Wikipedia and Open Source software communities have devoted significant attention to organizational structures and novel management practices.[3] Studies of political blogs and online activism instead have focused on applying quantitative sampling techniques (many of which assume a normal curve distribution) to make generalizations about the *full population* of bloggers or digital activists. This rush toward theory-testing skips a critical theory-building step, leading authors to "prove" or "disprove" theories that had not been clearly specified to begin with. Particularly when studying a digital landscape that is in the early phases of a diffusion process, such quantitative studies have a particularly brief shelf-life.

My role on the Sierra Club Board of Directors also introduced a degree of professional skepticism regarding publicly available data. Interest group studies often rely on GuideStar's database of I-990 forms to track the contours and funding levels of the interest group population. This is good data if you want to estimate and compare the overall budgets of nonprofit organizations. It is terribly limited if you are interested in detail, however. The conversations and debates I was involved in at the board level (regarding *our* work, *our* staff structure, *our* membership relations, and *our* fundraising challenges) were not traceable in public datasets. The public data simply cannot speak to **cost per member acquired** and **average lifetime giving rate**. This was a major and alarming trend, well known but occurring below the surface of public financial reporting.

Nonprofit organizations regularly pool their proprietary data in order to identify industry trends. As a Board member, I had access to that data. As a social scientist, I did not. This disjuncture highlighted the limitations imposed by proprietary data—trends like the decline of direct mail were completely unknown in the academic literature. What's more, they were *unknowable* based on the GuideStar database. Website and blog analysts face similar problems—individual bloggers and website managers have far more data at their disposal than the traffic and hyperlink data I harvest in the Blogosphere Authority Index. They develop organizational processes based upon data that cannot be accessed or evaluated by academics. This is a general limitation imposed on social scientific endeavors—even the most sophisticated analytic techniques still face the limitations of poor public data availability.

Given my existing role in the nonprofit advocacy community, I saw a natural opportunity to extend scholarly knowledge through a grounded theory approach. Bloggers and online advocacy professionals construct their work routines in response to proprietary data that will likely never be made public. They share this knowledge within their professional community and develop "best practices" on the basis of shared lessons. With only a few large-scale hubs of Internet-mediated advocacy, it seemed natural to treat these netroots organizations as a *professional field*. Rather than sampling from blog posts, blog readers, or digital tactics, I chose to look at how the new hub organizations compare to their legacy equivalents. My knowledge of legacy organizational practices, and my history of activity within the political advocacy world, made this design choice particularly advantageous. Netroots organizations have historically been tight-lipped and disinterested in speaking with academics. With an extensive existing network of social ties in the nonprofit advocacy community, I had an opportunity to interact with netroots organizational leaders more closely than my scholarly peers.

Case selection was based upon the self-evident realities imposed by power-law topography. Simply put, hub sites within a power-law distribution are easy to recognize. They receive overwhelming traffic levels, making them common knowledge among visitors and professionals alike. I selected MoveOn, DailyKos, and Democracy for America because they represented three clear hubs that employed variant organizational models. The Progressive Change Campaign Committee did not exist when I began this research, but observation of the netroots professional community made clear that it was a late-forming organization worthy of study as well.

For each of these cases, I employed a combination of content analysis, process tracing, elite interviews, and ethnographic participant observation. This included eight months of participant observation with Philly for Change (the Philadelphia affiliate of Democracy for America); attendance at YearlyKos 2007 and Netroots Nation 2008, 2009, and 2010; attendance at RootsCamp 2008 and 2010; attendance at Personal Democracy Forum 2009 and Politics Online 2008 and 2009; weekly in-person gatherings of "netroots" activists at Drinking Liberally events; and loosely structured informant interviews with high-ranking staff and volunteers in each organization. It also included substantial time reading and analyzing blog posts, MoveOn e-mail alerts, and online appeals from a variety of other organizations. The content analysis was based upon public data—mass e-mails and blog posts. Informant interviews began with an explanation of the project and a series of questions regarding the individual's professional background. He or she then responded to a set of questions regarding how the organization operated and the role that information technology played in the organization's inner workings. These prompts led to a range of subtopics, with interviews generally lasting between 45 minutes and 1 hour. Interviews with each organization continued until I had obtained coverage, meaning I had gained a clear understanding of their relevant processes and practices from multiple sources.

My own dual roles as political practitioner and political scientist were an unusual variant upon classical ethnographic techniques. Ethnographies are traditionally conducted by an external academic observer. Through months of interaction and observation, the ethnographer seeks to build a "rapport" with his or her research subjects, gaining some insight into community knowledge or practice. Within the ethnographic tradition, there are longstanding concerns regarding "going native," losing "critical distance," and altering the practices and activities of the group. In this case, though I was not myself a member of the polit-ical "netroots," my inside knowledge and network position with the Sierra Club rendered such external observer status impossible. My ties to the political advo-cacy realm long predate my ties to academia.

As one example, it has proven difficult for most academics to gain access to core MoveOn staff for lengthy elite interviews. My ability to conduct such inter-views was mediated through existing professional ties. One former MoveOn staffer was also a longtime Sierra Club colleague. I had met another at the Brower Youth Awards reception in 2000, where we had both been award recipients. Stephanie Taylor and I recognized each other from events like RootsCamp and Netroots Nation and had several friends in common. It is unlikely that these orga-nizational leaders would have been as giving of their time and insights if not for my existing status within the advocacy community. Attending Netroots Nation as a Researcher/Sierra Club Board Member likely prompts different conversa-tions than attending solely as a political science graduate student.

If personal network ties aided me in establishing formal, semi-structured interviews, the reservoir of cultural knowledge I had built up through years of participation in political associations and community organizing trainings pro-vided a subtler but broader asset. Ethnographers can often spend years seeking to understand the shared symbols and cultural artifacts of a community. The net-roots professional community is rooted in many of the same organizing traditions that I had been steeped in since high school. That baseline of cultural knowledge and shared symbols rapidly translates into a level of trust (what Richard Fenno terms "rapport"[4]) that might prove elusive for another social scientist.

Given the twin audiences of the project, including the goal of producing a study that would be of use to the practitioner community itself, I ensured accuracy by sending informants draft chapters and asking them (1) whether the quote and the context were accurate and (2) what general feedback or reaction they had to the theoretical and empirical claims I was making. It is for this reason that I use inter-viewees' real names in this study. All of the interviewees are public figures, trained in media relations and used to appearing in print. All quotations from interview sessions have been vetted with the interviewee. There are a variety of circumstances in which such free-flowing interaction with research subjects would be inappro-priate—in particular, if the researcher were producing a work of active criticism or had worries about glorifying the research subjects. My research question is aimed in a different direction, however. I have sought to answer these questions: "How has information technology affected political associations? How do the new orga-nizations operate differently than their predecessors?" That is very different than, for instance, "Are the new organizations achieving their goals?" For such a ques-tion, there is limited danger in either glorifying or vilifying the case examples (I am not attempting to address whether the organizations are *good* or *bad*), and substan-tial value in gaining additional nuanced explanation from my sources.

I augmented these individual interactions with the practitioner community through a series of presentations to that audience. These included conference presentations at Netroots Nation 2009, 2010, and 2011; Politics Online 2008 and 2009; Personal Democracy Forum 2009; and PowerShift 2009. Two additional presentations were particularly valuable: a February 2009 research presentation at the Sierra Club Board of Directors meeting and a November 2009 presentation to a group of technology consultants in New York City. Each of these presentations included a full enunciation of the "MoveOn Effect" thesis and the three advocacy group models. I received valuable feedback at each, and they served as an important robustness check, given the limitations imposed by proprietary data.

The challenge with a theory-building project such as this one is that it can ingrain the author's own biases. For this reason, I augmented the core qualitative, theory-building endeavor with two large data-generating efforts—the Blogosphere Authority Index and the Membership Communications Project. Both are open, public datasets, used to test major descriptive claims that came out of qualitative observational techniques. The following two sections explain the methodology from each, borrowing text from prior conference paper presentations where the datasets were initially discussed.

The Blogosphere Authority Index

[The following is excerpted from "Measuring Influence in the Political Blogosphere," published in the Institute for Politics, Democracy, and the Internet's *Politics and Technology Review*, March 2008. It describes the methodology behind the Blogosphere Authority Index tracking system. Some sections have been abbreviated or edited for clarity.]

Consider the following stylized example: blogger A posts infrequently on her personal site. This results in a small reader base and comparatively few hypertext links from around the blogosphere. Years ago, blogger A was a mentor to bloggers B, C, and D, though, and she now holds a key position within her party's establishment. The few people who frequent her blog are highly influential, either in the blogosphere or in more traditional political institutions. Blogger B posts once or twice a day on his individual blog, which was picked up by a major online news magazine last year. He has a journalistic background and specializes in developing new arguments or breaking new stories—he chooses to be a blogger because he likes to set his own deadlines, operate without an editor looking over his shoulder, and publish instantaneously. He often relies on blogger A for insights and tidbits that he researches and turns into original articles. He is among the most often-cited bloggers online, by liberals and conservatives alike. Blogger C posts 15–20 times per day. She rarely publishes original content, instead pouring over other blogs and writing short, pithy posts that tell her reader base about something interesting elsewhere on the web. She acts as a gatekeeper for her gigantic readership, who use her site as a roadmap to the rest of the Internet. Blogger D is the purveyor of one of the most active community blogs in the country. He posts eight times per day, with some original content and some "open threads" so that his community can keep their own discussion going. This community also publishes their own diaries, often 50 or so in a day. Political endorsements from this site mean dollars in a candidate's pocket. The membership recently spun off two new sites to support activity around universal health care and global warming, and the policy proposals from these sites have been adopted into congressional legislation.

Which blogger is most influential? This example is an illustration of four distinct areas of influence: *network centrality, link density, site traffic,* and *community activity.* To create a comprehensive ranking system, this paper identifies the best-available proxy for each of these types of influence, converts them to ordinal rankings, and then combines them into a single index of authority.

The Blogosphere Authority Index

The Blogosphere Authority Index (BAI) combines data from four measures of online influence into a single ranking system. Construction of the BAI is a two-stage process. The first stage involves collection of raw data on each of the influence measures. Some of this data is manually gathered through site visits. Some is gathered through publicly available tracking systems such as Technorati and Site-Meter. The BAI is structured to accept the best-available data source for each of the four metrics.

In the second stage, we convert this raw data into ordinal rankings. These rankings can be within the progressive or conservative blog "neighborhoods," or the raw scores of both neighborhoods can be combined to form a combined BAI. We then convert these individual ordinal rankings into a comprehensive ranking, leading to a final authority index. Data collection and conversion methods are described in greater detail below.

Stage 1:

The Authority Index combines four measures of influence: the Network Centrality Score, Hyperlink Authority Score, Site Traffic Score, and Community Activity Score.

NETWORK CENTRALITY SCORE

The *Network Centrality Score* (NCS) is an applied sociometric variable that is culled from blogrolls. Blogrolls are similar in nature to self-reports of friendship/readership networks, a common tool in social network analysis. Deletions from blogrolls are rare and usually accompanied by an uproar.[5] This biases the centrality score in favor of those blogs/bloggers who have been around the longest. It is a bias that *should* be captured, though. Jerome Armstrong (founder of MyDD) is described by his peer bloggers as "the true blogfather" because of the importance his site had when many were getting their start. This elder-statesman status is a type of power that doesn't track to current visits/activity. It also gives a hint as to *who* might be visiting his site. A site that receives 30 visits/day could be hugely important if those 30 visitors are front-page authors on the 30 largest sites, for instance. The centrality score, therefore, is meant as an indicator of accrued reputation over time. Beginning with network centrality also solves the problem of coding blogs as political/apolitical or liberal/independent/conservative. Adamic and Glance have demonstrated that the liberal and conservative blogospheres form largely independent neighborhoods.[6] If an elite blog self-identifies as conservative, but other conservative bloggers refuse to acknowledge it as such, can it be said to be part of the networked conservative blogosphere? This method treats the expansive blogosphere as consisting of network neighborhoods. The blogroll of a site is a means of self-reporting who one's "neighbors" are. In a world of 118 million+ blogs, this is a necessary simplifying assumption for scholars interested in identifying elite blogs within a particular category.

To construct the NCS, we begin with a seed site. This is the site that we have good reason to believe lies in or around the center of the blog network of interest. The selection of a seed site will have an effect on our findings, so this is an important decision. Conveniently, this hub will often be a well-known site. For this study, I chose to begin with DailyKos.com and HotAir.com. These two sites are listed as the progressive and conservative frontrunners by both Technorati.com and truthlaidbear.com.[7]

The NCS aggregates blogroll data within the network neighborhood. The data begins with the seed site blogroll. All listed blogs are then visited and their blogrolls are added to the dataset. A first-round tally is then created. Which sites are mentioned most often? Any sites in the top 25 that have not already had their blogrolls added are then visited in a second round of data collection. This continues for a third round if needed. This then produces a final set of tallies. Network Centrality Score is constructed by normalizing these tallies on a 0-to-1 scale. Add 1 to the tally of any site that provided a blogroll (some elite sites do not include a blogroll) to obtain N. This sets the highest possible score at 1.0, removing a bias against contributing sites (source sites do not blogroll themselves). Network Centrality Score is then equal to N/P, where P is the total population of blogs included in the coding scheme.[8]

The Network Centrality Score provides a population list for data collection on the other 3 measures. This is a necessary initial step, as SiteMeter and Technorati data are gathered by searching for sites by name. For the purposes of the other three data sources, I gathered data on the top 50 progressive and top 50 conservative blogs.

HYPERLINK AUTHORITY SCORE

The *Hyperlink Authority Score* (HAS) is derived directly from Technorati.com's authority tracking system. Technorati tracks the global blogosphere, using sophisticated web crawlers to measure link patterns and definitively describe which blogs are the most often cited. As previously noted, Technorati's top 100 tells us less *within* the political blogosphere than it used to because Technorati now tracks so many apolitical sites. It is somewhat akin to a public opinion poll that asks citizens which they prefer: Barack Obama, the Detroit Tigers, celebrity gossip, or puppies. With that said, Technorati measures link patterns at a depth that cannot be replicated, so the within-group measure is still a valuable indicator of importance.

To construct the HAS, search for the rankings of each blog in the population list (as determined by NCS rankings) in Technorati's overall system. These rankings must be individually accessed by entering http://www.technorati.com/blogs/[webaddress].

SITE TRAFFIC SCORE

The *Site Traffic Score* (STS) is the most obviously relevant and also the most challenging to accurately measure. SiteMeter.com directly measures the number of unique visitors a website receives every day. A high-traffic site should, *ceteris paribus*, be more important than a low-traffic site. Some bloggers, wary of the various link-tracking systems, rely exclusively on SiteMeter data to measure their success[9]. The problem, however, is that SiteMeter is an opt-in system, and over 25% of the sites in the dataset do not choose to include it. Previous scholars have used SiteMeter in their ranking systems, relying on the truthlaidbear.com traffic rankings, which aggregate SiteMeter data and simply make note that this is an incomplete system. These scholars try only to determine the population of elite political blogs without attempting to rank-order them. This study attempts to fill the gaps so we can use traffic rankings to gain greater analytic leverage.

To augment the standard SiteMeter data, I turn to another traffic-ranking system, Alexa.com. Alexa tracks visits to all websites rather than just blogs. It measures unique visits/month (a different datum than SiteMeter's visits/day) and offers higher-quality information on larger sites rather than smaller ones. I considered switching to Alexa rankings as a primary traffic ranking system, but many blogs in the study, particularly the lower-traffic ones, have low-quality or no data recorded by Alexa. Instead, I rank-ordered the sites with available SiteMeter data and then checked these sites against their comparative Alexa rankings to see if there was relative similarity between the two. Though the fit was not perfect, it was quite close, with the 9th-ranked site in SiteMeter being the 9th-largest Alexa site +/–1 in the rank order (the error signature gets larger as we go down the list, as the raw score gaps between the sites quickly shrink). This fit was the best available indicator, so I then performed "Alexa fills" for all sites that did not offer Site-Meter data. With an Alexa fill, we have no relevant raw score for the site, but we can estimate that it is larger than sites with lower Alexa scores and smaller than sites with higher ones. This was important for estimating the size of a few major sites, including HuffingtonPost.com, ThinkProgress.org, and TalkingPoints-Memo.com. I would characterize this technique as making the best of a bad data situation.[10]

The STS metric begins by recording SiteMeter data from all participating sites. Rank these sites and attempt to personally contact any bloggers who do not provide SiteMeter data to see if they will share it. Any remaining sites should receive an Alexa fill, triangulating their position in the rankings in comparison to SiteMeter-ranked blogs.

COMMUNITY ACTIVITY SCORE

The fourth and final data source is the *Community Activity Score* (CAS). Nearly all of the blogs in this study (88%) include a mechanism for readers to write comments in response to the author's post. This is the most basic form of user-generated content on the blogosphere, and it has been lauded as a major difference between blogging and traditional journalism. The particular value of the CAS is that it is a measure of engagement. Presumably, a reader who leaves a comment is likely to spend more time on the site and is more likely to become part of that site's community. The CAS balances out the historical bias of the NCS by giving additional weight to the blogs where active, vibrant conversation is happening today. To construct the CAS dataset, take a one-week snapshot of all postings for sites in the population set. Record the total number of reader-generated comments on these posts. Total Comments/Week serves as a site's CAS.

Stage 2:

At this point, we have four types of raw data recorded for the top 50 conservative and top 50 progressive sites. Each of these should be converted to "top 50" ordinal rankings. In stage 2, these rankings are combined into an aggregate score, adding the three best scores together and dropping the fourth from the study. This is to avoid unfairly biasing the study against sites whose architecture does not allow for reader comments and to minimize outlier effects that come from flaws within any of the four measures employed. Additionally, it minimizes the penalty against institutional sites like HuffingtonPost.com, and Newsbusters. com. Sites of this type receive depressed Network Centrality Scores because some bloggers list only traditional, individually based sites in their blogrolls. The final ranking equation is *Rank Final = Rank 1 + Rank 2 + Rank 3 + Rank 4—Worst Rank*. The best possible score is 3, indicating that a blog was first-ranked in three categories. The worst possible score is 150, indicating that a blog was last-ranked in all categories. This purpose of this study is to produce a list of the top 25 progressive and conservative blogs. Data on the top 50 was gathered in order to ensure that all potential members of the top 25 would be captured. The final output is a Blogosphere Authority Index of the two top 25 lists. A combined list was also constructed by combining the raw score data for the two network neighborhoods, constructing combined ordinal rankings, and then applying the same final ranking equation listed above.

The Membership Communications Project

[Excerpted and summarized from "Advocacy Group Activity in the New Media Environment, a paper presentation at the 2010 Political Communication APSA Preconference. Some sections have been edited for redundancy.]

The MCP dataset relies on a relatively simple, intuitive design, accessing publicly available membership communications from a large cluster of progressive advocacy organizations. On January 21st, 2010, I created a dummy e-mail account via Gmail. I then visited the websites of 70 advocacy organizations and signed up for any e-mail lists or outreach efforts provided through those sites. For the first two weeks of data collection, I used a broad descriptive classification scheme and then refined it to a set of seven categories based on observed patterns and commonalities between e-mails (described below). The purpose here is to do the basic descriptive work of categorizing what organizations contact their members about, at what frequency, and with what requests.

I encountered three primary hurdles in designing the dataset: (1) identification of an appropriate sample of political associations, (2) deciding what to do about conservative groups, and (3) accounting for limitations created by proprietary data and important e-mail lists that are left "unseen" by the analytic techniques employed. I discuss each hurdle below, to be followed by a description of the seven headings in the classification scheme and overall trends found in the data.

IDENTIFYING ORGANIZATIONS

As Jack Walker famously demonstrated, population definition is a permanent issue for students of American interest groups.[11] In practical terms, it was virtually impossible even in the 1980s to define the full universe of organizations. The population-definition problem is even more complicated in the current study for two reasons. First, I am interested in public interest advocacy groups—organizations that seek to mobilize some form of public pressure to affect public policy decisions out of concern for the public good. These "post-materialist" political associations are the most visible segment of the DC interest group community.[12] Yet the large majority of lobbying organizations and Political Action Committees (PACs) represent business or other private interests. Sampling from directories of Washington lobbying organizations or PAC spending reports thus does not present a solution. Unlike other recent work that focuses on documenting the lobbying community as a whole, I am interested solely in those groups that seek to galvanize an issue public to take action around their shared values.

Second, the Internet has facilitated novel structures for "netroots" political associations. Given my interest in including such groups in this study, it would be imprudent to assume that novel organization forms will appear in Washington directories. MoveOn has 5 million members, 38 staff members, and zero office space. The PCCC has 450,000 members, between 4 and 11 staff members, and no office space.[13] Interest group studies have traditionally been equated with studies of "the DC lobbying community." Though both groups have *some* presence in the nation's capital, their decision to eschew the substantial overhead costs associated with a large staff of policy experts and lobbyists may be indicative of a broader change in the field of Internet-mediated political associations. It is unclear whether the traditional indexes of DC interest groups appropriately capture this new generation of infrastructure-poor, communication-rich organizations.

To provide a workaround of sorts, I chose to rely on some high-profile moments in recent history to create a relevant convenience sample. In the aftermath of the America Coming Together 527 effort[14] in the 2004 presidential election, a large network of progressive/liberal major donors was unhappy with the results of their donations.

The list of groups eventually funded by the Democracy Alliance thus provides a network of interest in its own right. Funding from the Alliance not only represents a substantial investment of resources (creating a practical floor for the advocacy groups represented in the study), but also indicates that the groups fit together in an attempt at building a set of progressive institutions. Though support from the Democracy Alliance is not a necessary and sufficient condition for including an organization in the list of "public interest political associations," it is a highly suggestive place to start. Furthermore, though this direct donor list is not public information, the former Director of the Democracy Alliance published a helpful guide to the groups she/they felt were part of the new progressive infrastructure in her 2008 book *The Practical Progressive*. Technically, we do not know if the groups listed in this book represent the full population of supported organizations, but we *do* know that the list was assembled by a panel of 24 progressive "experts" with links to Payne and the Democracy Alliance. From the perspective of prominent public interest group leaders, this list provides a starting point for populating a study of the political Left. Payne's book lists a total of 81 organizations, though 32 of those organizations represented elements of progressive infrastructure that do not engage in direct mobilization (*The Nation* magazine and blogs like the Huffington Post and DailyKos, for instance).[15] In all, 49 of the 81 groups had some form of e-mail list to which a member or supporter could subscribe.

In addition to this list of 49 groups, I added 21 additional organizations that were either well-known members of the political Left (National Association for the Advancement of Colored People, National Organization for Women, Amnesty International, American Civil Liberties Union) or prominent "netroots" groups that had been founded since the book had been published (Organizing for America, Change Congress, Progressive Change Campaign Committee, Courage Campaign). This augmented list also included several environmental orgs (Greenpeace, Alliance for Climate Protection, 1Sky, 350.org, National Resources Defense Council, Environmental Defense Fund, Defenders of Wildlife) in preparation for a related study on that community. Note that those environmental orgs include very old groups (Sierra was founded in 1892) and very new groups (350.org was founded in 2007). The end of this appendix lists all of the groups included from the Democracy Alliance list, along with the 21 groups with which I augmented the list. I encourage the reader to peruse the appendix at this point and consider whether the compiled list seems appropriate.

For this study, I segment this broad list of progressive organizations into two groups based on founding date. Organizations founded after 1996 are considered members of the "new generation" of political associations, having been created to take advantage of the new communications landscape. Organizations founded prior to 1996 are considered "legacy" political associations.[16] The year 1996 provides a natural break in the data, as there are several organizations in the dataset founded in 1996, 1997, 1998, and 1999, but only one organization founded in the earlier 1990s. (FairVote was founded in 1992 under the name "Center for Voting and Democracy.") Forty organizations were founded post-1996, two of which contributed no e-mails to the dataset, while 30 organizations were founded pre-1996, four of which contributed no e-mails to the dataset. Of the 2,162 e-mails in the dataset, 911 come from legacy political associations, and 1,251 come from the new generation. This produces surprisingly similar averages for the two subsets, with the average legacy organization sending 30.4 e-mails over the past six months and the average new generation organization sending 31.3 e-mails in that timeframe.

In doing so, I am adopting an axiomatic assumption about organizational structure, rooted in Dimaggio and Powell's (1983) institutional isomorphism theory. Advocacy groups in a membership and fundraising environment will face pressures to develop isomorphic institutional structures. Groups from the direct-mail era will all have high-level departments in charge of direct-mail operations, for instance. Rather than classify organizations by subject era—grouping all civil rights organizations under one heading, grouping environmental organizations under another— I instead classify organizations by founding date. The questions I seek to answer specifically concern whether groups founded in the online communications regime operate differently than groups founded in earlier communications regimes (regardless of field of specialization).[17] Note that, since the MCP is an open data project, alternate segmentations of the list can be freely tested by members of the research community.

THE LEFT-RIGHT DIVIDE IN ORGANIZATIONAL COMMUNICATIONS

Absent from this study is any advocacy group representation from the political Right. Particularly during a time period when conservative grassroots mobilization appears to be on the rise through the "Tea Party" movement, this design choice requires explanation. I leave conservative advocacy organizations out of this study for two reasons: network structure and historical patterns.

[For explanation of network structure and communication flows, see Chapters 5 and 6.]

DATA COLLECTION

Having used the augmented Democracy Alliance list to identify a convenience sample, I then created a dummy account through Gmail, visited each organization's website, and signed up for any e-mail lists, online membership status, or action alert programs offered by the organization. Knowing that some organizations send more additional e-mails to the subset of members that take action, I clicked through and took the first online action offered by all groups as well. As messages came in to the account, I coded them based on nine variables: [date], [organization], [topic], [digest/e-newsletter], [action ask], [fundraising ask], [request for member input], [event advertisement], [media agenda link]. Each of these is discussed in greater detail below:

1. *Date.* Useful for treating the dataset as a time series and for observing the lifespan of an issue topic. Data collection began on January 21, 2010, and continued through July 21, 2010, providing six months of activity in total. The lowest point occurred during the week of the DC blizzard, when many organizations had to close their offices. Other low points were attributable to holidays (July 4th and Memorial Day). The high point occurred in the week leading up to final passage of the health care reform package in the House and the week following the Gulf oil spill. There is relatively little variance in the total traffic of e-mail from this set of organizations, an indication that communication protocols are well-established and fluctuations in communication frequencies are likely non-random.

2. *Organization.* Though the weekly volume of messages underwent only minor fluctuations, these messages were far from evenly distributed among organizations. Over the 26 weeks that the study was conducted, 6 organizations sent no

messages (AFL-CIO, Young Democrats, Rock the Vote, National Security Network, American Progressive Caucus Policy Foundation, and American Constitution Society for Law and Politics), and another 12 organizations sent fewer than one message per month (Bus Project, Alliance for Justice, Democracia Ahora, Public Campaign Action Fund, Gathering for Justice, Amnesty International, League of Young Voters, Progress Now, Women's Voices/Women's Vote, 21st Century Dems, Center for Progressive Leadership, and FairVote). Ten organizations sent more than two messages per week (Brennan Center (57), Leadership Conference on Civil Rights (59), PCCC (63), Organizing for America (75), Democracy for America (82), MoveOn (99), Center for Budget and Policy Priorities (110), Faith in Public Life (127), Sierra Club (145), and Campaign for Americas Future (288)). Campaign for America's Future alone sent out 13.3% of all messages in the dataset, primarily due to their twice-daily digest e-mails, "Progressive Breakfast" and "PM Update." Faith in Public Life likewise sent out a daily digest, "Daily Faith News," while the Center on Budget and Policy Priorities sent out frequent report releases and the Sierra Club sent out a variety of e-newsletters, as well as e-mailed versions of Executive Director Carl Pope's blog posts.[18] Figure 8.1 provides the distribution of group e-mails.

3. *Topic.* Here I categorized the messages by issue topic or by other dominant feature. The "Legal Services E-lerts" from the Brennan Center, for instance, is a series of alerts about legal services generally, and thus received that topical heading. Likewise, Faith in Public Life sent out "Daily Faith News" every weekday, listing faith-related headlines in the news. I relied on the dominant

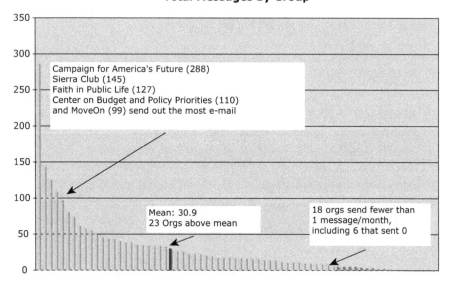

Figure 8.1 Total MCP Messages by Group

language of the e-mail to determine issue topic, so if the message was framed around health care, but also discussed the Recovery Act, it was coded as "Health Care." Likewise if a message was framed as "weekly e-news," it was simply recorded as "e-news." Topical headings are used in category 9 [media agenda] and in constructing affiliation network graphs. [Affiliation network graphs do not appear in the book but are part of a separate study based on the dataset.]

4. *Digest/E-newsletter.* The next five headings categorize the messages by their content type. Digest/e-newsletter is the largest category, encompassing 48.5% of the messages received (1,049 messages). It includes daily news digests from groups like Campaign for America's Future and Faith in Public Life, featuring links to news or blog posts of potential interest to their supporters. Also included are report releases from organizations like the Center on Budget and Policy Priorities and e-mailed versions of blog posts by groups like the Sierra Club. Note that these make up the top four most prolific organizations. A small set of groups use e-mail to frequently send informational updates to their membership, and those updates make up nearly half of the e-mail traffic from the organizations in the study. These e-mails generally do not attempt to mobilize the resources of any members, with only 126 action alerts (12.0%) and 108 fundraising, member input, or event announcements (10.2%). Nearly all of those action alerts, input and fundraising requests, and event announcements appeared in heavily formatted e-newsletters that include sidebar columns inviting readers to take action or announcing an upcoming event. All e-newsletters, digest e-mails, or other information-only messages are coded as a 1 in this column. All other messages are coded as a 0.

5. *Action Ask.* The "action ask" measure captures all e-mails that requested some action on the part of their membership. Rather than a binary category, this field recorded the type of action requested (sign petition/write letter/attend rally/call senator) and the target of the action (administration/Congress/corporation), recording all non-action e-mails with a 0. Of the messages, 836 included some form of action alert (38.7%), 710 of which were not contained in an e-newsletter. Eight organizations never sent an action alert, including Faith in Public Life and the Center on Budget and Policy Priorities, who sent the third and fourth most total messages in the dataset. Targets and action requests varied over the course of the six months of study. [Action alert figures in Chapters 2, 4, and 6 are based on this category of data.]

6. *Fundraising Ask.* Along with mobilizing the membership to take political action, mobilizing the membership to donate money represents a crucial activity for organizations. Particularly as direct-mail marketing is in industry-wide decline, e-mail-based fundraising provides a replacement revenue stream with lower overhead costs, faster turnaround, and the potential for dynamic message testing and sophisticated data mining. I recorded three distinct types of

fundraising e-mail. The first is a general request to become a member or supporter of the organization by donating to their work. Such an ask is virtually identical to the direct-mail type of fundraising appeal. The second is a request to support a specific action, such as giving $10 to put a television commercial on the air. Such fundraising is event-specific, introducing restrictions on its use for general organizational overhead costs. It is generally thought of as easier to raise but less useful to the organization. A third type of fundraising appeared frequently in the dataset as well. This was a form of "pass-through" fundraising, in which organizations urged their membership to donate directly to supported political candidates. These donations are bundled together so the candidate knows which advocacy group they are associated with, but they otherwise do not provide for organizational operating expenses. EMILY's List pioneered this style of fundraising, but many peer organizations choose instead to raise money for their own electoral campaigns, rather than bundling money and sending it to the candidates themselves. The links provided frequently lead to an ActBlue.com fundraising page, meaning that none of the money flows into the mobilizing organization's coffers. In this column, I record a "1" for general funding requests, a "2" for targeted funding requests, a "3" for pass-through funding requests, or a "0" if no funding request was present. In total, there were 214 general funding requests in the dataset, 56 targeted funding requests, and 80 pass-through funding requests.

7. *Member Input.* Online membership communication makes it theoretically possible for organizations to radically expand the degree of input they receive from members. In the absence of the Internet, membership deliberation can be prohibitively resource-intensive for a national organization, requiring either an expensive annual convention or a lengthy series of in-person membership meetings. Early scholars and practitioners had hopes that the speed and flexibility of e-mail and other online communications platforms would make organizations far more participatory.[19] Those hopes have mostly been dashed at this point, but the MCP provides a novel opportunity to gather empirical data on membership input. When do organizations solicit member input? Which organizations do so, and how frequently? This column codes user surveys, membership votes, and invitations to submit user-generated content as a 1, and all other messages as a 0. Only 70 such messages were sent in the six months of data collection (3.2%). A detailed exploration of this small-but-important class of e-mails is scheduled for a future study.

8. *Event Advertisement.* This column covers announcements of upcoming conferences, trainings, or other organizational events. Though this type of e-mail, coded as a bivariate 1 or 0, does not appear very frequently (217 messages/10.0%), one organization (New Organizing Institute) sent out *solely* event announcements during the six months of data collection, while another (Advancement Project) sent out only event announcements and a monthly e-newsletter.

9. *Media Agenda.* This last heading requires further exposition, as it is a novel design choice. As a test of the "headline chasing" claim, I compare the topic of organizational e-mails (listed in column 3) to the topics covered on the top two left-leaning news programs, *The Rachel Maddow Show* and *Countdown with Keith Olbermann.*[20] These two hour-length programs appear in the prime-time news slots on MSNBC (8 p.m. and 9 p.m., rebroadcast at 10 p.m. and 11 p.m.). Their hosts are liberal icons, frequently cited by the political netroots, with Olbermann occasionally blogging at DailyKos.com. If an e-mail topic received coverage on one of these programs on the day of, the day before, or the day after the date that the e-mail was sent, it is coded as a 1. Otherwise it is coded as a 0. Of the 2,162 e-mails in the dataset, 909 were tied to the media agenda in this manner.

I would stress at this point that I am *not* making the claim that these two television programs *set* the Left's media or political agenda. Though Maddow occasionally holds exclusive interviews that are newsworthy in their own right, and though Olbermann's occasional "special comments" likewise attract broader attention, for the most part these programs are *reflecting* the news of the day rather than *creating* it. An emerging research tradition documents the fragmentation of the news environment.[21] The current state of media fragmentation suggests that not only are the issues of the day *framed* differently, but also that different issues receive attention from left-leaning and right-leaning venues.

It is my contention that the audience of Maddow and Olbermann heavily overlaps with the membership/supporter base of progressive advocacy organizations. As such, the issues that, on a day-to-day basis, appear to the two programs' editorial staffs as being of high audience interest could be termed the issues that are at the top of the progressive media agenda. This relationship is depicted in the flow chart (Figure 8.2) below.

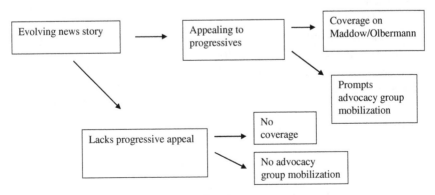

Figure 8.2 Headline-Chasing Process Flowchart

Daily coverage from the two programs was recorded according to topic area. Health care reform dominated coverage on the two shows between January 21 and March 31, 2010, generally as the lead story. Maddow demonstrated a preference for coverage of Don't Ask, Don't Tell hearings; coverage of the C Street House run by Christian organization "the Family," which houses several prominent members of Congress; and filibuster reform. Olbermann demonstrated a preference for criticizing Sarah Palin, organizers and activists in the Tea Party movement, Republican officials, and Fox News contributors. Both programs featured some coverage of financial reform, unemployment legislation, breaking news stories on disasters (Haiti and Peru earthquakes, plane crash into Austin IRS building), and Republican scandals. Both programs turned central attention from health care to extreme right-wing responses to the bill's passage in late March and early April. The BP oil spill then took center stage, receiving top billing on almost every program from April 30 to mid-July. As hypothesized, several Internet-mediated generalists (including MoveOn, PCCC, Democracy for America, Organizing for America, and Campaign for America's Future) sent out action alerts in response to the oil spill, having previously not focused on environmental or climate issues.

List of Organizations Included in the Study

From The Practical Progressive (50 groups)

21st Century Dems
Advancement Project
Alliance for Justice
American Constitution Society for Law and Politics
American Progressive Caucus Policy Foundation
Brennan Center for Justice
Bus Project
Campaign for Americas Future
Catholics in Alliance
Center on Budget and Policy Priorities
Center for Community Change
Center for Progressive Leadership
Century Foundation
Citizens for Tax Justice
Color of Change
Citizens for Responsibility and Ethics in Washington
Democracia USA
Democracy for America

Demos
Economic Policy Institute
EMILY's List
Fair Vote
Faith in Public Life
Free Press
The Gathering
Human Rights Campaign
Human Rights First
Leadership Conference on Civil Rights
League of Conservation Voters
League of Young Voters
Media Matters
Moms Rising
MoveOn
NARAL
National Council of La Raza
National Security Network
Planned Parenthood
Progress Now
Progressive Majority
Progressive States Network
Public Campaign
Rock the Vote
SEIU
Sierra Club
Sunlight Foundation
Truman Project
USAction/True Majority
Vote Vets
Women's Voices. Women Vote
Young Dems

Additional Organizations (20 groups)

Organizing for America
Courage Campaign
New Organizing Institute
EDF
NRDC
350.org
1Sky

Alliance for Climate Protection
PCCC
Greenpeace
NOW
ACLU
NAACP
IAVA
AFSCME
AFL-CIO
Amnesty International
Defenders of Wildlife
Change Congress
Open Left

Notes

Chapter 1

1. Kenneth Andrews and Bob Edwards (2004) offer a review of the "disconnected literatures on social movements, interest groups, and nonprofit organizations," noting that these parallel literatures are "too often fragmented and compartmentalized within disciplinary boundaries." In a similar vein, I use the terms "interest group," "political association," "political organization," "social movement organization," and "advocacy group" as interchangeable synonyms. Though each term is based in a divergent literature, their boundary definitions are vague and often indistinguishable. I treat the terms as synonyms both to make the text a bit more readable and to signal agreement with Andrews and Edwards that these intellectual traditions should be brought closer together.
2. Chamberlain 2011.
3. Bowers 2011.
4. Daniel Mintz, panel presentation at "The Wisconsin 14, The Recall, and the Impact of National Organizing in Wisconsin." Netroots Nation 2011, Minneapolis, MN.
5. Hohman 2011.
6. Gladwell 2010.
7. Earl and Kimport 2011.
8. "Organizing without Organizations" is the subtitle of Clay Shirky's 2008 book, *Here Comes Everybody.* "Theory 2.0" is a term coined by Earl and Kimport (2011).
9. See also Lupia and Sin 2003; Bimber, Flanagin, and Stohl 2005; Lev-On and Hardin 2008; and Karpf 2011b. Both are meant as responses to Mancur Olson's seminal 1965 book, *The Logic of Collective Action.*
10. Castells 2009, p. 58.
11. For a discussion of repertoires of contention, see McAdam, Tarrow, and Tilly 2001. For a discussion of online protest actions, see McCaughey and Ayers 2003. For a discussion of hybrid political scandals, see Chadwick 2011.
12. Earl and Kimport 2011, p. 32.
13. For a discussion of commons-based peer production, see Benkler 2006. For studies of the political economy of open source software, see Weber 2004, Kelty 2008, and Hindman 2007. For an analysis of Wikipedia, see Lih 2009, Reagle 2010, Karpf 2011b.
14. See Shulman 2009; Gladwell 2010; White 2010; and Morozov 2009, 2011 for illustrative examples of this critique.
15. Shulman 2009, pp. 25–26. See Karpf 2010b for a direct rebuttal.
16. Morozov 2011, p. 190. Morozov's broader argument concerns the threat that digital tools, poorly deployed, can pose in unstable regimes. On the broader point, I concur, but his writing paints digital engagement tools with a particularly broad brush.

17. Dahl 1957. The gendered pronoun "he" is an artifact of the times. I leave it unchanged here to emphasize just *how* deeply rooted this definition of political power is. There are contrasting definitions and a whole literature devoted to the subject—see Riker 1964, Nagel 1975, Tilly 1978, and Bachrach and Baratz 1962—but Dahl's simple definition remains both elegant and generally appropriate.
18. Margolis and Resnick 2000
19. Bimber and Davis 2003, p. 3.
20. Verba, Schlozman, and Brady 2010.
21. West 2005, p. 11.
22. Davis 2009.
23. Hindman 2008, p. 4.
24. Sunstein 2001.
25. Pariser 2011.
26. Howard 2006.
27. Turow 2008.
28. Mutz 2006. Also see Wojcieszak 2010.
29. Fiorina 2005. Also see Fiorina 1999.
30. Abramowitz 2010. Abramowitz cautions that this is true only if we weaken counter-majoritarian institutions, like the Senate filibuster, which prevent polarized parties from enacting their policy agenda and increasingly gridlock government.
31. Prior 2007.
32. Truman 1951, Dahl 1961. For critical reactions, see Lowi 1979, Olson 1965, Schattschneider 1960.
33. Baumgartner et al. 2009.
34. Walker 1991.
35. Neuman 1986, p 31.
36. Skocpol 2003.
37. See Bennett 2008b; Bennett, Wells, and Rank 2009.
38. Teles 2008
39. Hacker and Pierson 2010.
40. Masket 2011.
41. Exceptions include Bruce Bimber's landmark 2003 book, *Information and American Democracy*, Mario Diani's 2000 analysis of online political organizations, Lance Bennett's 2003 and 2004 studies of transnational social movement organizations, Andrew Chadwick's 2007 work on hybrid advocacy groups, and Matthew Kerbel's 2009 study of the netroots as a social movement.
42. PCCC mission statement: http://boldprogressives.org/home
43. Nichols 2010, Hayes 2010
44. Beutler 2010.
45. Arroyo 2010.
46. See Chadwick 2007 for a discussion of organizational hybridity.
47. Green 2009.
48. For a discussion of the informal party networks that play an increasingly important role in determining public policy decisions, see Masket 2010.
49. See Hindman 2008, Barabasi 2001, Watts 2003, Hindman et al. 2003, Shirky 2003, Drezner and Farrell 2008, and Karpf 2008a.
50. See Weinberger 2007 for a thought-provoking exploration of metadata, categorization schemes, and online information abundance.
51. Anderson 2006 famously and provocatively speculated on the implications of the long tail for music, commerce, and a host of other fields. Earl and Kimport focus their attention to power laws (pages 147–153) on the long-tail phenomenon as well.
52. See Rushkoff 2003, Gillmor 2006, Trippi 2005, Ratcliffe and Lebkowsky 2005.
53. Zysman and Newman 2007.

54. Christensen 1997.
55. Monitor Institute 2011.
56. Bimber 2003, Diani 2000, Chadwick 2007.
57. Bimber 2003, p. 7.
58. Howard 2006, Reagle 2010, Fenno 1978.
59. In 2011, MoveOn redesigned their website. It is no longer sparse, though the new content flows have not altered the organization's general model.
60. Kerbel and Bloom 2005.
61. Chadwick 2007 (p. 284) coins the term "sedimentary networks" in reference to online organizations like MoveOn.
62. See Kreiss forthcoming for a rich description of NOI status as a network forum.

Chapter 2

1. Critics of technologically deterministic language may object to my use of phrases like "led to" when ascribing MoveOn's successes to technological innovation. To be clear, I hold a "soft determinist" stance similar to those of Bimber (2003) and Howard (2006). The affordances of a new technology make certain activities easier and other activities harder. Political actors leverage these affordances and have agency in doing so. Technology is a necessary-but-not-sufficient condition for organizations like MoveOn.
2. See Baumgartner and Jones 1993 for a discussion of the interest group explosion. See Skocpol 2003 for a discussion of the shift in organization type.
3. Monitor Institute 2011, p. 9.
4. See Berry 1997 for a discussion of the "advocacy group explosion."
5. For a discussion of opportunity structures and resource mobilization, see Meyer and Imig 1993.
6. For a discussion of the use of direct mail by these membership groups, see Zald and McCarthy 1987.
7. See Nagel 1987; Salisbury 1969; and Clark and Wilson 1961 for a discussion of these various incentives.
8. Skocpol 2003, p. 220.
9. See Gray and Lowery 1996, Gray and Lowery 1997, Lowery and Gray 2004, and Bosso 2005 for applications of the population ecology model to interest group studies.
10. Minkoff, Aisenbrey, and Agnone 2008.
11. Clemens 1997.
12. See Berry 1984; Walker 1991; Berry 1999; Baumgartner and Jones 1993; Baumgartner et al. 2009; and Walker, McCarthy, and Baumgartner 2011 for key works on the interest group explosion.
13. Zetter 2004.
14. Clausing 1999.
15. http://www.moveon.org/about.html
16. Bai 2007.
17. Heaney and Rojas 2007.
18. The Bush in 30 Seconds competition was most noteworthy as a cautionary tale about the dangers of user-generated content in contentious politics. One of the hundreds of submitted videos featured a Bush–Hitler comparison and, seizing upon this single example, Republican opponents labeled MoveOn an extremist organization.
19. MoveOn 2008.
20. Diani 2000.
21. Hara 2008.
22. Hara 2008, p. 13.
23. Interview notes, Natalie Foster. July 8, 2008.

24. The organization does occasionally pay to provide work space for individual staffers. It does not, however, maintain any regional or national offices. Though several senior staff members live in Brooklyn, NY, for instance, they do not bear any costs in the New York real estate market.

25. See Fine 2006, Kanter and Fine 2010 for a discussion of networked nonprofits. The term is a variant on Woody Powell's classic 1990 piece, "Neither Market nor Hierarchy."

26. See Shirky 2008 for a simplified introduction to the birthday paradox in the context of digital networks.

27. We should be circumspect in judging this point. It is clearly evident that many MoveOn members do not view themselves as members. But it is equally evident that legacy organizations experience plenty of false positives (where a supporter believes he or she is a member, even if he or she hasn't sent a check in years) and false negatives (where a supporter sends a check but is unaware that he or she a member). Organizational membership, as a social construct, receives so little active speculation that the public definition of the term remains opaque. Organizational membership as a legal construct, meanwhile, has strict, exacting definitions, enforced both by nonprofit law and election law. It is in this sense—membership as legal definition—that I pursue the topic here.

28. Bai 2007, p. 81.

29. Within limits. Organizations must avoid mailing so broadly that they become classified as spam and have their messages rejected. These limits are well-known to list managers, however.

30. By "taking action," I adopt the working operational definition employed by advocacy groups themselves. Actions vary in intensity from a Facebook "like" to writing a letter to the editor or attending an in-person event. Higher-cost actions receive less participation but are more valuable. Organizations frequently stack these actions sequentially, creating a "ladder of engagement." The digital action repertoire has introduced modified forms of low-cost action, but these have clear parallels to the baseline actions used in pre-digital campaigns (signing an online petition plays the same first-step role as signing an offline petition).

31. The Analyst Institute, a Democratic think tank founded by former students of Donald Green and Alan Gerber's Center for the Study of American Politics, has worked with MoveOn in the past and actively promotes this "culture of testing" to legacy organizations.

32. Traditional organizations have long engaged in limited amounts of this testing with their direct-mail fundraising programs. The lowered transaction costs, however, mean that MoveOn can conduct several tests in a single day, immediately analyze the results, and incorporate them into their messages later that afternoon. Older groups, in contrast, face the barriers of more expensive direct mail and more time-consuming feedback, limiting them to a single test per month rather than several tests per day.

33. Data from Membership Communications Project.

34. See Lawrence 2000, Livingston and Bennett 2003, Bennett 2008.

35. This is a simple extrapolation from Zaller's (1992) well-established Reception-Acceptance-Sampling model of mass opinion.

36. See Earl and Kimport, pp. 49–51 for a discussion of warehouse sites.

37. Shulman 2009, White 2010.

38. Jon Stewart, *The Daily Show*, June 24, 2008. See http://www.youtube.com/watch?v=Sq30lapbC9c to view the "Alex" campaign commercial.

39. As one example, former White House Communications Director Nicole Wallace made this statement on *The Rachel Maddow Show* on July 12, 2011.

40. Gans 2004, p. 229.

41. Turow 2005, Napoli 2010, Boczkowski 2010.

42. Anderson 2011a, p. 555.

43. Anderson 2011a, p. 561.

44. Anderson 2011b.
45. The simple solution theoretically would be to obtain e-mail addresses for all dues-paying members. In practice, the combination of "spam" prevention systems and individual reticence to offer an e-mail address to the same organizations that have for years widely sold mailing address lists renders this solution impracticable.
46. Quoted in Pearce 2008. Mintz was Research and Development Director at the time of the interview in 2008. He is now MoveOn's Advocacy Campaign Director, as noted in Chapter 1.
47. See Bai 2007 for a first-person account of the deliberations.
48. This benefit was pointed out to me by Chris Warshaw, former political director of Democracy for America. DFA intentionally designed their local endorsement process to enable such "takeovers," under the belief that local campaign partisans are the people who are most likely to be active in local politics once the campaign has ended. Attempts to influence the endorsement process are thus the structural equivalent of recruitment drives.
49. In 2004, the Sierra Club faced a similar malicious takeover of its Board of Directors by anti-immigration activists (Barringer 2004). As Sierra Club volunteers mobilized to prevent the takeover attempt, they enlisted MoveOn to come to their aid. MoveOn sent out an e-mail to all of its environmentally interested members, urging them to vote for a slate of longtime Sierra Club volunteers if they happened to be members of the organization (full disclosure: I was one of the MoveOn-endorsed candidates in that election).
50. Zaller 1992.
51. My own introduction to these trends occurred through my role on the Sierra Club Board of Directors. I make use of the Monitor Institute data in this section out of respect for the confidential setting from which my own familiarity with the topic originated.
52. Monitor Institute 2011, p. 9. Who knew that the zoo had raccoon wheels?
53. Monitor Institute 2011, p. 10.
54. See McChesney and Pickard 2011 for an excellent compilation of recent research on news disruption.
55. Shirky 2011.
56. See Jones 2009.
57. They also have trouble paying off the debt from 1990s-era mergers and acquisitions. These debts, based on a presumption of continuous profit margins (see Carr 2010, Bennett 2008a) are one important limitation on the analogy between the news industry and nonprofit advocacy. The news industry has faced a faster and more pronounced crisis because of the profit expectation and history of debt-financed acquisitions.
58. Berry 1999, p. 26.
59. Percentage based on 1994 and generally accurate for the first realignment era. See Klein 1994, p. 16.
60. Ibid, p. 57.
61. Turow 2008, pp. 63–64. Turow is focused on commercial direct marketing firms. Nonprofit direct mail lags commercial trends, mimicking successful techniques developed in the commercial industry.
62. Personal correspondence, Deborah Sorondo. November 2008.
63. Bosso 2005, p. 111.
64. Berry 1999, p. 95
65. See Turow 2008, Howard 2005, Howard 2006.
66. This was a common phrase, spontaneously mentioned in multiple interviews. Names withheld, June through September, 2008.
67. Flannery, Harris, and Rhine 2008.
68. Flannery and Harris 2007, p. 5.
69. Personal correspondence, nonprofit name withheld. September 2008.
70. Monitor Institute 2011, p. 11.

71. This is a coding of message content, rather than clickthroughs or dollars raised. The latter data would be fascinating but is proprietarily held by each individual organization. For the purposes of this analysis, I chose to rely on public data so I could make a wider comparison across the organizational field.

72. See Hayward 2008 for a discussion of political bundling and its effects.

73. The multi-year gap in organization founding-year, coinciding with the introduction of the first web browser in 1993, made the 1993–1996 gap a natural breakpoint.

74. Arrayed in a Yates Chi-square test of independence yielded a value of 62.97, statistically significant at the p < 0.0001 level.

75. Minkoff, Aisenbrey, and Agnone 2008.

76. Strom 2009.

77. The disappearance of ACORN (Association of Community Organizations for Reform Now) follows a similar trajectory, with the loss of government funding leading to the dissolution of the organization. The role of conservative media entrepreneurs in that case make it far more complicated, however, and worthy of independent evaluation. See Dreier and Martin 2010 for further discussion.

Chapter 3

1. Moulitsas 2008, p. 15.

2. Bellantoni 2010.

3. Regardless of size comparisons, co-locating the conferences likely ensures increased media coverage for Right Online. Several netroots participants have suggested this plausible explanation to me.

4. As recorded on YouTube by username "ng1260," July 24, 2010: http://www.youtube.com/watch?v=jA8vFHZNZEE

5. Both the # and @ symbols are incorporated into the Twitter architecture, creating automatic hyperlinks to other content. "#" signifies a topic and takes a reader to a search of other posts with the same "hashtag." @ signifies a username and takes a reader to that user's profile.

6. August 4, 2007. "PoliticsTV @ Yearly Kos '07: Markos Moulitsas Keynote." http://www.youtube.com/watch?v=5jLuke2KBik

7. In the summer of 2010, DailyKos hired Chris Bowers to serve as their campaign director. He has since built the site's e-mail list, developing its capacity to operate like an Internet-mediated issue generalist. The e-mail program remains a secondary function of DailyKos, though. It is still primarily a blogging community.

8. See Herbst 1998 for a discussion of varying forms and representations of public opinion.

9. John Kelly at Morningside Analytics has provided one such example, with his blogosphere mapping tool (Etling, Kelly, Faris, and Palfrey 2010). Abe Gong's work (Gong 2011) provides another promising demonstration.

10. Rebecca Blood provides the oft-cited 23 blogs claim (2000); the 2009 statistic comes from Technorati's *State of the Blogosphere 2008* report.

11. Karpf 2010c.

12. Bloom and Kerbel 2006, Merry 2010.

13. Weber forthcoming.

14. Mayhew 1974, Pole 2009.

15. Margolis and Resnick 2000.

16. See also Barabasi 2003, Shirky 2003.

17. Barzilai-Nahon et al. 2011, Wallsten 2007.

18. Hindman 2008.

19. See Downie and Schudson 2009 for an extended discussion of digitally enabled journalism efforts.

20. Moulitsas 2008, p. 2.
21. The Trent Lott scandal was driven by blogging-as-citizen-journalism. The Republican Senate Minority Leader made a comment at the birthday celebration of former Senator Strom Thurmond (who ran for the presidency in 1948 on a segregationist Dixiecrat platform) that, if Thurmond had been elected president, "the country wouldn't have had all these problems over the years." Media coverage of the event largely ignored the comment, but bloggers seized on the phrase, pressuring mainstream media outlets to cover it. Lott eventually resigned his leadership post as a result. See Perlmutter 2008.
22. See Rheingold 2000 for a discussion of these early discussion boards. Also see Turner 2002.
23. Interview notes, "BooMan" 7/17/07 and Natasha Chart 9/15/07.
24. Davis 2009, p. 58.
25. Karpf 2009b.
26. As reported by SiteMeter.com: http://www.sitemeter.com/?a=stats&s=sm8dailykos. SiteMeter records unique visits per day rather than unique visitors per month, thus it provides a different metric than traffic ranking sites such as Hitwise, Quantcast, Compete, and Alexa. There are ongoing debates over which of these sites is "best" for research, but—since all of them are flawed—it is essentially a matter of personal preference.
27. Karpf 2008a.
28. As of July 2011. These employment levels will probably fluctuate in accordance with site growth and election year activity.
29. Payne 2008, p. 135.
30. Sides and Farrell 2011.
31. See Moulitsas 2011b.
32. The polling relationship was maintained through 2009 until a group of statisticians contacted Moulitsas with an independent study suggesting Research 2000 was potentially falsifying data. A lawsuit between Research 2000 and DailyKos is currently pending.
33. Andrews et al. 2010.
34. Bai 2007.
35. http://www.ginacooper.com/node/140
36. http://www.dailykos.com/storyonly/2009/5/14/123525/324
37. http://arjun-jaikumar.dailykos.com/
38. See Lovink 2007 for a critical appraisal of the great mass of political blogs. Comments per post are based on the initial Blogosphere Authority Index data collection in November 2007. Numbers have remained largely stable since DailyKos switched to the DK4 platform.
39. See Sunstein 2006, Weinberger 2007, Lev-On and Hardin 2008, and Karpf 2011b for a discussion of network effects.
40. $300,000 of this fundraising came through an ActBlue page set up specifically by kossacks after Tinklenberg's fundraising portal crashed from the web traffic surge. The total percentage of this $810,000 that came from DailyKos is unknowable without access to proprietary data, but the candidate himself publicly credited the DailyKos community for fundraising success. See Karpf 2010a for a complete case analysis.
41. http://www.mediaite.com/online/sarahpac-website-hit-list-image-that-included-target-on-giffords-district-kos-post-remains/
42. See Bruns 2008; Wallsten 2007, 2008; Perlmutter 2008; Gillmor 2006, 2010; Gil de Zuniga, Puig-i-Abril, and Rojas 2009
43. OpenLeft shut its digital doors in 2011, after founders Chris Bowers and Matt Stoller had left for higher-profile positions at different organizations.
44. Hindman 2008, p. 119.
45. Not all DailyKos editors provide photos on the site, and the front-page editorial group continually shifts. An exact count is difficult to obtain and sure to be out of date.

46. See Steinberg 2008 and Tenore 2011 for further description of Silver.
47. http://www.fivethirtyeight.com/2008/05/no-im-not-chuck-todd.html
48. In "Understanding Blogspace," I referred to this blog type as "individual blogs." Since multiple authors are often involved in the production of these blogs, that has led to some confusion, and I am thus revising the name here.
49. Note that online anonymity has two separate meanings. In this case, it refers to "being unknown," just as a single individual is anonymous in a crowd of people. Within the architecture of a blog comment thread, a more technical anonymity can exist. Web 2.0 software can choose one of three settings, allowing anonymous (nameless) comments, requiring registration and a pseudonym, or requiring users to verify their identity and use their real name. As a general rule, commenters tend to behave themselves and offer higher-quality participation when real names or pseudonyms are required. See Gillmor 2010, p. 42–43 for further discussion.
50. Kristol 2008.
51. Shirky 2008, p. 81.
52. Blumenthal 2008.
53. Karpf 2008a.
54. Karpf 2008a, 2008b, 2010b; Barzilai-Nahon et al. 2011a, 2011b; Benkler and Shaw 2010.
55. Benkler and Shaw (2010) identified a sample of 155 large political blogs on the left, right, and center. They were able to identify only 23 "center" blogs, noting "the fact that we found such a relatively small proportion of blogs in the center suggests that the most visible and heavily linked blogs remain strongholds of partisanship."
56. Lawrence, Sides, and Farrell 2010.
57. Abramowitz 2010.
58. One explanation of this finding may be the longstanding goal of "objectivity" in American news media. Whereas counter-institutional blogs on the left and right drew audiences that felt their ideas and opinions went unrepresented in the mainstream media, centrist blogs may have had less claim to such a critique. While the American Left believes the media displays a conservative or corporate bias, and the American Right believes the media displays a liberal bias, the American center displays little faith in the media but does not find it to be biased in one direction or the other (see Bennett 2008 for a discussion of media biases).
59. Using a Wilcoxan Mann-Whitney Rank Sum Test to test for non-parametric significance, these findings are significant at the 0.0001 level.
60. Ruffini 2009, 2010.
61. Conservative bloggers occupy positions at *Fox News, The Washington Times,* and *CNN* as well. The gap in institutional blogs cannot be easily explained through "liberal media bias."
62. Kerbel 2009, p. 46.
63. Bellantoni 2010.
64. Sunstein 2001, p 3.
65. Sunstein later modified and softened his critiques of the online information environment. See Sunstein 2006, 2007.
66. See Mutz 2002, 2006 for an overview of deliberative and participatory democracy.
67. Adamic and Glance 2005.
68. Hamilton, Madison, and Jay 1787.
69. Moulitsas, 2007.

Chapter 4

1. Shirky 2004.
2. Bai 2008, pp. 153–173, Kamarck 2006.

3. David Perlmutter uses the term "proto-blog" in a passing reference to refer to the Drudge Report in his 2008 book, *Blog Wars* (p. 58–60). I build upon and extend that concept in this chapter.

4. Intervew Notes, Jen Murphy. September 18, 2007.

5. Taussig 2007.

6. See Patel 2008a, 2008b.

7. Interview Notes, Hannah Miller. June 30, 2007.

8. Taussig 2007.

9. Wilson 1962, pp. 3–4, 13.

10. Skocpol 2003, p. 220.

11. The Sierra Club created its student-run arm, the Sierra Student Coalition, in part to help remedy this aging of the volunteer base in 1991. The results have been mixed. Several young leaders (including myself) joined the national volunteer ranks, but a clear generation gap persists at the local group and state chapter levels.

12. Interview Notes, Anne Dicker. August 27, 2007.

13. See Wolf 2004, Williams et al. 2004, Porter 2007.

14. Trippi 2004.

15. Fine 2006.

16. Shirky 2004, p. 234.

17. Paquet 2002.

18. Interview Notes, Anne Dicker.

19. Nielsen 2012.

20. This data comes from the Site Traffic Score raw data, collected as part of the Blogosphere Authority Index. It is gathered and made publicly available by SiteMeter.com.

21. Many of the major community blogs—including DailyKos, FireDogLake, and Open-Left—have recently added e-mail alerts to their mix of engagement tactics. A visitor will be greeted by a splash page, inviting them to sign up for action alerts, once per month. E-mail nonetheless remains a secondary activity for these quasi-interest group political blogs.

22. See Hindman 2005. I would technically disagree with this assertion. Though there are thousands of businesses quietly using the Internet for every eBay, Amazon, or CraigsList, I would argue that the greater impact comes from these new market disruptors. This disagreement is more a matter of perspective than empirics, however, and Hindman's point about backend streamlining is nonetheless quite useful.

23. Notice the juxtaposition here. Rather than a free e-mail newsletter, PFC chooses to spend a little money on printing so that their membership will receive something in harder-to-ignore hard copy.

24. Meeting notes, June 2008.

25. See De Tocqueville 1840, Dewey 1927, Barber 1984, Habermas 1989, Skocpol 2003.

26. See Pole 2009; Lawrence, Sides, and Farrell 2010 on blogs. See Gulati and Williams 2010, Wallsten 2010, and Klotz 2010 on YouTube. See Williams and Gulati 2008, Baumgarnter and Morris 2010, and Gueorguieva 2008 on social networks. See Boynton 2010 on Twitter.

27. Nielsen 2011.

28. The MCP study was conducted while I was a Postdoctoral Research Associate at Brown University's Taubman Center for Public Policy.

29. See boyd 2008, Watts 2003, p. 77 for a discussion of clustering in this context.

30. Groups can be either identity-based (Jewish Grandmas for Democracy) or place-based (Sarasotans for Democracy). In legal terms, these groups are not formally incorporated into DFA. This loose relationship simplifies issues of message control, particularly with regard to controversial endorsements.

31. Interview Notes, Chris Warshaw. May 18, 2007.

32. Interview Notes, Chris Warshaw. May 18, 2007.

33. Wellman 2001.

34. Trippi 2004, p. 59.
35. Trippi 2004, p. 59.
36. See Rheingold 2000, Turner 2002.
37. Perlmutter 2008, p. 58. Also see Wallsten 2011.
38. http://www.comscore.com/press/release.asp?press=2525
39. Cillizza 2008. Kevin Wallsten (2011) notes similar comments from many other main-stream journalists.
40. Perlmutter 2008, p. 58–60.
41. McCaughey and Ayers 2003.
42. http://www.youtube.com/watch?v=6lZMr-ZfoE4
43. Foster has also been Director of Online Organizing for Organizing for America and for the Sierra Club. At the time of our conversation, she was employed by the Sierra Club.
44. Natalie Foster, personal correspondence. May 16, 2008.
45. A more robust version of this argument, exploring the potential of distributed reputation tracking for offline activities, can be found in Karpf 2011a.
46. Jonathan Zittrain (2008), among others, has raised the concern that the iPhone represents a "tethered" Internet appliance, fundamentally different from the "generative" devices (computers in particular) that have been the primary tool through which individuals access the Internet. His argument about "generativity," presented in *The Future of the Internet . . . and How to Stop It*" is tangential to the subject of this particular study, but is well-worth consideration nonetheless.
47. Alexander 2010.
48. http://officialblog.yelp.com/2011/07/four-score-and-20-million-reviews-ago.html
49. Kee 2009.
50. Exley 2007a. Morris Fiorina offers a related thesis in his essay on "the Dark Side of Civic Engagement" (1999). Building from the Downsian tradition of rational choice analysis, Fiorina argues that rational citizens will sensibly decide not to engage in local political associations because the costs of doing so outweigh the policy gains they could hope to achieve through collective action. As a result, Fiorina argues, local associations tend to be dominated by people who receive an outsized psychological benefit from voicing their opinion or who have particularly strong opinions on the subject.
51. See Reagle 2010, Lih 2009.
52. See Resnick et al. 2006.
53. Lampe and Johnson 2005.
54. See Norris 2001, Warschauer 2004, Van Dijk and Hacker 2003.
55. Smith 2010.
56. Rosenstone and Hansen 1993. Verba, Schlozman, and Brady 1995
57. Kreiss 2011.
58. Nielsen 2012.
59. Karpf 2009a.
60. Rasmus Kleis Nielsen disputes this characterization, as Barry Goldwater's campaign was similar in size. Without entering that historical debate, we can at least note that the Obama campaign was larger than any other mobilization since the 1970s-era decline of the cross-class civic federations.
61. For a discussion of threshold models in the diffusion of innovation literature, see Valente 1996.
62. See Kingdon 1984, Baumgartner and Jones 1993.
63. See Chadwick 2007.
64. See Galvin 2010 for a discussion of historical attempts at presidential party-building.
65. I was not privy to the internal conversations that occurred amongst OFA strategists on January 17th. Whether this "dilemma of control" was a central conversation topic is unknown. I offer this analysis here because it was a point, clear at the time, which has frequently been overlooked in journalistic and scholarly treatments of OFA.

66. Melber 2010, p. 26–28.
67. Stewart 2010. This message was the first OFA health care-focused action alert in the MCP dataset.
68. Barber 1984.

Chapter 5

1. Teles 2008, p. 17. Teles credits Skowronek (1982) with coining this term and also draws parallel to Epp's (1998) "support structure for legal change."
2. Walker, McCarthy, and Baumgartner 2011.
3. See Kreiss forthcoming and Turner 2002, respectively, for discussions of the New Organizing Institute in particular and network forums in general.
4. http://livingliberally.org/living/about accessed online, March 2, 2011.
5. See Nielsen 2012, Chapter 2.
6. This claim is based on personal observation as a member of the Sierra Club Board of Directors—November 2004 was not a happy Board meeting. Also see Sullivan 2005 or Bai 2007.
7. Bai 2007, p. 26.
8. Hacker and Pierson 2010, p. 7.
9. Edited Transcript of the Hudson Institute panel on "How Vast the Left Wing Conspiracy." http://www.hudson.org/files/pdf_upload/Transcript_2006_11_30.pdf, p. 8.
10. See Edsall 2005, Vandehei and Cillizza 2006 for further details.
11. Recent scholarship by Steven Teles (2008) arrives at complementary conclusions.
12. Bai 2007, p. 97. These membership requirements may have fluctuated since the time of Bai's writing.
13. Brookes 2008.
14. See Bai 2007, Edsall 2005, Vandehei and Cillizza 2006, Stein 2006, and Payne 2008.
15. Moulitsas 2008, pp. 2–3.
16. Van Slyke and Clark 2010, p. 20.
17. Bowers and Stoller 2005, p. 2.
18. Teles 2008, p. 17.
19. NOI and ActBlue both technically have member lists that they e-mail with donation requests. The distinction is a term-of-art, and certainly debatable. I consider them NMAOs because the constellation of stakeholders in their work is far different from that of netroots generalists or legacy political associations.
20. Fullenwider 2010.
21. Exley 2007b.
22. Username "neworganizinginst," 2009.
23. See Turner 2002 for a discussion of network forums in the broader "cyberculture" community. Also see Kreiss 2012, who is responsible for initially making this connection.
24. http://neworganizing.com/ accessed on July 23, 2011. These two quotes were the subject lines of tip-of-the-day e-mails on July 19th and 20th, 2011.
25. Ganz's coauthors include Theda Skocpol, providing an interesting network tie between practitioner and academic thought that animate this particular book. See Ganz 2009; Skocpol, Ganz, and Munson 2000.
26. See Alexander 2010. Full disclosure: the Camp Obama trainings were based upon the Leadership Development Project curriculum that Ganz developed with the Sierra Club. In my volunteer role with the Sierra Club, I was a member of that development team, working directly with Marshall while delivering the curriculum to New Mexico Sierra Club volunteer leaders.
27. Lupia and Sin 2003.
28. Shulman 2009, p. 26. Also see Earl 2010, Earl et al. 2010.

29. Bimber, Flanagin, and Stohl 2005.
30. . . . Just try asking an electoral field organizer how "rational" they are feeling on election eve. The response will prove entertaining.
31. See Terdiman 2004, Mosk 2007, Schatz 2007, and Wayne 2007.
32. Arroyo 2011.
33. Karpf 2010a.
34. Karpf 2010a.
35. See Hayward 2008 for a discussion of political bundling.
36. http://blog.actblue.com/blog/2009/07/actblue-technical-services.html
37. MoveOn nonetheless frequently makes use of ActBlue on a project-specific basis.
38. Ed Walker (2009) and Caroline Lee (2010) examine a fourth noteworthy development: the outsourcing of industry "Astroturf" campaign functions. Such activities occur among a different cluster of new media vendors. Though a fascinating and troubling topic in its own right, I do not cover it here because I believe it falls just barely outside the confines of the current study.
39. Posted to Twitter by username "SalsaLabs," February 3, 2010, 8:43 a.m. Salsa Labs was a project of Democracy in Action at that time and has since been spun off into a separate company.
40. Shulman 2009, p. 29.
41. Sifry 2010.
42. Montgomery and Nyhan 2010, p. 12.
43. Many of these vendors employ some form of non-compete clause in their employment contracts, meaning that staffers cannot move from, for instance, Blue State Digital to Salsa Labs. Former Blue State Digital staffers are attractive candidates for New Media Director or Communications Director positions at nonprofits, however.
44. Dimaggio and Powell 1983, Wasserman and Faust 1995.
45. See Nielsen 2011 for a discussion of Catalist's role as a central data vendor for Democratic Field Campaign operations in the 2010 congressional elections.
46. Dulio 2004. Also see Medvic 2001, Sabato 1981, Luntz 1988, and Thurber 2000.
47. Von Hippel 2005, p. 1.
48. Von Hippel, p. 2.
49. Dulio 2004.
50. Atrios's site, "Eschaton," regularly ranks between 3rd and 5th on the Blogosphere Authority Index. He also had been immortalized on *The West Wing*, one of only two real-life individuals to be depicted on the program.
51. http://livingliberally.org/living/about accessed February 10, 2011.
52. http://livingliberally.org/drinking accessed February 10, 2011. Chapter activity is measured through monthly surveys, and the list is kept current by removing chapters if they stay inactive for several months.
53. Interview notes, February 10, 2011.
54. Pinto 2007.
55. Pinto 2007, Sullivan 2008.
56. Gladwell 2010.
57. McAdam 1990.
58. See Marwell and Oliver 1993 for a theory of social networks and collective action, McAdam 1990 for a discussion of network ties in the context of the civil rights movement, Granovetter 1973 for the classic introduction to weak-tie studies, and Earl 2010 for a discussion of protest-related diffusion on the web.
59. Barry Wellman likewise has demonstrated that most online ties serve to augment offline connections. See Wellman et al. 2003, Wellman 2004 for one example, though this point reverberates through several articles and presentations emerging from Wellman's Net-Lab research team. One might attempt to salvage Gladwell's argument by stipulating that

he is referring only to social media sites such as Twitter and Facebook, rather than to Internet communication as a whole or to Internet-mediated organizations that use those tools along with others. It requires a rather selective reading of Gladwell and the discussion stemming from his article to reach such a conclusion, however. The author is clearly equating Internet-mediated political engagement with "Facebook activism."

60. Due to flaws in *The New Republic*'s archive system, Zengerle's article is not accessible online. See Scherer 2006 for coverage of the incident.
61. Schulman 2007.
62. Klein, E. 2010.
63. See Karpf 2010c for a case study of the "Weigelgate" scandal.
64. Klein, J. 2010.
65. Michael Calderone appears to be the first person to publicly coin this term, in a 2009 Politico article on JournoList.
66. As I have never been a member of either TownHouse or JournoList, I cannot confirm whether this is the exact language used on either list. It is commonly used on various other backchannels, however.
67. Chait 2010.
68. Breitbart 2010.
69. Barzilai-Nahon 2008.
70. Castells 2009.
71. Fallows 2010.
72. See Barabasi 2003 for a discussion of these dynamics.
73. Sargent 2010.
74. Barlow 1996. See Morrison 2011 for a discussion of the statement's history, importance, and effects.
75. In the course of conducting interviews for this book, I received at least a half-dozen invitations to join TownHouse if I'd like, often prefaced by the Yogi Berra quote. I demurred based primarily on the assessment that I was receiving enough e-mail already.
76. Nielsen 2011.

Chapter 6

1. See Jamieson and Cappella 2008 for a discussion of the history and impacts of political talk radio.
2. This trend was particularly noteworthy in blog-related studies circa 2006–2008, providing the impetus for creation of the Blogosphere Authority Index. See Karpf 2008a for a literature review.
3. See Dimaggio and Powell 1983.
4. Van Jones deserves credit for coining the phrase "meta-brand" in reference to the Tea Party at Netroots Nation 2011. It is better terminology than I had previously used.
5. See Tily 1978, McAdam 1999, and Tarrow 2011.
6. Klotz 2004, p. 77.
7. Bowers and Stoller 2005.
8. Adamic and Glance 2005, Ackland 2005.
9. Grossman 2004.
10. See Karpf 2008a for further explanation.
11. See Karpf 2009 for further discussion.
12. Ruffini 2009, 2010.
13. http://www.time.com/time/specials/packages/article/0,28804,1879276_1879093_1879090,00.html
14. Catanese 2010b.
15. http://www.rightmarch.com/about.htm accesses online December 18, 2008.

16. In a 2005 interview with Politics Online Internet radio (www.politicsonline.com/content/main/interviews/2005/greene/greene.doc), Bill Greene of RightMarch claimed an e-mail list of 2 million members but was noticeably circumspect in doing so. The organization has been tight-lipped about its membership, tactics, and successes. Speaking editorially from my time in the nonprofit world, this is often a sign that an organization has little to brag about.

17. *Mother Jones Online* July, 2007. http://www.motherjones.com/interview/2007/07/david_all.html?welcome=true

18. Note that this MoveOn figure conflicts with MoveOn's own reporting of over $90 million raised. The difference likely is because much of MoveOn's fundraising was bundled directly to the candidates. Nonetheless, this may indicate that RightMarch's total fundraising is similarly underrepresented by the Center's data.

19. RightMarch data available at http://www.opensecrets.org/pacs/lookup2.php?cycle=2008&strID=C00386482 MoveOn data available at http://www.opensecrets.org/pacs/lookup2.php?strID=C00341396

20. Harkinson 2007.

21. Kane and Weisman 2008.

22. Luo 2008.

23. Ward 2008.

24. Catanese 2010a.

25. Odom 2010.

26. Odom 2011a.

27. Odom 2011b.

28. Sifry 2006.

29. www.slatecard.com, accessed online December 19, 2008

30. RightRoots.com, accessed online July 25, 2011. You read that correctly. In mid-2011, RightRoots is updating the website for the *2010 election*.

31. See Davis 2009, Perlmutter 2008, Bowers and Stoller 2005.

32. Surely, many liberal and centrist elites fundamentally misunderstand the new media environment as well. Those elites have often hired new staff and consultants, though. Conservative elites have been less quick to reward successful strategists.

33. Ruffini 2009, 2010. Also see Smith 2011.

34. Micah Sifry identified 607 such groups listed on Meetup.com (Sifry 2010b). Tea Party organizations have boasted that there are thousands, but provide no data to support such claims. Meetup group listings are only a partial indicator, overcounting groups that were announced but failed to meet or disbanded, while undercounting groups that self-organize outside of the Meetup.com system.

35. Zernike 2010, p. 156.

36. For a discussion of the Koch brothers' major role in funding conservative movement infrastructure, see Mayer 2010.

37. See Walker 2009. Astroturf is a term-of-art that lacks rigorous boundary conditions. While extreme cases of Astroturfing are easy to spot—corporations hiring "demonstrators" and paying them a daily wage to show up at a hearing—the phrase carries a pejorative connotation and is generally applied to question the authenticity of opposition efforts at citizen mobilization. Progressives call FreedomWorks an Astroturf organization; conservatives apply the same label to many unions.

38. http://mediamatters.org/research/200912220009

39. http://mediamatters.org/research/200912220009

40. Glen Beck's affiliation with Fox News ended in the summer of 2011.

41. Many Tea Party members are indeed Independents, but they vote almost universally for Republicans on Election Day. See Parker 2010, Zernike and Thee-Brenan 2010.

42. McGirr 2001, Rozell and Wilcox 1995.

43. McGirr 2001.
44. Rozell and Wilcox 1995; Green, Rozell, and Wilcox 2003.
45. Murakami 2008.
46. See Paquet 2002, Shirky 2008.
47. Teachout and Streeter 2008, p. 19–20.
48. Ibid.
49. Nielsen 2009.
50. Harkinson 2007, p. 35.
51. Catanese 2010a.
52. Interview notes. December 13, 2008.
53. Harkinson 2007, pp. 34–35.
54. See Perlstein 2001, McGirr 2001.
55. Note to quantitatively oriented researchers: to my knowledge, no studies have been conducted on the correlation between social movement activism and trends in pet ownership. This represents an obvious and entertaining gap in the literature. Come on, someone needs to run those regressions!
56. Zernike, p. 38.
57. Piore and Sabel 1984, Tapscott and Williams 2006, 2010.
58. Henke 2008.
59. See Carmines and Stimson 1989 for a discussion of the two parties' transition along civil rights issues.
60. Armstrong and Moulitsas 2007.
61. Smith and Rainie 2008, p. 20.
62. Tarrow 2011, p. 54.
63. Truman's *The Governmental Process* (1951) is a landmark pluralist text. Rosenberg's *The Hollow Hope* (1991) discusses how major Supreme Court decisions affect the landscape of political mobilization. Taeku Lee (2002) and Lowery & Gray et al. (2005) provide divergent commentary on counter-mobilization as well. The term itself, "counter-mobilization," can refer to divergent activities across research literatures. I use the term here specifically in reference to the temporal setting that a partisan ideological network faces.
64. Turner 1991, p. 220.
65. Teles 2008, pp. 148–149.
66. And, I would note, the Progressive Change Campaign Committee has built its membership base by carving out a niche as the venue for progressive discontent with the Obama administration.
67. Mayhew 1974, p. 49.
68. Or, on a micro-level, through Federal Elections Commission decisions. One such judicial change, *Citizens United v Federal Elections Commission* (2010) indeed made quite a substantial difference for political organizations in the 2010 election. Dramatically altering campaign finance law, the altered rules spurred the creation of several large-scale political associations and the abandonment of others.
69. See Green and Gerber 2000, 2004.
70. Harnden 2008.
71. Kerbel 2009.
72. One corollary of this thesis, then, is that scholars interested in the Internet's impact on political campaigning should *not* be treating all campaigns as equal. There has been a trend in the literature toward quantitative research that counts the total number of candidate websites that include specific communications technologies—YouTube or Face-Book or blogs (Gulati and Williams 2007, Williams and Gulati 2008, Williams and Gulati 2010, Bloom and Kerbel 2006, Klotz 2010). This technocentric research agenda fails to distinguish between the types of campaigns that we should expect to feature innovations and the types we should expect to stand pat.

73. Armstrong and Moulitsas 2007.
74. Moulitsas 2011a.
75. Dulio 2004.
76. Gibson and Rommele make a similar argument in their 2001 analysis of "professionalized campaigning" among European parties.
77. Sullivan 2005.
78. Kamarck 2006, Bai 2007.
79. Shulman 2007, p. 34.
80. Vargas 2008.
81. Ruffini 2008.
82. Interview notes, Jon Henke. April 21, 2009.
83. Leading conservative blogger Michelle Malkin is also an Oberlin alumnus. I consider this point to be the single biggest unsolved puzzle in my multi-year study of technology and politics. (Just a little joke for any readers committed enough to read all the footnotes!)
84. The first "saboteurs" were Dutch peasants who would break machines by throwing their wooden shoes, or "sabots" into the machinery. Thus "digitized wooden shoes" is a term meant to evoke the earliest, less-deadly meaning of the word.
85. Ambinder 2008.
86. http://ideas.rebuildtheparty.com/pages/general/suggestions/68216?page=31
87. See http://wonkette.com/tag/rebuild-the-party
88. Username "anonymous office zombie," 2008.
89. www.sadlyno.com/about, Accessed December 18, 2008.
90. See Coleman and Galub 2008, Coleman 2011 on hackers and the 4Chan community.
91. Breitbart 2009.
92. Gillmor 2010.
93. Moulitsas 2008, p. 173.
94. Ibid, p 175.
95. Limbaugh 2008. "Chaos Hijacks Democrat Primary." http://www.rushlimbaugh.com/home/daily/site_050508/content/01125108.guest.html
96. A competing, more ideologically based explanation would be that the modern American conservative movement embodies the same "paranoid style" Richard Hofstadter described in 1964.

Chapter 7

1. Kranzberg 1986.
2. Trippi 2004; Rheingold 2002; Ratcliffe and Lebkowsky 2005; Rushkoff 2003; and Fine, Sifry, Rasiej, and Levy 2008.
3. Davis 2009.
4. Schlozman, Verba, and Brady 2010.
5. Hindman 2009.
6. Hargattai 2008.
7. Hindman 2009.
8. See Prior 2007 for a discussion of the "knowledge gap" and Relative Entertainment Preferences.
9. And as Eli Pariser (2011) notes, the selecting can be taken out of a citizen's hands. Increasingly sophisticated predictive filtering mechanisms on sites like Google and Facebook seek to optimize and personalize the news diet. Individuals who rarely click on political stories will be treated to fewer political headlines, even if they generally would like to remain informed.
10. Anderson 2006, Shirky 2008, also see Benkler 2006.
11. Schudson 1998.

12. Key 1958, Aldrich 1995.
13. Gibson and Rommele 2001, Anstead and Chadwick 2008, Diani 2000.
14. Turow 2008.
15. See Howard 2006.
16. Howard 2010, Faris 2008.
17. Bennett 2003, 2004.
18. Morozov 2011.
19. Wojcieszak and Mutz 2009, Wojcieszak 2010, Sunstein 2006.
20. Anderson 2010, Boczkiewski 2004.
21. For a discussion of the multi-tiered, "hourglass architecture" of the Internet, see Zittrain 2008, pp. 67–71.
22. There is some controversy over when and where Mead actually made this statement. No clear citation trail is present.
23. Blumer 1948.
24. Zaller 1992.
25. Blumer p. 545. Emphasis in original.
26. Schattschneider 1960, p. 66.
27. Lee 2002, p. 83.
28. Herbst 1998 p. 13.
29. Gosnell 1927.
30. Green and Gerber 2000, 2004.
31. Brewer 2010. MoveOn's Daniel Mintz suggested the term "advocacy inflation" in the comment section of my blog. It is a much better term than the one I had been using, and he deserves credit for the coinage.
32. Tarrow 2011, p. 54.
33. Moulitsas 2008, pp. 15, 22.
34. Shirky 2004, p. 233.
35. Kreiss forthcoming.
36. See Nielsen 2012.
37. This occurs at a crowding threshold that is almost universally higher than individuals would expect. Every election season features exasperated voters saying "Stop calling me! Forget it, I'm not going to vote anymore." There is little evidence that fewer Get Out the Vote calls would yield better results, though.
38. See Pierson 2004, or Orren and Skowronek 2004 for an overview of path dependence and American Political Development.
39. Skowronek 1993.
40. See Boynton 2010.
41. Creed 2010.
42. Username "ablake34," 2010.
43. Lessig 2009, Jenkins 2006, also see Sinnreich 2010.
44. Bennett 2008; Bennett, Wells, and Rank 2009.
45. See Perlmutter 2008, Gueorguieva 2008, Scherer 2006.
46. Lizza 2006.
47. See Karpf 2010a for a full argument.
48. For a discussion of public goods problems, see Olson 1965 or Lupia and Sin 2003. Also see Lev-On and Hardin 2008.
49. Shirky 2009.
50. Starr 2009.
51. There are some good experimental attempts at replicating these functions online. Global Voices Online provides crowdsourced international journalism. ProPublica offers a "pro-am" version of investigative reporting. Several attempts at "hyperlocal" online journalism are currently underway. See Downie and Schudson 2009 for a more complete discussion.

52. See Entman 1989, Hamilton 2004, and Bennett 2008a.
53. Abramowitz 2010.
54. Mutz 2006, Adamic and Glance 2005.

Appendix

1. Hendler was the co-chair of WebSci'09 in Athens, Greece. This was one of his remarks on stage, jotted down through the fog of jetlag.
2. Barabasi 2003, Hindman et al. 2003, Shirky 2003, Lev-On and Hardin 2008.
3. Benkler 2006, Weber 2004, Lih 2009.
4. See Richard Fenno's methodological essay in *Home Style* (1978) for a further discussion of "rapport."
5. For an illustrative example of "blogroll purges," see http://www.boomantribune.com/story/2007/3/21/91449/7914
6. Adamic and Glance 2005, p. 14.
7. Note: The original BAI used MichelleMalkin.com rather than Hotair.com. Both sites are operated by Malkin. Later iterations started from Hotair because Malkin invested heavily in driving traffic to that site.
8. *P* can vary drastically depending on the blogroll size of the seed site.
9. Duncan Black, interview, Philadelphia, PA, October 20, 2007.
10. Additionally, the Alexa fill cannot be applied to institutional blogs hosted by a larger media site (Slate.com, WashingtonPost.com, etc.) because Alexa provides traffic statistics only at the domain level. For those sites (Glenn Greenwald, for instance), no STS can be recorded.
11. Walker 1991.
12. Berry 1999.
13. 450,000 at the time the MCP dataset was created. It has since grown to over 750,000.
14. "527" refers to a line in the tax code. 527 groups are organizations that engage in Independent Expenditure Campaigns during election cycles, under guidance established by the Bipartisan Campaign Reform Act of 2002.
15. DailyKos launched an e-mail program in August 2010, after the MCP data collection period had concluded.
16. These terminology decisions reflect some important realities. First, it would be inappropriate to term the new generation "Internet-mediated organizations" since, as Bimber (2003), Chadwick (2007), and others have noted, older organizations have themselves adopted Internet-mediated tools. Second, the "legacy" organizations include groups founded in the direct-mail era and groups founded in the earlier era described by Skocpol (2003). Groups like the Sierra Club (founded 1892) underwent major structural adaptations in response to the new membership and fundraising regimes of the 1970s (Andrews et al. 2010).
17. This choice also alleviates some otherwise-difficult classification problems. Should Color of Change be considered a "civil rights organization" or an "Internet-mediated organization," for instance? It was developed as a spinoff of MoveOn to better respond to the particular interests of the African American community. A strong argument could be made for both.
18. Technically, Pope ceased to be Executive Director of the Sierra Club midway through the data collection period. He took a new position as Chairman of the organization, and continued unchanged in posting to his "Taking the Initiative" blog.
19. Fine 2006, Trippi 2004.
20. *Countdown with Keith Olbermann* eventually stopped being broadcast on MSNBC. It has moved to Current TV and been replaced by *The Last Word with Lawrence O'Donnell*.
21. Jamieson and Cappella 2010, Sunstein 2001, Xenos and Kim 2008.

Bibliography

Abramowitz, Alan. 2010. *The Disappearing Center: Engaged Citizens, Polarization, and American Democracy.* New Haven, CT: Yale University Press.

Ackland, Robert. 2005. "Mapping the U.S. Political Blogosphere: Are Conservative Bloggers More Prominent?" Submission to *BlogTalk.* Retrieved from http://incsub.org/blogtalk/images/robertackland.pdf

Adamic, Lada, and Natalie Glance. May 2005. "The Political Blogosphere and the 2004 US Election: Divided They Blog." Presented at Conference on Knowledge Discovery in Data, Japan. Retrieved from http://portal.acm.org/citation.cfm?doid=1134271.1134277

Aldrich, John. 1995. *Why Parties? The Origin and Transformation of Political Parties in America.* Chicago, IL: University of Chicago Press.

Alexander, Jeffrey. 2010. *The Performance of Politics: Obama's Victory and the Democratic Struggle for Power.* New York: Oxford University Press.

Alexander, Leigh. October 18, 2010. "Apple's App Store Reaches 300,000 Total Applications." *Gamasutra.com.* Retrieved from http://www.gamasutra.com/view/news/31033/Apples_App_Store_Reaches_300000_Total_Applications

Ambinder, Marc. November 6, 2008. "Young Republicans Push Internet Organizing Priority." *The Atlantic* online. Retrieved from http://marcambinder.theatlantic.com/archives/2008/11/young_republicans_push_interne.php

Anderson, Chris. 2006. *The Long Tail.* New York: Hyperion Books.

Anderson, C.W. 2010. "Journalistic Networks and the Diffusion of Local News: The Brief, Happy News Life of the 'Francisville Four,'" *Political Communication* 27(3), 289–309.

Anderson, C.W. 2011a. "Between Creative and Quantified Audiences: Web Metrics and Changing Patterns of Newswork in Local US Newsrooms." *Journalism* 12(5), 550–566.

Anderson, C.W. 2011b. *"What Aggregators Do."* Paper Presentation, Workshop on Social Media as Politics by Other Means. Rutgers University, April 11, 2011.

Andrews, Kenneth T., and Bob Edwards. 2004. "Advocacy Organizations in the U.S. Political Process." *Annual Review of Sociology* 30, 479–506.

Andrews, Kenneth T., Marshall Ganz, Matthew Baggetta, Hahrie Han, and Chaeyoon Lim. 2010. "Leadership, Membership, and Voice: Civic Associations That Work." *American Journal of Sociology* 115 (4), 1191–1242.

Anstead, Nick, and Andrew Chadwick. 2008. "Parties, Election Campaigning, and the Internet: Toward a Comparative Institutional Approach." In Andrew Chadwick and Philip Howard, eds., *Routledge Handbook of Internet Politics* (pp. 56–71). New York: Routledge Press.

Armstrong, Jerome, and Markos Moulitsas. 2007. *Crashing the Gates: Netroots, Grassroots, and the Rise of People-Powered Politics.* White River Junction, VT: Chelsea Green Publishing.

Arroyo, Adrian. February 23, 2010. "ActBlue and the Legislative Process." Retrieved from http://blog.actblue.com/blog/2010/02/actblue-and-the-public-option.html

Arroya, Adrian. January 27, 2011. "On the PCCC." Blog post, *ActBlue.com*. Retrieved from http://blog.actblue.com/blog/2011/01/pccc.html?utm_source=feedburner&utm_medium=feed&utm_campaign=Feed:+actblue+(The+ActBlue+Blog)

Bachrach, Peter, and Morton Baratz. 1962. "The Two Faces of Power." *American Political Science Review* 56 (4), 947–952.

Bai, Matthew. 2007. *The Argument: Billionaires, Bloggers, and the Battle to Remake Democratic Politics.* New York: Penguin Press.

Barabasi, Albert-Laszlo. 2003. *Linked.* New York: Plume Books.

Barber, Benjamin. 1984. *Strong Democracy: Participatory Politics for a New Age.* Berkeley, CA: University of California Press.

Barlow, John Perry. 1996. "A Declaration of Independence of Cyberspace." Retrieved from http://w2.eff.org/Censorship/Internet_censorship_bills/barlow_0296.declaration

Barringer, Felicity. April 22, 2004. "Establishment Candidates Defeat Challengers in Sierra Club Voting." *The New York Times.* Retrieved from http://www.nytimes.com/2004/04/22/us/establishment-candidates-defeat-challengers-in-sierra-club-voting.html

Barzilai-Nahon, Karine. 2008. "Toward a Theory of Network Gatekeeping: A Framework for Exploring Information Control," *Journal of the American Society for Information Science and Technology* 59 (9), 1493–1512.

Barzilai-Nahon, Karine, Jeff Helmsley, Shawn Walker, and Muzammil Hussain. 2011. "Fifteen Minutes of Fame: The Place of Blogs in the Life Cycle of Viral Political Information," *Policy & Internet* 3 (1), Article 2.

Barzilai-Nahon, Karine, and Jeff Helmsley. 2011. "Democracy.com: A Tale of Political Blogs and Content." 44th Hawaiian International Conference on System Sciences, Hawaii, January 2011.

Baumgertner, Frank, Jeffrey Berry, Marie Hojnacki, David Kimball, and Beth Leech. 2009. *Lobbying and Policy Change.* Chicago, IL: University of Chicago Press.

Baumgartner, Frank, and Bryan Jones. 1993. *Agendas and Instability in American Politics.* Chicago, IL: University of Chicago Press.

Baumgartner, Jody, and Jonathan Morris. 2010. "MyFaceTube Politics: Social Networking Websites and Political Engagement in Young Adults." *Social Science Computer Review* 28 (1), 24–44.

Bellantoni, Christina. July 24, 2010. "Conservative Counter-Event Boasts Bigger Size Than Netroots (But It's Not)." *Talking Points Memo.* Retrieved from http://tpmdc.talkingpointsmemo.com/2010/07/conservative-counter-event-boasts-bigger-size-than-netroots.php

Benkler, Yochai. 2006. *The Wealth of Networks.* New Haven, CT: Yale University Press.

Benkler, Yochai, and Aaron Shaw. 2010. "A Tale of Two Blogospheres: Discursive Practices on the Left and Right." Berkman Center for Internet & Society. Retrieved from http://cyber.law.harvard.edu/publications/2010/Tale_Two_Blogospheres_Discursive_Practices_Left_Right

Bennett, W. Lance. 2003. "Communicating Global Activism: Strengths and Vulnerabilities of Networked Politics." *Information, Communication, and Society* 6 (2), 143–168.

Bennett, W. Lance. 2004. "Global Media and Politics: Transnational Communication Regimes and Civic Cultures." *Annual Review of Political Science* 7, 125–148.

Bennett, W. Lance. 2008a. *News: The Politics of Illusion* (8th Edition). New York: Longman Publishing.

Bennett, W. Lance. 2008b. "Changing Citizenship in the Digital Age." In W.L. Bennett (Ed.), *Civic Life Online: Learning How Digital Media Can Engage Youth* (pp. 1–24). Cambridge, MA: MIT Press.

Bennett, W. Lance, Chris Wells, and Allison Rank. 2009. "Young Citizens and Civic Learning: Two Paradigms of Citizenship in the Digital Age." *Citizenship Studies* 13 (2), 105–120.

Berry, Jeffrey. 1984. *The Interest Group Society.* New York: Little, Brown.

Berry, Jeffrey. 1997. *The Interest Group Society* (3rd Edition). New York: Longman.

Berry, Jeffrey. 1999. *The New Liberalism*. Washington, DC: Brookings Institution Press.

Beutler, Brian. February 23, 2010. "How Outside Groups and Vulnerable Dems Gave the Public Option a New Pulse." *Talking Points Memo*. Retrieved from http://tpmdc.talkingpointsmemo.com/2010/02/how-outside-groups-and-vulnerable-dems-gave-the-public-option-a-new-pulse.php?ref=actblueblg

Bimber, Bruce. 2003. *Information and American Democracy*. Cambridge, UK: Cambridge University Press.

Bimber, Bruce, and Richard Davis. 2003. *Campaigning Online*. Oxford: Oxford University Press.

Bimber, Bruce, Andrew Flanagin, and Cynthia Stohl. 2005. "Reconceptualizing Collective Action in the Contemporary Media Environment." *Communication Theory* 15 (4), 365–388.

Blood, Rebecca. September 7, 2000. "Weblogs: A History and Perspective." *Rebecca's Pocket*. Retrieved from http://www.rebeccablood.net/essays/weblog_history.html

Bloom, Joel David, and Matthew Kerbel. 2006. "Campaign Blogs in 2004 and Beyond: The Care, Feeding and Harvesting of Online Communities of Supporters." Paper presentation at the 2006 annual meeting of the American Political Science Association, Philadelphia, PA.

Blumenthal, Mark. 2008. "The Poblano Model." *National Journal*. Retrieved from http://www.nationaljournal.com/njonline/mp_20080507_8254.php

Blumer, Herbert. 1948. "Polling and Public Opinion." *American Sociological Review* 13 (5), 542.

Bosso, Christopher. 2005. *Environment Inc: From Grassroots to Beltway*. Lawrence, KS: University Press of Kansas.

Boczkowski, Pablo. 2004. *Digitizing the News: Innovation in Online Newspapers*. Cambridge, MA: MIT Press.

Boczkowski, Pablo. 2010. *News at Work: Imitation in an Age of Information Abundance*. Chicago, IL: University of Chicago Press.

Bowers, Chris. June 29, 2011. "What Victory in Wisconsin Will Mean for All of Us." *DailyKos.com*. Retrieved from http://www.dailykos.com/story/2011/06/29/989875/-What-victory-in-Wisconsin-will-mean-for-all-of-us?via=search

Bowers, Chris, and Matthew Stoller. 2005. "The Emergence of the Progressive Blogosphere." Research report, *New Politics Institute*. Retrieved from http://ndn-newpol.civicactions.net/sites/ndn-newpol.civicactions.net/files/The-Emergence-of-the-Progressive-Blogosphere.pdf

boyd, danah. July 15, 2008. "Can the iPhone Hit Crucial Network Density for Noticeable Cluster Effects?" Blog post. Retrieved from: http://www.zephoria.org/thoughts/archives/2008/07/15/can_the_iphone.html

Boynton, Bob. April 2010. "Politics Moves to Twitter: How Big Is Big and Other Such Distributions." Paper presented at the Midwest Political Science Association Annual Meeting, Chicago, IL.

Breitbart, Andrew. March 30, 2009. "Online activists on the right, unite!" *Washington Times Online*. Retrieved from http://www.washingtontimes.com/news/2009/mar/30/rules-for-conservative-radicals/?page=2

Breitbart, Andrew. June 29, 2010. "Reward: $100,000 for the full 'JournoList' archive; Source fully protected." Blog post, Bigjournalism.com. Retrieved from http://bigjournalism.com/abreitbart/2010/06/29/reward-100000-for-full-journolist-archive-source-fully-protected/

Brewer, Jake. October 25, 2010. "The Tragedy of Political Advocacy." Blog post, *Huffington Post*. Retrieved from http://www.huffingtonpost.com/jake-brewer/the-tragedy-of-political_b_773734.html

Brookes, Julian. October 23, 2008. "An Interview with Erica Payne, Author of The Practical Progressive." *Huffington Post*. Retrieved from http://www.huffingtonpost.com/julian-brookes/an-interview-with-erica-p_b_137206.html

Bruns, Axel. 2008. *Blogs, Wikipedia, Second Life, and Beyond: From Production to Produsage*. New York: Peter Lang

Calderone, Michael. March 17, 2009. "JournoList: Inside the Echo Chamber." *Politico.com.* Retrieved from http://www.politico.com/news/stories/0309/20086.html

Carr, David. October 5, 2010. "At Sam Zell's Tribune, Tales of a Bankrupt Culture." *The New York Times.* Retrieved from http://www.nytimes.com/2010/10/06/business/media/06tribune.html

Castells, Manuel. 2009. *Communication Power.* New York: Oxford University Press.

Catanese, David. August 19, 2010a. "Liberty.com Aims to Top MoveOn." *Politico.com.* Retrieved from http://www.politico.com/news/stories/0810/41262.html

Catanese, David. August 20, 2010b. "MoveOn Unfazed By New Group." *Politico.com.* Retrieved from http://www.politico.com/news/stories/0810/41291.html

Chadwick, Andrew. 2006. *Internet Politics.* Oxford: Oxford University Press.

Chadwick, Andrew. 2007. "Digital Network Repertoires and Organizational Hybridity." *Political Communication* 24(3), pp. 283–301.

Chadwick, Andrew. 2011. "The Political Information Cycle in a Hybrid News System: The British Prime Minister and the 'Bullygate' Affair." *The International Journal of Press/Politics* 16(1), pp. 3–29.

Chait, Jonathan. June 28, 2010. "The Secrets of Journolist." Blog post, *The New Republic.* Retrieved from http://www.tnr.com/blog/jonathan-chait/75877/the-secrets-journolist

Chamberlain, Charles. March 2nd, 2011. "Wisconsin T.V. ad—Going on offense." Mass membership e-mail, Democracy for America.

Christensen, Clayton M. 1997. *The Innovator's Dilemma.* New York: Harper Business Books.

Cillizza, Chris. September 17, 2008. "Drudge-ology 101: McCain, Obama and Media Bias," in *Washington Post Online: The Fix.* Retrieved from http://voices.washingtonpost.com/the-fix/2008/09/drudge-ology_101_softening_tow.html?nav=rss_blog

Clark, Peter, and James Q. Wilson. 1961. "Incentive Systems: A Theory of Organizations." *Administrative Science Quarterly* 6, 219–266.

Clausing, Jeri. Jan. 8, 1999. "Anti-Impeachment Web Site Tallies Millions in Pledges," *New York Times.* Retrieved from http://emoglen.law.columbia.edu/CPC/archive/campaigns/move-on-website-gets-pledges.html

Clemens, Elisabeth. 1997. *The People's Lobby: Organizational Innovation and the Rise of Interest Group Politics in the United States, 1890–1925.* Chicago, IL: University of Chicago Press.

Coleman, Gabriella. April 6, 2011. "Anonymous: From the Lulz to Collective Action." Retrieved from http://mediacommons.futureofthebook.org/tne/pieces/anonymous-lulz-collective-action

Coleman, Gabriella, and Alex Golub. 2008. "Hacker Practice: Moral genres and the Cultural Articulation of Liberalism." *Anthropological Theory* 8 (3), 255–277.

Creed, Ryan. September 19, 2010. "Maher Airs Christine O'Donnell 'Witchcraft' Video." *ABC News Online.* Retrieved from http://abcnews.go.com/News/bill-maher-airs-christine-odonnell-witchcraft-video/story?id=11674862

Dahl, Robert. 1957. "The Concept of Power." *Behavioral Science* 2 (3), 201–215.

Dahl, Robert. 1961. *Who Governs?* New Haven, CT: Yale University Press

Davis, Richard. 2009. *Typing Politics.* New York: Oxford University Press.

De Tocqueville, Alexis. 1840. *Democracy in America.* Garden City, NY: Doubleday Books.

Dewey, John. 1927. *The Public and Its Problems.* Athens, OH: Swallow Press.

Diani, Mario. 2000. "Social Movement Networks Virtual and Real." *Information, Communication and Society* 3 (3), 386–401.

Dimaggio, Paul, and Walter Powell. 1983. "The Iron Cage Revisited: Institutional Isomorphism and Collective Rationality in Organizational Fields." *American Sociological Review* 48, 147–160.

Downie, Len, and Michael Schudson. October 19, 2009. "The Reconstruction of American Journalism." *Columbia Journalism Review.* Retrieved from http://www.cjr.org/reconstruction/the_reconstruction_of_american.php?page=1

Dreier, Peter, and Christopher R. Martin. 2010. "How ACORN Was Framed: Political Controversy and Media Agenda Setting." *Perspectives on Politics* 8, (3), 761–792.

Drezner, Daniel, and Henry Farrell. 2008. "The Power and Politics of Blogs." *Public Choice* 134 (1–2), 15–30.

Dulio, David. 2004. *For Better or Worse? How Political Consultants are Changing Election in the United States.* Albany, NY: SUNY Press

Earl, Jennfer. 2010. "Dynamics of Protest-Related Diffusion on the Web." *Information, Communication, & Society* 13 (2), 209–225.

Earl, Jennifer, Katrina Kimport, Greg Prieto, Carly Rush, and Kimberly Reynoso. 2010. "Changing the World One Webpage at a Time: Conceptualizing and Explaining Internet Activism." *Mobilization* 15 (4), 425–446.

Earl, Jennifer, and Katrina Kimport. 2011. *Digitally Enabled Social Change.* Cambridge, MA: MIT Press.

Edsall, Thomas. August 7, 2005. "Rich Liberals Vow to Fund Think Tanks." *Washington Post.* Retrieved from http://www.washingtonpost.com/wp-dyn/content/article/2005/08/06/AR2005080600848.html

Entman, Robert. 1989. *Democracy without Citizens.* New York: Oxford University Press.

Epp, Charles R. 1998. *The Rights Revolution: Lawyers, Activists, and Supreme Courts in Comparative Perspective.* Chicago, IL: University of Chicago Press.

Etling, Bruce, John Kelly, Robert Faris, and John Palfrey. 2010. "Mapping the Arabic Blogosphere: Politics and Dissent Online." *New Media & Society* 12, 1225–1243.

Exley, Zack. 2007a. "Can the Internets Make Me President?" Blog post. Retrieved from http://www.neworganizing.com/wiki/index.php/Can_the_Internets_make_me_president%3F

Exley, Zack. July 12, 2007b. "A New Kind of Nonprofit." Blog post, *ZackExley.com.* Retrieved from http://zackexley.com/category/new-organizing-institute/

Fallows, James. July 21, 2010. "On Today's Hot Media Stories." *Atlantic.com.* Retrieved from http://www.theatlantic.com/politics/archive/2010/07/on-todays-hot-media-stories-sherrod/60210/

Farrell, David. 2011. *Electoral Systems: A Comparative Introduction* (2nd Edition). New York: Palgrave MacMillan.

Faris, David. September 2008. "Revolutions without Revolutionaries? Network Theory, Facebook, and the Egyptian Blogosphere." *Arab Media & Society* 6, 1–11.

Fenno, Richard. 1978. *Home Style: House Members in Their Districts.* New York: Little, Brown.

Fine, Allison. 2006. *Momentum: Igniting Social Change in the Connected Age.* San Francisco, CA: Jossey-Bass.

Fine, Allison, Micah Sifry, Andrew Rasiej, and Joshua Levy. 2008. *Rebooting Democracy.* New York: Personal Democracy Forum.

Fiorina, Morris. 1999. "Extreme Voices: A Dark Side of Civic Engagement." In Skocpol and Fiorina (Eds.), *Civic Engagement in American Democracy* (pp. 395–426). Washington, DC: Brookings Institution Press.

Fiorina, Morris, Samuel Abrams, and Jeremy Pope. 2005. *Culture War? The Myth of a Polarized America.* New York: Longman.

Fisher, Dana. 2006. *Activism, Inc.* Stanford, CA: Stanford University Press.

Flannery, Helen, and Rob Harris. 2007. "2006 donorCentrics™ Internet Giving Benchmarking Analysis." *Target Analysis Group, Inc.* Retrieved from www.targetanalysis.com

Flannery, Helen, Rob Harris, and Carol Rhine. 2008. "Index of National Fundraising Performance" *Target Analytics.* Retrieved from www.targetanalysis.com

Foot, Kirsten, and Steven Schneider. 2006. *Web Campaigning.* Cambridge, MA: MIT Press.

Fullenwider, Kyla. 2010. "Q&A: A West Point for Community Organizers." *Good Magazine.* Retrieved from http://www.good.is/post/q-a-a-west-point-for-community-organizing/

Galvin, Daniel. 2010. *Presidential Party Building: Dwight D. Eisenhower to George W. Bush.* Princeton, NJ: Princeton University Press.

Gans, Herber, 2004. *Deciding What's News: A Study of CBS Evening News, NBC Nightly News, Newsweek and Time.* Evanston, IL: Northwestern University Press.

Ganz, Marshall. 2009. *Why David Sometimes Wins: Leadership, Organization, and Strategy in the California Farm Worker Movement.* New York: Oxford University Press.

Gibson, Rachel, and Andrea Rommele. 2001. "Changing Campaign Communications: A Party-Centered Theory of Professionalized Campaigning." *Harvard International Journal of Press/Politics* 6 (4), 31–43.

Gil de Zúñiga, Homero, Eulàlia Puig-i-Abril, and Hernando Rojas. 2009. "Weblogs, Traditional Sources Online and Political Participation: An Assessment of How the Internet Is Changing the Political Environment." *New Media & Society* 11 (4), 553–574.

Gillmor, Dan. 2006. *We the Media: Grassroots Journalism For the People, By the People.* Sebastopol, CA: O'Reilly Media.

Gillmor, Dan. 2010. *Mediactive.* New York: Creative Commons. Retrieved from http://mediactive.com/book/

Gladwell, Malcolm. October 4, 2010. "Small Change: Why the Revolution Will Not Be Tweeted." *The New Yorker.* Retrieved from http://www.newyorker.com/reporting/2010/10/04/101004fa_fact_gladwell?currentPage=all

Gong, Abe. 2011. "An Automated Snowball Census of the Political Web." Paper Presentation at JITP Conference on "The Future of Computational Social Science." May 16, University of Washington, Seattle.

Gosnell, Harold. 1927. *Getting-Out-the-Vote: An Experiment in the Stimulation of Voting.* Chicago, IL: University of Chicago Press.

Granovetter, Mark. 1973. "The Strength of Weak Ties." *American Journal of Sociology* 78 (6), 1360–1380.

Gray, Virginia, and David Lowery. 1996. *The Population Ecology of Interest Representation: Lobbying Communities in the American States.* Ann Arbor, MI: University of Michigan Press.

Gray, Virginia, and David Lowery. 1997. "Life in a Niche: Mortality Anxiety among Organized Interests in the American States." *Political Research Quarterly* 50 (1), 25–47.

Green, Adam. April 9, 2009. "Profiles in Bad Online Organizing: Part 1 (DSCC)." Blog post, *OpenLeft.com.* Retrieved from http://www.openleft.com/diary/12745/profiles-in-bad-online-organizing-part-1-dscc

Green, Donald, and Alan Gerber. 2000. "The Effects of Canvassing, Telephone Calls, and Direct Mail on Voter Turnout: A Field Experiment." *American Political Science Review* 94 (3), 653–663.

Green, Don, and Alan Gerber. 2004. *Get Out the Vote! How to Increase Voter Turnout.* Washington, DC: Brookings Press.

Green, John, Mark Rozell, and Clyde Wilcox (Eds.). 2003. *The Christian Right in American Politics: Marching to the Millennium.* Washington, DC: Georgetown University Press.

Grossman, Lev. December 19, 2004. "Blogs Have Their Day." *Time Magazine.* Retrieved from http://www.time.com/time/subscriber/personoftheyear/2004/poyblogger.html

Gueorguieva, Vassia. 2008. "Voters, MySpace, and YouTube: The Impact of Alternative Communication Channels on the 2006 Election Cycle and Beyond." *Social Science Computer Review* 26 (3), 288.

Gulati, Girish, and Christine Williams. 2007. "Closing the Gap, Raising the Bar: Candidate Web Site Communication in the 2006 Campaigns for Congrtess." *Social Science Computer Review* 25 (4), 443–465.

Gulati, Girish, and Christine Williams. 2010. "Congressional Candidates' Use of YouTube in 2008: Its Frequency and Rationale," *Journal of Information Technology & Politics* 7 (2–3), 93–109.

Habermas, Jurgen. 1989. *The Structural Transformation of the Public Sphere.* Cambridge: Polity Press.

Hacker, Jacob, and Paul Pierson. 2010. *Winner-Take-All Politics: How Washington Made the Rich Richer—and Turned Its Back on the Middle Class.* New York: Simon and Schuster.

Hamilton, James. 2004. *All the News That's Fit to Sell*. Princeton, NJ: Princeton University Press.

Hamilton, Alexander, James Madison, and John Jay. 1787. *The Federalist Papers*. New York: Soho Books.

Hampton, Keith, Lauren Sessions, Eun Ja Her, and Lee Rainie. 2009. "Social Isolation and New Technology." *Pew Internet & American Life Project*. Retrieved from http://www.pewinternet.org/~/media//Files/Reports/2009/PIP_Tech_and_Social_Isolation.pdf

Hara, Noriko. 2008. "Internet Use for Political Mobilization: Voices of Participants." *First Monday* 13 (7). Retrieved from http://firstmonday.org/htbin/cgiwrap/bin/ojs/index.php/fm/rt/printerFriendly/2123/1976

Hargattai, Eszter. 2008. "The Digital Reproduction of Inequality." In David Grusky (Ed.), *Social Stratification* (pp. 936–944). Boulder, CO: Westview Press.

Harkinson, Josh. August 2007. "RightOn: Conservative Netroots." *Mother Jones*, 34–35.

Harnden, Tom. July 18, 2008. "John McCain 'Technology Illiterate' Doesn't Email or Use Internet." *London Telegraph*. Retrieved from http://www.telegraph.co.uk/news/newstopics/uselection2008/johnmccain/2403704/John-McCain-technology-illiterate-doesnt-email-or-use-internet.html

Hayes, Chris. February 25, 2010. "CPR for the Public Option." *The Nation*. Retrieved from http://www.thenation.com/article/cpr-public-option

Hayward, Allison. 2008. "Is That a Bundle in Your Pocket, Or?. . ." *The Forum* 6 (1), Article 12. Retrieved from http://www.bepress.com/forum/vol6/iss1/art12/

Heaney, Michael, and Fabio Rojas. 2007. "Partisans, Nonpartisans, and the Antiwar Movement in the United States." *American Politics Research* 35, 431–464.

Henke, Jon. June 3, 2008. "The Online Right." Blog post. Retrieved from http://thenextright.com/jon-henke/the-online-right

Herbst, Susan. 1998. *Reading Public Opinion: How Political Actors View the Democratic Process*. New York: Cambridge University Press.

Hindman, Matthew, Kostas Tsioutsiouliklis, and Judy Johnson. March 2003. "'Googlearchy': How a Few Heavily-Linked Sites Dominate Politics on the Web." Paper presented at the Annual Meeting of the Midwest Political Science Association, Chicago, IL.

Hindman, Matthew. 2005. "The Real Lessons of Howard Dean: Reflections on the First Digital Campaign." *Perspectives on Politics* 3 (1), 121–128.

Hindman, Matthew. 2007. "'Open-Source Politics' Reconsidered: Emerging Patterns in Online Political Participation." In Viktor Mayer-Schonberger and David Lazer (Eds.), *Governance and Information Technology: From Electronic Government to Information Government* (pp. 183–207). Cambridge, MA: MIT Press.

Hindman, Matthew. 2008. *The Myth of Digital Democracy*. Princeton, NJ: Princeton University Press.

Hofstadter, Richard. November 1964. "The Paranoid Style in American Politics." *Harper's Magazine*, 77–86.

Hohman, James. February 26, 2011. "Daniels Defends Labor Position." *Politico.com*. Retrieved from http://www.politico.com/news/stories/0211/50248.html

Howard, Philip N. 2005. "Deep Democracy, Thin Citizenship: The Impact of Digital Media in Political Campaign Strategy." *Annals of the American Academy of Political and Social Science* 597, 153–170.

Howard, Philip N. 2006. *New Media and the Managed Citizen*. New York: Cambridge University Press.

Howard, Philip N. 2010. *The Digital Origins of Dictatorship and Democracy*. New York: Oxford University Press.

Jamieson, Kathleen Hall, and Joseph Cappella. 2010. *Echo Chamber: Rush Limbaugh and the Conservative Media Establishment*. New York: Oxford University Press.

Jenkins, Henry. 2006. *Convergence Culture: Where Old and New Media Collide*. New York: NYU Press.

Jones, Sidney. May 22, 2009. "Online Classifieds" Survey Report, Pew Internet and American Life Project. Retrieved from http://pewinternet.org/Reports/2009/7—Online-Classifieds.aspx?r=1

Kahn, Richard, and Douglass Kellner. 2004. "New Media and Internet Activism: From the Battle of Seattle to Blogging." *New Media and Society* 6, 87–95.

Kamarck, Elaine. 2006. "Assessing Howard Dean's Fifty State Strategy and the 2006 Midterm Elections," *The Forum* 4 (3). Retrieved from http://www.bepress.com/forum/vol4/iss3/art5

Kane, Paul, and Jonathan Weisman. January 20, 2008. "A Conservative Answer to MoveOn: Political Advocacy Group Formed by Former Bush Aides Plans a Broad Agenda." *The Washington Post*, A05. Retrieved from http://www.washingtonpost.com/wp-dyn/content/article/2008/01/19/AR2008011902309_pf.html

Kanter, Beth, and Allison Fine. 2010. *The Networked Nonprofit*. San Francisco, CA: Jossey-Bass.

Karpf, David. 2008a. "Measuring Influence in the Political Blogosphere." *Politics and Technology Review*, George Washington University's Institute for Politics, Democracy, & the Internet, 33–41.

Karpf, David. 2008b. "Understanding Blogspace." *Journal of Information Technology and Politics* 5 (4), 369–385.

Karpf, David. January 17, 2009a. "Obama Unveils 'Organizing for America'. Hold onto Your Hats, This Just Got Interesting." Blog post, *ShoutingLoudly.com*. Retrieved from http://www.shoutingloudly.com/2009/01/17/obama-unveils-organizing-for-america-hold-onto-your-hats-this-just-got-interesting/

Karpf, David. May 20, 2009b. "A Few Things Political Scientists Need to Stop Getting Wrong about the Political Blogosphere." Blog post, *ShoutingLoudly.com*. Retrieved from http://www.shoutingloudly.com/2009/05/20/a-few-things-political-scientists-need-to-stop-getting-wrong-about-the-blogosphere/

Karpf, David. 2010a. "Macaca Moments Reconsidered: Electoral Panopticon or Netroots Mobilization?" *Journal of Information Technology and Politics* 7 (2), 143–162.

Karpf, David. 2010b. "Online Political Mobilization from the Advocacy Group's Perspective: Looking Beyond Clicktivism." *Policy & Internet* 2 (4). Retrieved from http://www.psocommons.org/policyandinternet/vol2/iss4/art2/

Karpf, David. September 2010c. "Beyond Citizen Journalism: Weigelgate, JournoList, and the Shifting Media Ecology of America." Paper presentation, American Political Science Association Annual Meeting. Washington, DC.

Karpf, David. 2011a. "Implications of the Mobile Web for Online-Offline Reputation Systems." *IEEE Intelligent Systems* 26 (1), 40–47.

Karpf, David. 2011b. "Open Source Political Community Development: A Five-Stage Adoption Process." *Journal of Information Technology and Politics* 8 (3), 323–345.

Kee, Tameka. April 27, 2009. "Yelp Closes Traffic Gap with CitySearch." Blog post. Retrieved from http://www.paidcontent.org/entry/419-yelp-closes-the-traffic-gap-with-citysearch

Kelty, Chris. 2008. *Two Bits: The Cultural Significance of Free Software*. Durham, NC: Duke University Press.

Kerbel, Matthew. 2009. *Netroots: Online Progressives and the Transformation of American Politics*. Boulder, CO: Paradigm Publishers.

Kerbel, Matthew, and Joel David Bloom. 2005. "Blog for America and Civic Involvement." *Harvard International Journal of Press/Politics* 10 (3), 3–27.

Key, V.O. 1958. *Politics, Parties, and Pressure Groups* (4th Edition). New York: Crowell.

Kingdon, John. 1984. *Agendas, Alternatives, and Public Policy*. New York: Longman Publishers.

Klein, Ezra. June 25, 2010. "On JournoList, and Dave Weigel." *WashingtonPost.com*. Retrieved from http://voices.washingtonpost.com/ezra-klein/2010/06/on_journolist_and_dave_weigel.html

Klein, Joe. July 22, 2010. "On Journolist." Blog post, *Time.com*. Retrieved from http://swampland.blogs.time.com/2010/07/22/on-journolist/

Klein, Kim. 1994. *Fundraising for Social Change* (3rd Edition). Berkeley, CA: Chardon Press.

Klotz, Robert J. 2004. *The Politics of Internet Communication*. Lanham, MD: Rowman and Littlefield.

Klotz, Robert. 2010. "The Sidetracked 2008 YouTube Senate Election." *Journal of Information Technology and Politics* 7 (2–3), 110–123.

Kranzberg, Melvin. 1986. "Technology and History: 'Kranzberg's Laws.'" *Technology and Culture* 27 (3), 544–560.

Kreiss, Daniel. Forthcoming. *Taking Our Country Back: The Crafting of Networked Politics from Howard Dean to Barack Obama.* New York: Oxford University Press.

Kristol, William. February 11, 2008. "Obama's Path to Victory." *The New York Times.* Retrieved from http://www.nytimes.com/2008/02/11/opinion/11kristol.html?_r=1

Lampe, Cliff, and Eric Johnston. November 2005. "Follow the (Slash) dot: Effects of Feedback on New Members in an Online Community." Proceedings of the International Conference on Supporting Group Work, GROUP '05, Sanibel Island, FL.

Lawrence, Regina. 2000. *The Politics of Force: Media and the Construction of Police Brutality.* Berkeley, CA: University of California Press.

Lawrence, Eric, John Sides, and Henry Farrell. 2010. "Self-Segregation or Deliberation? Blog Readership, Participation and Polarization in American Politics." *Perspectives on Politics* 8 (1), 141–157.

Lee, Caroline W. 2010. "The Roots of Astroturfing." *Contexts* 9 (1), 73–75.

Lee, Taeku. 2002. *Mobilizing Public Opinion: Black Insurgency and Racial Attitudes in the Civil Rights Era.* Chicago, IL: University of Chicago Press.

Lessig, Lawrence. 2009. *Remix: Making Art and Commerce Thrive in the Hybrid Economy.* New York: Penguin Books.

Lev-On, Azi, and Russell Hardin. 2007. "Internet-based Collaborations and Their Political Significance." *Journal of Information Technology and Politics* 4 (2), 5–27.

Lih, Andrew. 2009. *The Wikipedia Revolution.* New York: Hyperion Books

Limbaugh, Rush. 2008. "Chaos Hijacks Democrat Primary." Blog post. Retrieved from http://www.rushlimbaugh.com/home/daily/site_050508/content/01125108.guest.html

Livingston, Steven, and W. Lance Bennett. 2003. "Gatekeeping, Indexing, and Live-Event News: Is Technology Altering the Construction of News?" *Political Communication* 20, 363–380.

Lizza, Ryan. April 24, 2006. "George Allen's Race Problem." *The New Republic.* Retrieved from http://www.tnr.com/article/george-allens-race-problem

Lovink, Geert. 2007. *Zero Comments.* New York: Routledge Press.

Lowery, David, and Virginia Gray. 2004. "A Neopluralist Perspective on Research on Organized Interests." *Political Research Quarterly* 57 (1), 163–175.

Lowery, David, Virginia Gray, Jennifer Wolak, Erik Godwin, and Whitt Kilburn. 2005. "Reconsidering the Counter-Mobilization Hypothesis: Health Policy Lobbying In the American States." *Political Behavior* 27 (2), 99–132.

Lowi, Theodore. 1979. *The End of Liberalism.* New York: Norton.

Luntz, Frank. 1988. *Candidates, Consultants, and Campaigns.* Boston, MA: Blackwell Press.

Luo, Michael. April 12, 2008. "Great Expectations for a Conservative Group Seem All but Dashed." *The New York Times.* Retrieved from http://www.nytimes.com/2008/04/12/us/politics/12freedom.html?_r=1

Lupia, Arthur, and Gisella Sin. 2003. "Which Public Goods Are Endangered?: How Evolving Communication Technologies Affect the Logic of Collective Action" *Public Choice* 117 (3–4), 315–331.

Margolis, Michael, and David Resnick. 2000. *Politics as Usual: The Cyberspace "Revolution."* New York: Sage Press.

Marwell, Gerald, and Pam Oliver. 1993. *The Critical Mass in Collective Action: A Micro-social Theory.* New York: Cambridge University Press.

Masket, Seth. 2011. *No Middle Ground: How Informal Party Organizations Control Nominations and Polarize Legislatures.* Ann Arbor, MI: University of Michigan Press.

Mayer, Jane. August 30, 2010. "Cover Operations: The Billionaire Brothers Who Are Waging a War Against Obama." *The New Yorker.* Retrieved from http://www.newyorker.com/reporting/2010/08/30/100830fa_fact_mayer

Mayhew, David. 1974. *Congress: The Electoral Connection.* New Haven, CT: Yale University Press.

McAdam, Doug. 1990. *Freedom Summer.* New York: Oxford University Press.

McAdam, Doug. 1999. *Political Process and the Development of Black Insurgency, 1930–1970.* Chicago, IL: University of Chicago Press.

McAdam, Doug, Sidney Tarrow, and Charles Tilly. 2001. *Dynamics of Contention.* New York: Cambridge University Press.

McCaughey, Martha, and Michael Ayers. 2003. *Cyberactivism: Online Activism in Theory and Practice.* New York: Routledge.

McChesney, Robert, and Victor Pickard. 2011. *Will the Last Reporter Please Turn Out the Lights: The Collapse of Journalism and What Can Be Done to Fix It.* New York: The New Press.

McGirr, Lisa. 2001. *Suburban Warriors.* Princeton, NJ: Princeton University Press.

Medvic, Stephen. 2001. *Political Consultants in U.S. Congressional Elections.* Columbus, OH: Ohio State University Press.

Melber, Ari. 2010. "Year One of Organizing for America: The Permanent Field Campaign in a Digital Age." *Personal Democracy Forum.* Retrieved from http://techpresident.com/files/report_Year_One_of_Organizing_for_America_Melber.pdf

Merry, Melissa. 2010. "Blogging and Environmental Advocacy: A New Way to Engage the Public?" *Review of Policy Research* 27 (5), 641–656.

Meyer, David, and Douglas Imig. 1993. "Political Opportunity and the Rise and Decline of Interest Group Sectors." *Social Science Journal* 30 (3), 253–271.

Minkoff, Debra, Silke Aisenbrey, and Jon Agnone. 2008. "Organizational Diversity in the U.S. Advocacy Sector." *Social Problems,* 55 (4), 525–548.

Monitor Institute. April 2011. "Disruption: Evolving Models of Engagement and Support. A National Study of Member-Based Advocacy Groups." Retrieved from http://www.monitorinstitute.com/disruption/

Montgomery, Jacob, and Brendan Nyhan. June 2010. *"The Party Edge: Consultant-Candidate Networks in American Political Parties."* Proceedings of the 2010 Political Networks Conference, Duke University, Durham, NC.

Morozov, Evgeny. May 19, 2009. "The Brave New World of Slacktivism." *Foreign Policy.* Retrieved from http://neteffect.foreignpolicy.com/posts/2009/05/19/the_brave_new_world_of_slacktivism

Morozov, Evgeny. 2011. *The Net Delusion: How Not to Liberate the World.* New York: Penguin Press.

Morrison, Aimee Hope. 2011. "An Impossible Future: John Perry Barlow's 'Declaration of the Independence of Cyberspace'" *New Media & Society* 11 (1–2), 53–71.

Mosk, Matthew. March 11, 2007. "Donations Pooled Online Are Getting Candidates' Attention." *Washington Post.* Retrieved from http://www.washingtonpost.com/wp-dyn/content/article/2007/03/10/AR2007031001185_pf.html

Moulitsas, Markos. 2007. "Keynote Address: YearlyKos convention." Retrieved from http://www.youtube.com/watch?v=5jLuke2KBik

Moulitsas, Markos. 2008. *Taking on the System.* New York: Penguin Group.

Moulitsas, Markos. February 7, 2011a. "DLC Is Done." *Dailykos.com.* Retrieved from http://www.dailykos.com/story/2011/02/07/941918/-DLC-is-done?via=search

Moulitsas, Markos. June 9, 2011b. "DK4 Update and Response to More Community Concerns." Blog post, *DailyKos.com.* Retrieved from http://www.dailykos.com/story/2011/01/09/934528/-DK4-update-and-responses-to-more-community-concerns

MoveOn Staff. December 2008. "MoveOn Post-Election Report." Retrieved from http://s3.moveon.org/pdfs/moveon_postelectionreport_ah14.pdf

Murakami, Michael. 2008. "Divisive Primaries: Party Organizations, Ideological Groups, and the Battle over Party Purity." *PS: Political Science & Politics* 41 (4), 918–923.

Mutz, Diana. 2002. "Cross-Cutting Social Networks: Testing Democratic Theory in Practice." *American Political Science Review* 96 (2), 111–126.

Mutz, Diana. 2006. *Hearing the Other Side: Deliberative Versus Participatory Democracy.* New York: Cambridge University Press.

Nagel, Jack H. 1975. *The Descriptive Analysis of Power*. New Haven, CT: Yale University Press.

Nagel, Jack H. 1987. *Participation*. Englewood Cliffs, NJ: Prentice Hall.

Napoli, Phillip. 2010. *Audience Evolution: New Technologies and the Transformation of Media Audiences*. New York: Columbia University Press.

Neuman, W. Russell. 1986. *The Paradox of Mass Politics*. Cambridge, MA: Harvard University Press.

Nichols, Jon. December 30, 2010. "Slide Show: Progressive Honor Roll." *The Nation*. Retrieved from http://www.thenation.com/slideshow/157350/slide-show-progressive-honor-roll-2010

Nielsen, Rasmus Kleis. 2009. "The Labors of Internet-Assisted Activism: Overcommunication, Miscommunication, and Communication Overload. *Journal of Information Technology & Politics* 6 (3), 267–280.

Nielsen, Rasmus Kleis. 2011. "Mundane Internet Tools, Mobilizing Practices, and the Coproduction of Citizenship in Political Campaigns." *New Media and Society* 13, 755–771.

Nielsen, Rasmus Kleis. 2012. *Ground Wars*. Princeton, NJ: Princeton University Press.

Nielsen, Rasmus Kleis, and Cristian Vaccari. "Twitter in the Midterms." *Rasmuskleisnielsen.net*. Retrieved from http://rasmuskleisnielsen.net/2010/11/15/twitter-in-the-midterms/

Norris, Pippa. 2001. *Digital Divide: Civic Engagement, Information Poverty, and the Internet Worldwide*. New York: Cambridge University Press.

Odom, Eric. September 2, 2010. "Let's Get This New TV Ad Slamming Harry Reid on the Air." Mass e-mail correspondence. Accessible through MCP dataset.

Odom, Eric. February 8, 2011a. "The Oath to 'Support and defend the Constitution.'" Mass e-mail correspondence. Accessible through MCP dataset.

Odom, Eric. February 14, 2011b. "Happy Valentine's Day! Unless You Live in Iran. . . . " Mass e-mail correspondence. Accessible through MCP dataset.

Olson, Mancur. 1965. *The Logic of Collective Action*. Cambridge, MA: Harvard University Press.

Orren, Karen, and Stephen Skowronek. 2004. *The Search for American Political Development*. New York: Cambridge University Press.

Paquet, Sebastian. October 9, 2002. "Making Group-Forming Ridiculously Easy." Blog post. Retrieved from http://radio.weblogs.com/0110772/2002/10/09.html

Patel, Mary F. February 13, 2008a. "Pyramid Scheming." *Philadelphia City Paper*. Retrieved from http://citypaper.net/articles/2008/02/14/pyramid-scheming

Patel, Mary F. March 5, 2008b. "Doc v Farnese v Dicker v Fumo." *Philadelphia City Paper*. Retrieved from http://citypaper.net/articles/2008/03/06/doc-v-farnese-v-dicker-v-fumo

Payne, Erica. 2008. *The Practical Progressive: How to Build a Twenty-First Century Political Movement*. New York: Public Affairs.

Pearce, Seth. 2008. "Daniel Mintz Is Living Liberally." Blog post. Retrieved from http://livingliberally.org/talking-liberally/blog/Daniel-Mintz-Living-Liberally

Perlmutter, David. 2008. *Blog Wars*. New York: Oxford University Press.

Perlstein, Rick. 2001. *Before the Storm: Barry Goldwater and the Unmaking of the American Consensus*. New York: Nation Books.

Pierson, Paul. 2004. *Politics in Time: History, Institutions, and Social Analysis*. Princeton, NJ: Princeton University Press.

Pinto, Nick. January 18, 2007. "Drinking Liberally: A New Strategy for Progressive Politics." *AlterNet.org*. Retrieved from http://www.alternet.org/story/46614/?page=entire

Piore, Michael, and Charles Sabel. 1984. *The Second Industrial Divide: Possibilities for Prosperity*. New York: Basic Books.

Pole, Antoinette. 2009. *Blogging the Political: Politics and Participation in a Networked Society*. New York: Routledge Press.

Porter, Noah. 2007. "Real Challenges, Virtual Challengers: The Democracy for America Movement." Doctoral Dissertation, University of South Florida. Retrieved from http://gradworks.umi.com/3292528.pdf

Powell, Walter W. 1990. "Neither Market nor Hierarchy: Network Forms of Organization." *Research in Organizational Behavior* 12, 295–336.

Prior, Markus. 2007. *Post-Broadcast Democracy: How Media Choice Increases Inequality in Political Involvement and Polarizes Elections*. New York: Cambridge University Press.

Putnam, Robert. 2000. *Bowling Alone: The Collapse and Revival of American Community*. New York: Simon and Schuster.

Ratcliffe, Mitch, and Jon Lebkowsky (Eds.). 2005. *Extreme Democracy*. Creative Commons: Lulu.com.

Reagle, Joseph. 2010. *Good Faith Collaboration: The Culture of Wikipedia*. Cambridge, MA: MIT Press.

Resnick, Paul, Richard Zeckhauser, John Swanson, and Kate Lockwood. 2006. "The Value of Reputation on eBay: A Controlled Experiment." *Experimental Economics* 9, 79–101.

Rheingold, Howard. 2000. *The Virtual Community: Homesteading on the Electronic Frontier* (2nd Edition). Cambridge, MA: MIT Press.

Rheingold, Howard. 2003 *Smart Mobs: The Next Social Revolution*. Cambridge, MA: Basic Books.

Riker, William. 1964. "Some Ambiguities in the Notion of Power." *American Political Science Review* 58 (20), 341–349.

Rosenberg, Gerald. 1991. *The Hollow Hope: Can Courts Bring About Social Change?* Chicago, IL: University of Chicago Press.

Rosenstone, Steven, and John Mark Hansen. 1993. *Mobilization, Participation, and Democracy in America*. New York: Longman Classics.

Rozell, Mark, and Clyde Wilcox (Eds.). 1995. *God at the Grassroots: The Christian Right in the 1994 Elections*. Lanham, MD: Rowman & Littlefield.

Ruffini, Patrick. 2008. "Change Won't Come From the Top Down." Blog Post, *TheNextRight.com*. Retrieved from http://www.thenextright.com/patrick-ruffini/change-wont-come-from-the-top-down

Ruffini, Patrick. September 17, 2009. "Rising Rightroots and Declining Netroots Now at Parity (or Better)." Blog post, *TheNextRight.com*. Retrieved from http://www.thenextright.com/patrick-ruffini/rising-rightroots-and-declining-netroots-now-at-parity-or-better

Ruffini, Patrick. September 28, 2010. "Why the Right Is Winning Online in 2010." Blog post, *TheNextRight.com*. Retrieved from http://thenextright.com/patrick-ruffini/why-the-right-is-winning-online-in-2010

Rushkoff, Douglass. 2003. *Open Source Democracy: How Online Communication Is Changing Offline Politics*. New York, NY: Demos Press.

Sabato, Larry. 1981. *The Rise of Political Consultants*. New York: Basic Books.

Salisbury, Robert. 1969. "An Exchange Theory of Interest Groups." *Midwest Journal of Political Science* 13 (1), 1–32.

Sargent, Greg. July 22, 2010. "Tucker Carlson: We Will Not Publish Full J-List Emails." Blog post, *WashingtonPost.com*. Retrieved from http://voices.washingtonpost.com/plumline/2010/07/tucker_carlson_we_will_not_pub.html

Schattschneider, E.E. 1960. *The SemiSovereign People*. Orlando, FL: Harcourt, Brace, Jovanovich Publishers.

Schatz, Amy. September 28, 2007. "Local Politics, Web Money." *The Wall Street Journal*. Retrieved from http://online.wsj.com/public/article/SB119092762951941696.html#

Scherer, Michael. June 22, 2006. "Bloggers' double-super-secret smoky room." *Salon.com*. Retrieved from http://www.salon.com/news/politics/war_room/2006/06/22/townhouse/index.html

Schlozman, Kay Lehmann, Sidney Verba, and Henry Brady. 2010. "Weapon of the Strong? Participatory Inequality and the Internet." *Perspectives on Politics* 8 (2), 487–509.

Schudson, Michael, 1998. *The Good Citizen*. Cambridge, MA: Harvard University Press.

Schulman, Daniel. July/August 2007. "Politics 2.0: Fight Different." *Mother Jones*. Retrieved from http://motherjones.com/politics/2007/06/politics-20-fight-different

Shirky, Clay. 2003. "Power Laws, Weblogs, and Inequality." Reprinted in Ratcliffe and Lebkowsky (Eds.), *Extreme Democracy*. 2005. Stanford, CA: Creative Commons. Retrieved from http://extremedemocracy.com

Shirky, Clay 2004. "Exiting Deanspace." Reprinted in Ratcliffe and Lebkowsky (Eds.), *Extreme Democracy*. 2005. Stanford, CA: Creative Commons. Retrieved from http://extremedemocracy.com

Shirky, Clay. 2008. *Here Comes Everybody: The Power of Organizing without Organizations*. New York: Penguin Press.

Shirky, Clay. 2009. "Newspapers and Thinking the Unthinkable." Blog post. Retrieved from http://www.shirky.com/weblog/2009/03/newspapers-and-thinking-the-unthinkable/

Shirky, Clay. 2011. "Why We Need the New News Environment To Be Chaotic." Blog post. Retrieved from http://www.shirky.com/weblog/2011/07/we-need-the-new-news-environment-to-be-chaotic/

Shulman, Stuart. 2009. "The Case Against Mass E-mails: Perverse Incentives and low Quality Public Participation in U.S. Federal Rulemaking." *Policy & Internet* 1 (1), 23–53.

Sides, John, and Henry Farrell. 2011. "The Kos Bump: The Political Economy of Campaign Fundraising in the Internet Age." Paper Presentation, Midwest Political Science Association Annual Meeting, Chicago IL.

Sifry, Micah. August 2, 2006. "RightRoots vs Netroots?" Blog post. Retrieved from http://www.personaldemocracy.com/node/973

Sifry, Micah. December 30, 2010a. "Interview: Jascha Franklin-Hodge, Blue State Digital Partner, on Being Acquired by Global Giant WPP." *TechPresident.com*. Retrieved from http://techpresident.com/blog-entry/interview-jascha-franklin-hodge-blue-state-digital-partner-being-acquired-global-giant-wp

Sifry, Micah. September 25, 2010(b). "Tea Party vs Netroots; Rs vs Ds: Whose Online Base is Bigger?" Blog post, *TechPresident.com*. Retrieved from http://techpresident.com/blog-entry/tea-party-vs-netroots-rs-vs-ds-whos-online-base-bigger

Sinnreich, Aram. *Mashed Up: Music, Technology, and the Rise of Configurable Culture*. Amherst, MA: University of Massachusetts Press.

Skocpol, Theda. 2003. *Diminished Democracy: From Membership to Management in American Civic Life*. Norman, OK: University of Oklahoma Press.

Skocpol, Theda, Marshall Ganz, and Ziad Munson. 2000. "A Nation of Organizers: The Institutional Origins of Civic Voluntarism in the United States. *American Political Science Review* 94 (3), 527–546.

Skowronek, Stephen. 1982. *Building a New American State: The Expansion of National Administrative Capacities 1877–1920*. New York: Cambridge University Press.

Skowronek, Stephen. 1993. *The Politics Presidents Make*. Cambridge, MA: Harvard University Press.

Smith, Aaron. July 7, 2010. "Mobile Access 2010." Research Report, Pew Internet & American Life Project. Retrieved from http://pewinternet.org/Reports/2010/Mobile-Access-2010.aspx

Smith, Aaron. January 27, 2011. "Twitter and Social Networking in the 2010 Midterm Elections." Research Report, Pew Internet & American Life Project. Retrieved from http://pewresearch.org/pubs/1871/internet-politics-facebook-twitter-2010-midterm-elections-campaign

Smith, Aaron, and Lee Rainie. June 15, 2008. "The Internet and the 2008 Election." Research Report, Pew Internet & American Life Project. Retrieved from http://www.pewinternet.org/Reports/2008/The-Internet-and-the-2008-Election.aspx

Starr, Paul. March 4, 2009. "Goodbye to the Age of Newspapers (Hello to a New Era of Corruption." *The New Republic*.

Stein, Rob. November 2006. "Edited Transcript: How Vast the Left Wing Conspiracy?" Panel presentation, Bradley Center for Philanthropy and Civic Renewal, Washington, DC. Retrieved from http://www.hudson.org/files/pdf_upload/Transcript_2006_11_30.pdf

Steinberg, Adam. October 12, 2008. "The Spreadsheet Psychic." *New York Magazine*. Retrieved from http://nymag.com/news/features/51170/

Stewart, Mitch. February 6, 2010. "Pass Health Reform Now." Mass e-mail correspondence.

Strom, Stephanie. December 8, 2009. "Civil Liberties Group Loses $20 Million Donor." *The New York Times*. Retrieved from http://www.nytimes.com/2009/12/09/us/09aclu.html

Sullivan, Amy. 2005. "Fire the Consultants!" *Washington Monthly*. Retrieved from http://www.washingtonmonthly.com/features/2005/0501.sullivan.html

Sullivan, Courtney. June 1, 2008. "Every Thursday Night, Liberal Politics and Pints." *The New York Times*. Retrieved from http://www.nytimes.com/2008/06/01/nyregion/01drinking.html?_r=1

Sunstein, Cass. 2001. *Republic.com*. Princeton, NJ: Princeton University Press.

Sunstein, Cass. 2006. *Infotopia: How Many Minds Produce Knowledge*. New York: Oxford University Press.

Sunstein, Cass. 2007. *Republic.com 2.0*. Princeton, NJ: Princeton University Press.

Tapscott, Donald, and Anthony Williams. 2006. *Wikinomics: How Mass Collaboration Changes Everything*. New York: Portfolio Books.

Tapscott, Donald, and Anthony Williams. 2010. *Macrowikinomics: Rebooting Business and the World*. New York: Portfolio Books.

Tarrow, Sidney. 2011. *Power in Movement: Social Movements and Contentious Politics* (3rd Edition). New York: Cambridge University Press.

Taussig, Doron. March 14, 2007. "Re-formers: Who Are These Strange Beings Who Want to Save City Hall," *Philadelphia City Paper*. Retrieved from http://www.citypaper.net/articles/2007/03/15/reformers

Teachout, Zephyr, and Thomas Streeter. 2007. *Mousepads, Shoe Leather, and Hope: Lessons from the Howard Dean Campaign for the future of Internet Politics*. Boulder, CO: Paradigm Publishers.

Technorati. 2009. *State of the Blogosphere 2008*. Research Report. Retrieved from http://technorati.com/blogging/state-of-the-blogosphere/

Teles, Steven M. 2008. *The Rise of the Conservative Legal Movement*. Princeton, NJ: Princeton University Press.

Tenore, Mallary Jean. February 21, 2011. "FiveThirtyEight's Nate Silver adjusts to New York Times, 6 months after joining the newsroom." *Poynter Online*. Retrieved from http://www.poynter.org/latest-news/top-stories/120212/fivethirtyeights-nate-silver-adjusts-to-new-york-times-as-a-blogger-6-months-after-joining-the-newsroom/#comment-153966115

Terdiman, Daniel. September 28, 2004. "ActBlue Lets Anyone Be PAC Man." *Wired*. Retrieved from http://www.wired.com/politics/law/news/2004/09/65082

Thurber, James. 2000. *Campaign Warriors: The Role of Political Consultants in Elections*. Washington, DC: Brookings Institution Press.

Tilly, Charles. 1978. *From Mobilization to Revolution*. New York: Random House.

Trippi, Joe. 2005. *The Revolution Will Not Be Televised: Democracy, the Internet, and the Overthrow of Everything*. New York, NY: Harper Collins.

Truman, David. 1951. *The Governmental Process*. New York: Knopf.

Turner, Fred. 2002. *From Counterculture To Cyberculture: Stewart Brand, The Whole Earth Network, and the Rise of Digital Utopianism*. Chicago, IL: University of Chicago Press.

Turner, Tom. 1991. *Sierra Club: 100 Years of Protecting Nature*. New York: Abrams Books.

Turow, Joseph. 2005. "Audience Construction and Culture Production: Marketing Surveillance in the Digital Age." *The Annals of the American Academy of Political and Social Science* 597 (1), 103.

Turow, Joseph. 2008. *Niche Envy: Marketing Discrimination in the Digital Age*. Cambridge, MA: MIT Press.

Username "ablake34," October 4, 2010. *YouTube* video. Retrieved from http://www.youtube.com/watch?v=uxJyPsmEask

Username "anonymous office zombie." November 12, 2008. Retrieved from http://wonkette.com/404325/american-people-give-republican-party-major-responsibility-big-ale-on-truck-nutz#comments

Username "neworganizinginst." January 26, 2009. "Zack Exley, President of NOI, Speaks about the NOI Mission." *YouTube* video. Retrieved from http://www.youtube.com/watch?v=bQ6RbXeKxEw

Valente, Thomas. 1996. *Network Models of the Diffusion of Innovations*. New York: Springer.

Van Dijk, Jan, and Ken Hacker. 2003. "The Digital Divide as a Complex and Dynamic Phenomenon." *The Information Society,* 19 (4), 315–326.

Van Slyke, Tracy, and Jessica Clark. 2010. *Beyond the Echo Chamber.* New York: New Press.

VandeHei, Jim, and Chris Cillizza. July 17, 2006. "A New Alliance of Democrats Spreads Funding." *The Washington Post.* Retrieved from http://www.washingtonpost.com/wp-dyn/content/article/2006/07/16/AR2006071600882.html

Vargas, Jose Antonio. November 25, 2008. "Republicans Seek to Fix Short-Sitedness." *Washington Post,* pg C01. Retrieved from http://www.washingtonpost.com/wp-dyn/content/article/2008/11/24/AR2008112403004.html?hpid=artslot

Verba, Sidney, Kay Lehman Schlozman, and Henry Brady. 1995. *Voice and Equality: Civic Voluntarism in American Politics.* Cambridge, MA: Harvard University Press.

Von Hippel, Eric. 2005. *Democratizing Innovation.* Cambridge, MA: MIT Press.

Walker, Edward. 2009. "Privatizing Participation: Civic Change and the Organizational Dynamics of Grassroots Lobbying Firms." *American Sociological Review* 74 (1), 83–105.

Walker, Edward, John McCarthy, and Frank Baumgartner. 2011. "Replacing Members with Managers? Mutualism among Membership and Nonmembership Advocacy Associations in the United States." *American Journal of Sociology* 116 (4), 1284–1337.

Walker, Jack L. 1991. *Mobilizing Interest Groups in America: Patrons, Professions, and Social Movements.* Ann Arbor, MI: University of Michigan Press.

Wallsten, Kevin. 2007. "Political Blogs: Transmission Belts, Soapboxes, Mobilizers, or Conversation Starters?" *Journal of Information Technology and Politics* 4 (3), 19–40.

Wallsten, Kevin. 2008. "Agenda Setting and the Blogosphere: An Analysis of the Relationship between Mainstream Media and Political Blogs." *Review of Policy Research* 24 (6), 567–587.

Wallsten, Kevin. 2010. "Yes We Can: How Online Viewership, Blog Discussion, Campaign Statements, and Mainstream Media Coverage Produced a Viral Video Phenomenon." *Journal of Information Technology and Politics* 7 (2–3), 163–181.

Wallsten, Kevin. March–April, 2011. "The Most Powerful Journalist in America? The Drudge Report and Media Coverage of the 2008 Campaign." Paper Presentation, Midwest Political Science Association Annual Meeting, Chicago, IL.

Ward, Jon. December 8, 2008. "Exclusive: Freedom's Watch to Close." *The Washington Times.* Retrieved from http://washingtontimes.com/news/2008/dec/08/freedoms-watch-shut-end-month/

Warschauer, Mark. 2004. *Technology and Social Inclusion: Rethinking the Digital Divide.* Cambridge, MA: MIT Press.

Wasserman, Stanley, and Katherine Faust. 1995. *Social Network Analysis: Methods and Applications.* New York: Cambridge University Press.

Wayne, Leslie. November 29, 2007. "A Fund-Raising Rainmaker Arises Online." *The New York Times.* Retrieved from http://www.nytimes.com/2007/11/29/us/politics/29actblue.html?_r=2&scp=1&sq=ActBlue&st=nyt&oref=slogin

Watts, Duncan. 2003. *Six Degrees: The Science of a Connected Age.* New York: Norton.

Weber, Steven. 2004. *The Success of Open Source.* Cambridge, MA: Harvard University Press.

Weber, Matthew. Forthcoming. "The Long-term Effects of Hyperlinking in a Community of News Organizations." *Journal of Computer-Mediated Communication.*

Weinberger, David. 2007. *Everything Is Miscellaneous.* New York: Holt Paperbacks.

Wellman, Barry. 2001. "Computer Networks as Social Networks." *Science* 293 (5537), 2031–2034.

Wellman, Barry. 2004. "Connecting Community: On and Offline." *Contexts* 3 (4), 22–28.

Wellman, Barry, Anabel Quan-Haase, Jeffrey Boase, Wenhong Chen, Keith Hampton, Isabel Diaz, and Kakuko Miyata. 2003. "The Social Affordances of the Internet for Networked Individualism." *Journal of Computer-Mediated Communication* 8 (3). Retrieved from http://jcmc.indiana.edu/vol8/issue3/wellman.html

West, Darrell. 2005. *Digital Government: Technology and Public Sector Performance.* Princeton, NJ: Princeton University Press.

White, Micah. August 12, 2010. "Clicktivism Is Ruining Leftist Activism." *The Guardian Online.* Retrievedfromhttp://www.guardian.co.uk/commentisfree/2010/aug/12/clicktivism-ruining-leftist-activism

Williams, Christine, Bruce Weinberg, and Jesse Gordon. September 2004. "When Online and Offline Politics 'Meetup:' An Examination of the Phenomenon, Presidential Campaign and Its Citizen Activists. Paper presented at the Annual Meeting of APSA, Chicago, IL.

Williams, Christine, and Girish Gulati. 2008. "The Political Impact of Facebook: Evidence from the 2006 Midterm Elections and the 2008 Nomination Contest." *Politics and Technology Review* 1 (1), 11–24.

Williams, Christine, and Girish Gulati. 2010. "Congressional Candidates' Use of YouTube in 2008: Its Frequency and Rationale." *Journal of Information Technology and Politics* 7 (2), 93–109.

Wilson, James Q. 1962. *The Amateur Democrat.* Chicago, IL: University of Chicago Press.

Wolf, Gary. 2004. "How the Internet Invented Howard Dean." *Wired.* Retrieved from http://www.owlnet.rice.edu/~comp300/documents/HowtheInternetInventedDean.pdf

Wojcieszak, Magdalena. 2010. "'Don't Talk to Me': Effects of Ideologically Homogeneous Online Groups and Politically Dissimilar Offline Ties on Extremism." *New Media & Society* 12 (4), 637–655.

Wojcieszak, Magdalena, and Diana Mutz. 2009. "Online Groups and Political Discourse: Do Online Discussion Spaces Facilitate Exposure to Political Disagreement?" *Journal of Communication* 59 (1), 40–56.

Xenos, Michael. 2008. New Mediated Deliberation: Blog and Press Coverage of the Alito Nomination, *Journal of Computer-Mediated Communication* 13 (2), 485–503.

Zald, Mayer, and John McCarthy. 1987. *Social Movements in an Organizational Society.* New Brunswick, NJ: Rutgers University Press.

Zaller, John. 1992. *The Theory and Nature of Mass Opinion.* New York: Cambridge University Press.

Zernike, Kate. 2010. *Boiling Mad.* New York: MacMillan.

Zernike, Kate, and Megan Thee-Brenan. April 14, 2010. "Poll Finds Tea Party Backers Wealthier and More Educated." *The New York Times.* Retrieved from http://www.nytimes.com/2010/04/15/us/politics/15poll.html

Zetter, Kim. July 26, 2004. "MoveOn Moves Up in the World." *Wired Magazine.* Retrieved from http://www.wired.com/politics/law/news/2004/07/64340?currentPage=all

Zittrain, Jonathan. 2008. *The Future of the Internet (And How to Stop It).* New Haven, CT: Yale University Press.

Zysman, John, and Abraham Newman. 2007. *How Revolutionary Was the Digital Revolution?* Stanford, CA: Stanford University Press.

Index